SOCIAL SCIENCE STUDIES CAHIERS DES SCIENCES SOCIALES

No. 5

INDUSTRY AND EDUCATION
A Century of Canadian Development

by

O. J. FIRESTONE
Professor of Economics
University of Ottawa

UNIVERSITY OF OTTAWA PRESS
OTTAWA, ONTARIO, CANADA
1969

INDUSTRY AND EDUCATION

A CENTURY OF CANADIAN DEVELOPMENT

PREFACE

At this time when various levels of governments are required to spend increasingly higher proportions of their revenues on education, studies like the one presented in this book by Dr. O. J. Firestone are most helpful. His analysis which covers the first century since Canadian Confederation and deals with the changing relationship between education and economic development, leads the author to certain general conclusions which will no doubt attract the attention of all those who are interested in the progress of our country.

The patrons of the arts and of other cultural activities of past centuries understood that material progress offered society increased opportunities in other fields, allowing among other things philosophers, artists and composers the freedom to employ their talents. Affluence encouraged the creation of artistic, literary and philosophic work enriching mankind and strengthening the foundation of our civilization.

At present, public authorities have taken on a major role as the patrons of cultural advancement. One can only hope that their vision will continue to broaden. In this process, they may be assisted by studies like the present one which assembles evidence to show that continuing education is indispensable and in fact in most instances may bring a better return on investment in human capital than in physical capital.

This study, while comprehensive, could be extended, and further aspects could be examined. In fact, subsequent studies may make it desirable to modify some of the conclusions arrived at on the basis of preliminary evidence obtained.

The problems facing universities which must be solved are numerous and complex. Too often, unfortunately, decisions must be made without being able to base them on studies conducted with scientific reasoning. The latter is the most important aspect of research in all university disciplines. The academic organization of our universities and their place in the community can be determined in the final analysis only after a careful examination of the needs of tomorrow's society and according to the requirements appropriate to each discipline.

vii

Universities aspire to assist human beings to achieve completeness. Indeed, such well-rounded individuals can make a major contribution to the economic development of their country. There is need to blend an understanding of the contribution which education makes to enhance human qualities with that to raise productivity, bringing beneficial results to the individual and society as a whole. Dollar expenditures and monetary returns are only one set of criteria. Human happiness and social advancement are even more important. Enlightened decision-makers in education understand this dual objective. They realize that wise decisions can best be made by taking into account the facts of a given situation, seen in perspective, allowing for the diverse views that may be held, to find equitable and judicious solutions to pressing problems.

By congratulating the author on his excellent contribution to a field so vital to the well-being of our country, I invite him earnestly to continue his research and cite him as an example to others, more and more numerous, who would be well-equipped to follow a path that Dr. O. J. Firestone has opened up in Canada.

Dr. Roger GUINDON, O.M.I.,
Rector,
University of Ottawa.

Ottawa, September 1968.

PRÉFACE

Au moment où les divers échelons de gouvernements sont appelés à investir un pourcentage de plus en plus élevé de leurs ressources respectives dans l'éducation à tous ses niveaux, des études comme celle du Dr O. J. Firestone sont indispensables. L'analyse qu'il a faite du premier siècle de la Confédération canadienne pour en dégager les relations entre l'éducation d'une part et l'essor économique d'autre part, l'amène à certaines conclusions générales qui retiendront sans doute l'attention de tous ceux qui s'intéressent au progrès de notre pays.

Les mécènes des siècles passés avaient compris qu'une part de leurs biens matériels devait assurer aux philosophes, artistes ou compositeurs les conditions requises à l'exercice de leurs talents. Ce faisant, ils favorisaient la production d'œuvres artistiques, littéraires et philosophiques dont l'humanité tout entière s'est enrichie et qui forment les assises de notre civilisation. De nos jours, ce sont les pouvoirs publics qui jouent presque exclusivement le rôle de mécènes. On ne peut que souhaiter que leur vision soit éclairée par des études qui, comme celle-ci, les rassurent, s'il en est besoin, sur le fait que l'on obtient un meilleur rendement des placements dans le capital humain que dans le capital matériel.

Cette étude sur les grands ensembles devra être prolongée et précisée. Il se peut que certains aspects doivent être corrigés à la lumière d'études ultérieures qui révéleront d'autres variables dont il faudra tenir compte.

Les problèmes auxquels les universités doivent trouver des solutions sont nombreux et complexes. Trop souvent, hélas, les décisions doivent être prises sans qu'on ait l'avantage de les baser sur des études conduites avec la rigueur scientifique qui préside aux recherches dans toutes les disciplines universitaires. La planification académique de nos universités et leur insertion dans la communauté ne peut se faire véritablement qu'à la suite d'un examen attentif des besoins de la société de demain et selon des exigences propres à chaque discipline.

Les universités ambitionnent de former des hommes complets qui, certes, pourront jouer un rôle important dans l'essor

ix

*économique de leur pays. Mais il est nécessaire de bien com-
prendre que l'éducation contribue à la fois au développement
des qualités humaines et à l'augmentation de la productivité,
répandant son influence bienfaisante sur les individus et sur
l'ensemble de la société. Les dépenses encourues et le rendement
en dollars ne constituent qu'un des critères; le bonheur humain
et le progrès social sont encore plus importants. Les chefs
éclairés qui ont à prendre des décisions en matière d'éducation
sont conscients de ce double but à atteindre. Ils comprennent
que la meilleure façon de prendre de sages décisions, c'est
d'analyser une situation donnée dans son ensemble, compte tenu
des divers points de vue afin de trouver une solution équitable
aux problèmes urgents.*

*En félicitant l'auteur de son excellente contribution en un
domaine aussi vital au bien-être de notre pays, je l'invite
instamment à poursuivre ses recherches et je le donne en
exemple à ceux qui, de plus en plus nombreux et bien équipés,
devront s'engager dans la voie que le Dr O. J. Firestone vient
d'ouvrir au Canada.*

Roger GUINDON, o.m.i.
Recteur,
Université d'Ottawa.

Ottawa, septembre 1968.

TABLE OF CONTENTS

PAGE

Preface by Rev. Dr. Roger Guindon vii

Préface par le R.P. Roger Guindon ix

Introduction XV

Part I

INDUSTRIAL DEVELOPMENT

Chapter 1. Industry and Economic Progress 3
Employment and Income, Capital Spending, Exports,
Profits, Direct Benefits, Industrial Development
in Perspective.

Chapter 2. Confederation and the Industrial Revolution   15
Pre-Industrial Period, Will to Industrialize,
Challenge of Confederation.

Chapter 3. First Half Century 21
Industrial Takeoff — Handicaps Notwithstanding,
Great Depression, "Reciprocity of Tariffs",
Progress in the Midst of Adversity, Broadening
the Industrial Base, World War I.

Chapter 4. Second Half Century 31
Interwar Period, World War II, Postwar Reconstruction,
New Resources Impetus, Korean War and Adjustment,
Slowdown in Economic Growth, Strong Expansion Again.

Chapter 5. International Orientation and Competition ..   41
Degree of Manufacturing, Increasing Competition,
Changing Position in World Markets, Response to
Postwar Challenges, Devaluation of Canadian Dollar,
World Trends, Raising Productivity, Government
Encouragement, Encouragement of Business.

Chapter 6. Foreign Control and Ownership 55
Liberal Policies, Net International Indebtedness,
Extent of Control, Risks and Rewards, Canadian
Dilemma, Political Attitudes, United States Action,
Guide-lines.

Chapter 7. Role of Government 65
Canadian Philosophy of Industrial Development,
Effect on the Balance of Payments,
A Task Force of Eight Economists,
Government Assistance to Industrial Development,
C. D. Howe: A Great Nation Builder, Federal Measures,
New Role of Provincial Governments.

Chapter 8.   Whither Canadian Industry ?   77
Blessings and Toil, Balanced Growth, Continental
Approach, National Survival.

Chapitre 9.   Sommaire (en français)   81

Part II

EDUCATION AND ECONOMIC DEVELOPMENT

Chapter 10.   Concepts of Economic Growth,
Development and Progress   89
Variety of Meaning of Economic Growth, Essential
Features of Economic Development, Interrelationship
between Economic Growth and Economic Development,
Definition of Economic Progress, Interrelationship
between Economic Development and Economic Progress,
Economic Growth and Labour Force Quality.

Chapter 11.   The "Stages" Framework   99
Delineation of Stages, Traditional Society, Preconditions
for Take-Off, Take-Off, Drive to Maturity,
Age of High Mass-Consumption.

Chapter 12.   A Century of Economic Development   119
Extent of Progress, Snowball Effect,
Productivity Improvements.

Chapter 13.   Structural Changes   125
Structural Changes Defined, Changes in Industrial
Structure, Changes in Structure of Output, Changes in
Structure of Consumer Spending, Education and
Structural Changes.

Chapter 14.   Economic Implications of Education   137
Education and Civilization, Education and Economic Choice,
Dissemination of Education, Continuing Education,
Matching Supply and Demand, Education — Consumption
or Investment, Productive and Social Investment, Education
and Economic Development, Education and Consumer
Sovereignty, Policy Implications, Analytical Implications.

Chapter 15.   Dual Effects of Education   155
Different Types of Duality, Contribution to Capacity
to Consume, Contribution to Capacity to Produce,
Supply and Demand Effects, Cultural and Social Factors,
Quantitative Assessment.

Chapter 16.   Education Industry   169
Characteristics, Teachers, Students and Expenditures,
Educational Explosion, Knowledge Explosion.

Chapter 17.   Education and Stages of Economic
     Development _____ 177
     Education and Poverty, Public Support of Education,
     First Stage, Second to Fourth Stage, Fifth Stage, Differentials
     in Rates of Growth, Reasons for Differentials,
     Industrialization and Education, Take-Off in Education.

Chapter 18.   Effect on Labour Force and Earnings _____ 197
     Educational Attainments, Greater School Enrolment in
     Aggregate, Greater School Enrolment and School Age
     Population, Greater Number of School Years, Greater
     Number of School Days, Greater Emphasis on Higher
     Learning, Greater Quality of Teaching, Effects on
     Past Earnings, Effects on Anticipated Earnings,
     Return on Educational Investment.

Chapter 19.   Effect of Net Migration _____ 223
     Extent of Net Migration, Effect on Stock of Education,
     Valuation of Educational Capital.

Chapter 20.   United States Influence _____ 229
     Education and Productivity Differentials, Education and
     Income Differentials, Reasons for Differentials, Offset to
     Lagging Education, Negative and Positive Effects.

Chapter 21.   Education and Economic Growth _____ 239
     Cause and Consequence, Quantifying Education's
     Contribution to Economic Growth, Industrial and Human
     Development, Conclusion.

Chapitre 22.   Sommaire (en français) _____ 249

Appendix A.   Basic Tabular Material _____ 261

Appendix B.   Notes on Sources and Quality of Estimates 273

List of Tables _____ 285

Index of Subjects _____ 287

INTRODUCTION

This book is the result of two studies. One is an examination of the industrial development of Canada during her first century of nationhood, 1867-1967, presented in Part I. The other, presented in Part II, includes an assessment of the relationship of education and economic growth, economic development and economic progress in aggregate, in structural and micro-economic terms on the basis of one hundred years of Canadian experience.

Canada has reached an advanced stage of technological maturity and high levels of productivity and incomes. She is now one of the eight leading industrialized nations, with her people enjoying a standard of living surpassed only by that of the United States. Canada has reached the stage of great affluency and full industrialization during the last two decades. Hence this country has only recently joined the circle of "have" nations.

For most of her history, during 262 years as colonial territory and during the first 80 years as a nation, Canada has continuously struggled to develop a viable base for economic, social and individual advancement. Frequently, such efforts were frustrated by the harsh realities of a northern climate, long distances, natural barriers, large stretches of wasteland, internal struggles and adverse economic and political pressures emanating from abroad.

That Canada has succeeded in doing as well as she has, was in part due to the use of her bountiful natural resources, the determination of her people and a measure of good fortune. But memories are still fresh of hard times, of struggling for a livelihood and of converting a largely primary industry-oriented country to a predominantly secondary industry and service-oriented economy. It is a new experience for Canada to have reached the level of a highly productive nation which participates on a fairly large scale in world trade, international finance and economic aid.

Thus Canada is a developed country where the memories are still vivid of the frustrations of underdevelopment. In endeavouring to industrialize their country and to educate and train their people, Canadians faced many trials and tribulations as they moved from one stage of economic development to another. The goal, of course, was to arrive at the stage all societies seem to aim at — that of full industrialization, a high degree of affluency and an opportunity to provide their citizens with adequate opportunities for creative self-expression and material welfare.

There is no suggestion that the experiences of Canadians and their efforts to industrialize their economy, and to enhance the quality of human capital through education, provide an object lesson which some less developed nations could consider if they faced difficulties similar to those encountered in this country. Each country has its distinct physical, locational and economic features, and its people have distinct ethnic, cultural, social and political characteristics. There exists what Rostow has called "the uniqueness of each nation's experience". And this means that the experience of one country cannot be adapted to the problems of another country without the risk of over-simplification and misapplication.

There are, however, two broad conclusions that appear to be of general applicability and that can be gleaned from one hundred years of Canadian economic development.

One is that economic development is gradual and continuous, interruptions and setbacks notwithstanding, with the rate of progress snowballing once Canada reached the stage of full technological maturity. Whenever inbalances in the economic growth process occurred, public pressures developed to bring about a better balance and a more equitable distribution of the fruits of economic progress, with such pressures growing as the public became better educated and more aware of alternative choices open to society.

Still, in the midst of plenty, there exists a great deal of poverty affecting one Canadian in five, a proportion similar to that prevailing in the United States, the wealthiest country in the world. Hence, with all the skills that Canadians have acquired to conquer nature and to maximize production, a solution to the problem of providing adequate opportunities for all has so far eluded the best intentioned decision-makers active in the political and economic life of the nation.

The other is that the key to rapid Canadian economic progress was the human factor: the skills of the people, their initiative, enterprise and creativeness. While Canadians also owe a great debt to other nations for having been able to draw on their scientific and technical knowledge, and human and financial capital, in the final analysis Canadians had to stand on their own two feet. And they had to educate and train their young people to levels adequate to cope with the most complex issues of a scientific age.

What Canadians have learnt over the last century is that education and economic growth go hand in hand. And as the evidence presented in this book indicates, the take-off in education in Canada came much later than the take-off in economic development, about half a century later. In the intervening period, this country relied heavily on know-how and trained people from abroad until the economy with growing affluence and expanding resources was able to meet most of the requirements from domestic sources.

Looking back, it becomes clear that many of the setbacks and frustrations experienced in Canada could have been avoided or could have been reduced in intensity if earlier generations had the knowledge of the economic, social and political implications of the trial and error methods they employed.

Is there anything that less developed countries can learn from a century of Canadian efforts to industrialize their economy and the role that education has played in this process ? The answer is: Yes — a little. In the main it is this: Economic and social progress can be speeded up when a nation knows what it wants to do and if it is willing to do all in its power to work unitedly and steadfastly towards achieving such goals, making effective use of its own resources and those of other countries, made freely available in a spirit of international cooperation. Growing affluence does not only reduce the wretchedness of poverty; it also increases the equality of economic opportunity and the freedom to dissent. There is of course much more to the subject and this book deals with a number of aspects, both in theoretical and applied terms, drawing on one hundred years of Canadian experience.

Part I of this book is based on a study entitled "Industrial Development" a shortened version of which was incorporated as

Chapter 14 of *The Canadians, 1867-1967*, edited by J. M. S. Careless and R. Craig Brown, published by the MacMillan Company of Canada Limited, Toronto, 1967. With the kind permission of the MacMillan Company of Canada the full original text, with minor editorial changes, is reproduced in this book. The helpful suggestions for editorial improvements made by Mr. J. W. Bacque of the MacMillan Company of Canada are gratefully acknowledged.

Part II of this book is based on a paper entitled "Education and Economic Development — The Canadian Case", given at the Tenth General Conference of the International Association for Research in Income and Wealth, Maynooth College, Ireland, August 20-26, 1967. A shortened version of this paper has been published in the *International Review*, December 1968. The text presented here is an extended version of the paper originally given, revised in the light of comments received and incorporating new data and additional information which had become available. The use of the original text of the paper, as revised, is published with the kind permission of the International Association for Research in Income and Wealth.

The paper was one of several presented at the session of the Association dealing with "Education and National Accounts", chaired by Professor Dudley Seers.

Professor Edward E. Denison acted as the leading discussant of the paper and offered a number of constructive comments. Several other participants at the conference made helpful observations including Miss Phyllis Deane, Miss Mary Jean Bowman and Professor Thomas Brinley. Account of many of the observations made by these and other participants of the conference was taken in revising the original paper and this assistance is gratefully acknowledged.

Miss V. Martin and Mr. T. R. Vout offered editorial suggestions and Mrs. L. Rowntree looked after the typing of the manuscript. Father L. Lanctôt, O.M.I., undertook the French translation of the summary of Part I in Chapter 9 and the summary of Part II in Chapter 22 and he was kind enough to see the book through the press. My sincere thanks go to all those who helped.

O. J. FIRESTONE
Professor of Economics

Ottawa, September 1968

PART I

Industrial Development

> "The character of the [Canadian] people is sufficiently different from that of the United States to make even her industrial development bear a stamp of its own." [1]

---

[1] James BONAR, "Industrial Development : Introduction", in *Canada and Its Provinces*, Edinburgh University Press, 1913, Vol. IX, p. 6.

CHAPTER 1

Industry and Economic Progress

Canada, with a population of over 20 million people, two-thirds of one per cent of the world's population, is one of the leading trading and industrial countries. Canadian goods and services are sold in all corners of the globe — with trade crossing oceans, mountains and man-made barriers, both economic and political.

Canada is the world's fifth largest trading nation in terms of total exports. She is among the eight leading industrial nations of the world — in terms of Gross Domestic Product originating in manufacturing — and the fourth on a per capita basis following the United States, Western Germany and France, but ahead of the United Kingdom, U.S.S.R., Japan and Italy. [2] As a result of great advances in industrial and trade development, Canadians have experienced for most of the post-war period a particularly rapid rate of economic growth, making possible for them to expand their productive capacity materially while at the same time enjoying a rising standard of living.

How have Canadians been able to achieve all this in the life of three generations, starting as they did from modest beginnings, a group of widely dispersed settlers with limited material and financial resources facing dangers from the south and uncertainty from across the ocean ?

One reason was their determination to make a go of developing their natural and human resources. The other was their willingness to be pragmatic, to improvise and to compromise, all with the objective of maintaining their political independence and bettering the fate of their people.

As Canada's population became more numerous and as the economy became more productive, Canadians began to take an increasing interest in international affairs and to shoulder growing responsibilities in the economic and political arena.

---

[2] Special estimates based on data relating to 1963, taken from the *Yearbook of National Accounts Statistics, 1964,* and from *Monthly Bulletin of Statistics,* October 1965, New York, United Nations, 1965.

Canadians realized early in their history as a new nation that economic progress at home and an increasing contribution in world affairs depended on economic strength and political stability.

Both could not be achieved without a struggle to overcome the adverse forces of a reluctant nature and of human passions. Part of the struggle was the effort to make Canada a truly industrial nation. This then was the great challenge Canadians faced : How to produce in this country the most complex products that modern science and advanced technology could fashion ? How to process at home the multitude of valuable natural resources that make up Canada's storehouse ? How to fabricate as many products as possible drawing on the raw materials, sources of energy and human resources available in this country ? How to meet the demand of the Canadian market for most manufactured products ? How to serve growing international markets in supplying increased quantities of processed materials and finished goods of a quality and at a price that could compete with the best that other countries had to offer ?

This part of the book tells the story of a century of Canada's industrial development : How industrial progress contributed materially to the economic growth of the country and enabled Canadians to lead a better and fuller life; how the benefits spread, both at home and abroad; how industrialization was achieved — the problems that Canadians faced and how they overcame them; the successes and the failures, the hopes and the aspirations and the role played by individuals, management and labour, and governments in this process.

This is also the story of the dilemma Canadians face as they enter their second century of nationhood and the road they are travelling, as the rate of progress of their country gathers momentum making it possible for future generations to achieve greater things than past generations, with each generation moving from strength to strength on the solid and broadening base built by their forefathers.

Canada's manufacturing industries comprise a heterogeneous group of business firms whose single common characteristic is that this industry converts raw materials into a more advanced stage of processing or fabricating. Thus manufacturing covers the processing of minerals and non-ferrous metals, the milling of wheat, the conversion of logs into pulp and paper, the production of synthetic materials, chemicals, iron and steel products and the creation of a variety of finished and fully fabricated items covering a wide range of consumer goods and capital goods. Hence manufacturing covers the production of both finished and unfinished goods whether for final use by individuals, business, governments and institutions, or for integration into other production processes.

EMLOYMENT AND INCOME

In 1967, the Canadian manufacturing industry provided jobs for about 1.8 million persons comprising about one-quarter of all those employed in this country. The gross value of manufacturing production amounted to some $40 billion in 1967 approaching some two-thirds of Canada's Gross National Product valued at about $62 billion. Net value added to manufacturing was of the order of $18 billion, close to 30 per cent of the Gross National Product. [3] In terms of wages and salaries, manufacturing industries contributed about 29 per cent to total earnings. Putting it in general terms, Canadian manufacturing industries provided jobs for one out of four Canadians. One of every three dollars earned originated directly in Canada's secondary industries.

During the first half century of Canada's nationhood, primary industries, particularly agriculture, were the main sources of gainful employment and income. But the situation changed following the significant industrial efforts exerted during World War I, with manufacturing becoming the most important single source of income earned in Canada. Still in terms of numbers of persons working, agriculture was to remain the main source of employment for another two decades.

It took another war, World War II, to transform Canada's economic structure. This country came out of the war as a major industrialized nation with manufacturing by far the most important and most dynamic source of economic activity, employment and income. In the last two decades, manufacturing industries have become the pace setter in Canadian economic progress. Rising productivity made it possible to pay workers

---

[3] In terms of Gross Domestic Product at factor cost, Canadian manufacturing industries contributed a slightly lesser proportion.

higher wages while at the same time the number of hours worked per week were reduced. Increased profits made it possible to reward management and investors adequately and to attract increasing amounts of capital for further plant expansion and productive improvements.

As workers were able to get higher wages and salaries and obtained better working conditions in manufacturing industries, other sectors of the economy had to follow suit in order to keep their work force. And such sectors as agriculture that could not compete with the attractions and rewards of urban factory employment lost large numbers of farm workers to cities and towns. Between 1945 and 1967 the agricultural labour force was reduced by about one-half from some 1.2 million to a little over 600,000, with an equivalent number of workers being absorbed additionally in urban manufacturing plants. Employment in secondary industries rose from 1.1 million in 1945 to 1.8 million in 1967.

CAPITAL SPENDING

Manufacturing industries are among the greatest spenders on expanding and improving their capital facilities next to public utilities, which during most years in the postwar period have made larger capital expenditures than any other sector. The distribution of capital expenditures in 1966 was as follows: [4]

	Amount $ Mill.	Per Cent
Public Utilities	2,892	19.4
Manufacturing Industries	2,803	18.8
Housing	2,181	14.6
Primary Industry	2,084	14.0
Government Departments	2,022	13.6
Commercial and Financial Services and Construction	1,729	11.6
Institutional Services	1,186	8.0
Total	14,897	100.0

[4] Data are from DOMINION BUREAU OF STATISTICS and DEPARTMENT OF TRADE AND COMMERCE, *Private and Public Investment in Canada, Outlook 1967*, Ottawa, 1966, p. 11.

EXPORTS

Manufacturing industries have developed largely to cater to Canada's domestic market. But increasingly Canadian manufacturing industries have striven to obtain a growing share of expanding export markets. In these efforts Canadian industries have experienced some setbacks from time to time. Still about two-thirds of Canada's merchandise export trade, amounting to $8.5 billion in 1965, was comprised of fully or partially manufactured products. This represented about 17 per cent of the gross value of Canada's total manufacturing output.

In other words, Canadian industry relied for 83 cents out of every dollar on sales to domestic consumers, with the other 17 cents being earned by selling abroad.

PROFITS

No other industry produces as substantial a profit for both Canadian and foreign investors, as does the manufacturing industry. In 1966, for example, secondary industries generated corporation profits amounting to $2,133 million or 44.6 per cent out of a total of $5,187 million. The wholesale and retail trade sectors, with $716 million, or 13.8 per cent came next, followed by the finance, insurance and real estate sectors, with $643 million or 12.4 per cent. Then came the transportation, storage and communications industry with $584 million or 11.2 per cent, and the mining (including oil and natural gas) industry with $570 million or 11.0 per cent. The remaining group of "other" industries accounted for $361 million or 7.0 per cent. [5]

DIRECT BENEFITS

To restate, the main contribution resulting from Canadian industrial development so far referred to:

1. Substantial increases in the number of job opportunities.

2. High real incomes.

3. Greater productivity.

4. Reduction in the number of hours worked per week.

---

[5] Data are from DOMINION BUREAU OF STATISTICS, *National Accounts, Income and Expenditures, 1966,* Ottawa, 1967, p. 33.

5. Major source of capital spending, essential to continuing economic growth.

6. Contributing two-thirds to Canada's merchandise exports in the form of partially and fully manufactured products.

7. Greater profits generated than any other sector in the economy.

8. Pacesetter in economic progress by offering an example to other sectors of the economy of how to maximize output with a minimum of input, bringing increasing rewards to those engaged in manufacturing activity.

The dynamic character of manufacturing industries in economic development is much more complex than would be suggested by a simple listing of the major contributions, such as those mentioned above. The very fact that manufacturing industries employ more people than any other sector in the economy providing the greatest single source of income earned, means that the industry not only produces output but it also creates the income that results in the demands for its products from consumers and business, thus contributing to economic growth. Manufacturing industries represent also the most important single group of taxpayers thus making an essential contribution to the fiscal soundness of the country.

Hence, rapid industrial expansion over the last century has brought this country two direct benefits: it has provided Canadians with an opportunity to earn a better livelihood and it has supplied them with a greater quantity and variety of goods that are symbolic of rising standards of living in modern society.

But Canada's industrialization has many wider ramifications going beyond economic and material enhancement so highly valued in North America.

It made it possible for Canadians to play a greater role in international affairs, both politically and economically. Canadians are able to speak in increasingly firmer tones, backing up their words by deeds, whether this means more intensive trade discussions, greater economic aid to less developed countries, financial support to international institutions, or military supplies and personnel for United Nations peace missions.

It made it possible for Canadians to play their proper part in two world wars and in brush fire wars such as the Korean War that required support of the cause for freedom in terms of men, materials, and money.

It made it possible for Canadians to embark on a comprehensive program of income redistribution, social security and welfare largely paid for out of rising productivity.

It made it possible for Canadians to expand the range of government services in areas vital to human betterment and economic progress, such as education, health and urban development.

And finally, it gave Canadians a sense of achievement and inner strength to withstand the trials and tribulations of internal discontent and international bickering.

The greatness of the achievement speaks for itself — and in its mirror the complaints of Canada's detractors pale into insignificance.

What in fact did Canadians achieve in the last century? Here are some of the highlights of their industrial achievements.

INDUSTRIAL DEVELOPMENT IN PERSPECTIVE

One of Canada's outstanding social scientists, a great teacher and a distinguished civil servant, O. D. Skelton, once observed: "With Confederation a new stage in the industrial development of the Northern half of this continent began." [6]

Great were the hopes to build a strong and united nation in one of the largest countries of the world, endowed with great riches of natural resources, waiting to be developed by an energetic and independently-minded people. Have these expectations been fulfilled in Canada's first century as a nation?

In economic terms the achievements are truly gigantic. In human terms the results are gratifying. In political terms the results are reassuring, if account is taken of the need to adapt the political and constitutional system to changing aspirations and desires for national and cultural fulfilment.

---

[6] O. D. SKELTON, "General Economic History, 1867-1912", in *Canada and Its Provinces,* Edinburgh University Press, 1913, Volume IX, p. 95.

But success did not come easily. There were many national disappointments, economic setbacks, business failures, political defeats and human unrest. The story of some of the problems faced and tackled by Canadians with varying success over time, is told as Part I proceeds.

Here are some of the highlights of Canada's economic achievements over a century — to an important extent the result of successful continuing and persistent efforts to industrialize the country.

In 1867 Canada had a population of 3.5 million people, a labour force of 1.1 million, a Gross National Product of the order of $400 million and merchandise exports of some $50 million. [7]

Manufacturing operations were of a simple nature. Canada was still waiting to realize the full benefits of the industrial revolution which had made the United Kingdom a great industrial and trading nation. Still, Canadian manufacturing industries provided jobs for some 170,000 people, about 16 per cent of the total number of persons working, 1,060,000. The gross value of goods manufactured was of the order of $170 million and the net value added in manufacturing, [8] about $85 million equivalent to approximately 20 per cent of the Gross National Product.

At the time of Confederation, the average person working in manufacturing earned about $217 per year, or approximately 75¢ per day. He usually worked between ten and twelve hours a day, six days a week and only some were able to shave off an hour or two on Saturday. [9]

---

[7] The data for 1867 are special estimates based largely on two studies by the author. The estimates are of necessity approximate and subject to a number of limitations. The interested reader is referred to the two publications mentioned : *Canada's Economic Development, 1867-1953,* London, Bowes and Bowes, 1958; and "Development of Canada's Economy, 1850-1900", in *Trends in the American Economy in the Nineteenth Century,* Studies in Income and Wealth, Vol. 24, by the Conference on Research on Income and Wealth, a Report of the National Bureau of Economic Research, Princeton University Press, 1960, pp. 217-252. (See also Table 1 in Appendix A and Appendix B.)

[8] This approximates the amount contributed by manufacturing to Canada's national income, after eliminating duplications.

[9] The number of hours worked per day in some manufacturing industries in the United States was placed between 13 and 14 for 1830, and between 10 and 11 for 1884. Working conditions in Canadian industrial establishments were similar to those prevailing in the United

Now here is the picture in approximate terms 100 years later. [10]

Canada's population in mid-1967 numbered 20½ million, the labour force 7.8 million, persons working 7.5 million, while Gross National Product for the year as a whole amounted to about $62 billion and merchandise exports to over $11 billion.

To complete the perspective and to restate: Manufacturing industries provided jobs for about 1.8 million persons, close to 25 per cent of the total number of persons employed. Gross value of manufacturing production amounted to some $40 billion and net value added to approximately $18 billion or close to 30 per cent of the Gross National Product.

The average hourly wage in manufacturing in 1967 amounted close to $2.40, with the number of hours worked per week slightly above 40 hours, on the basis of a five-day week, usually with two weeks' paid holidays and numerous other fringe benefits.

This then is the record of a century's achievement:

1. Canada's population increased sixfold.

2. Jobs increased by better than sevenfold.

3. Gross National Product in current dollars rose over 150 times and in real terms over 30 times.

4. Merchandise exports in current dollars rose over 200 times and in real terms over 40 times.

5. Gross value of manufacturing production in current dollar terms rose close to 250 times and in real terms about 50 times.

6. Employment in manufacturing increased more than tenfold.

States even though the development of Canadian industry in many sectors was considerably behind that of the United States. The American data are from Edward ATKINSON, "What Makes the Rate of Wages ?", in *Canadian Economics,* Proceedings of the Conference of the British Association for the Advancement of Science, held in Montreal in 1884, Montreal, Dawson Brothers, 1885, p. 279.
[10] The figures for 1967 are in the main estimates based on DOMINION BUREAU OF STATISTICS, *Canadian Statistical Review,* Vol. 41, No. 4, January 1968. (See also Table 1 in Appendix A.)

7. Output in real terms per man-year in manufacturing increased about five times.

8. Number of hours worked per week in manufacturing was reduced by two-fifths.

9. Average weekly earnings per person working in manufacturing industries in current dollar terms increased 21 times and in real terms about 4 times.

Or to put it differently: A Canadian working in manufacturing in 1867 would have earned 75¢ a day. By working six days a week, his total earnings would be $4.50. In 1967 his great-grandson would be earning about $19 a day for a weekly pay of $95, not counting overtime pay and numerous fringe benefits.

Over the last century the general price level in Canada has risen about fivefold. [11] This means that in 1967 the average Canadian working man had to earn $5 for every dollar his ancestor earned in 1867 to be able to buy the same quantity of goods and services — though, of course, he would have the benefit of a considerable improvement in the quality and variety of goods and services that have occurred over the last century. Allowing then for price changes, the average Canadian working in a factory in 1967 would have earnings 4 times those of his ancestor in 1867, not counting the fringe benefits, shorter hours of work, better working conditions and the higher quality of goods and services he would be able to buy with his earnings. Thus in terms of human satisfaction the average Canadian factory worker in 1967 would be considerably better off than can possibly be portrayed with crude statistics reflecting a century of economic progress.

Over half a century ago a senior Canadian civil servant wrote an economic treatise to lend substance to Sir Wilfrid Laurier's famous pronouncement that "the twentieth century would be the century of Canada". [12] This was the conclusion

[11] See Table 1 in Appendix A.
[12] Statement by the Right Hon. Sir Wilfrid Laurier, *House of Commons Debates*, Ottawa, February 21st, 1905, p. 1421. On another occasion, while speaking in Toronto, on October 14th, 1904, Sir Wilfrid Laurier made the same point but this time emphasizing the development aspect of Canadian economic growth: "The 20th century shall be the century of Canada and of Canadian development" (see *Canadian Annual Review of Public Affairs, 1904*, edited by J. Castell HOPKINS, Toronto, Annual Review Publications Company Ltd., 1905, p. 184).

offered: "There will be in Canada as in other industrial countries occasional years of depression when little progress will be made, but the development of the manufacturing industry will keep pace with the general growth of the country." [13]

As the record of achievement over the last century shows, this forecast was not optimistic enough. For Canada's industrial progress has been even more rapid than that of the economy as a whole with many of the material and human benefits widely spread across the country. But progress has been uneven and industrialization has proceeded in fits and starts.

As was pointed out in a study prepared for the Royal Commission on Canada's Economic Prospects:

> The growth of secondary industry has traditionally been greatest in periods when the Canadian economy has been expanding buoyantly. In peace time such periods of rapid expansion have typically been associated with the growth of our resource and export industries, with heavy derived investment, rising consumer incomes, and with large inflows of capital, skills, and manpower from abroad. In the complicated growth process which has occurred, the expansion of secondary industry of course has played a large part, but such growth appears [. . .] to have stemmed largely in the first instance from other sectors of the economy. [. . .] Nevertheless, the share of national output accounted for by secondary industry has increased in the long run because this sector has gained more than any other from the expansion of the Canadian economy. New secondary industries established at times of rapid growth as the 1900's, the 1920's and the Second World War have usually acquired the technical ability, capital, and skills necessary to survive more competitive conditions, so that when the market expanded further they were able to take full advantage of it. [14]

---

[13] Watson GRIFFIN, *Canada, the Country of the Twentieth Century*, Report to Sir George E. Foster, Minister of Trade and Commerce, Ottawa, November 1st, 1915, p. 207.
[14] D. H. FULLERTON and H. A. HAMPSON, *Canadian Secondary Manufacturing Industry*, Study prepared for the Royal Commission on Canada's Economic Prospects, Ottawa, Queen's Printer, May 1957, p. 163.

CHAPTER 2

Confederation and the Industrial Revolution

The Industrial Revolution in the late eighteenth century had made Great Britain a great industrial nation, with some other nations in Western Europe and the young United States in North America following her lead in the first half of the nineteenth century. The Industrial Revolution was founded on a combination of iron, steel and steam, requiring the availability of "large resources of coal and iron in reasonably close proximity to one another. The technology of production on which it was based required very great amounts of heat and power, and these could be supplied, in the quantities required and with the engineering and scientific knowledge then available, only by coal. Since coal was a weight-losing material, industrial processes using large quantities of coal tended to be located near the coal source, thus minimizing transportation costs." [1]

PRE-INDUSTRIAL PERIOD

In the middle of the nineteenth century Canada lacked the essential ingredients to benefit from the Industrial Revolution that made it possible for a number of nations to speed up their rate of economic growth and bring substantial material rewards to their people. The Canadian economy was in a "pre-industrial" period, "characterized by the use of wind, water, and animals as sources of energy and wood as the basic construction material, with economic activity located primarily close to food supplies." [2]

Thus Canada in the pre-Confederation period was largely a raw material exporting country, meeting just as many other undeveloped nations and colonial territories, the needs of a few industrialized nations, foremost Great Britain, for industrial raw materials and food stuffs.

The British preferential tariffs encouraged the four colonies in North America that were to become Canada, to exchange

---

[1] W. T. EASTERBROOK and Hugh G. J. AITKEN, *Canadian Economic History*, Toronto, Macmillan Company of Canada Limited, 1956, pp. 516 and 517.
[2] *Ibid.*, p. 517.

primary products for manufactured goods. Even if Canadians had known that they had all the resources needed to develop into an important industrial nation at that early stage in their history, the simple laws of economics would have made it clear to them that rapid industrialization at that time was premature in the light of the international trading pattern and market structure then prevailing. For the four colonies, Nova Scotia, New Brunswick, and the Canadas (Quebec and Ontario), though they had politically matured, were economically not ready to tackle the complex task of rapid industrialization, of the type undertaken by other more developed countries. The four colonies were isolated from each other. They lacked essential means of transportation and communication. They did not share in the manufacturing and technical knowledge and the managerial experience that had been built up and was being accumulated at a rapid pace in industrialized countries. They did not have the capital required to build up essential facilities or the foreign exchange to import the large quantities of machinery and equipment needed. And above all, they did not have an adequate incentive to develop their secondary industries on a broad scale.

Why should Canadians build up their secondary industries when they did well in selling raw materials and agricultural products abroad and when they were able to buy manufactured products from other countries more cheaply than they could produce themselves ?

WILL TO INDUSTRIALIZE

Thus the economic and political conditions, the state of knowledge of the arts and the attitude prevailing in Canada in the mid-nineteenth century mitigated against the industrial development of this country. But four things happened to change both the economic and political climate, and the will to industrialize.

The first was that as a raw material and food exporting nation, the Canadian economy was subject to the vagaries of substantial external fluctuations in demand and prices. Thus the four colonies were particularly vulnerable to changes in international trading conditions. The industrial structure of their country was such that they could take little compensatory action if threatened by rising unemployment and loss of income due to declining sales abroad.

The second was that the remaining British colonies in North America, which had grown to rely on the mercantile privileges supplied to them by British navigation laws and trade preferences, were suddenly faced with a major policy change. The adoption by the British of "free trade" policies meant the loss of many of the trade advantages that the North American colonies had enjoyed. Further, the British Government served notice to the colonies that with the assumption of responsible government they had to take on appropriate fiscal and defence responsibilities. These changes "marked the end of the sheltered world the colonies had known". [3]

The third was that relationships were changing between the North American colonies and the United States. Faced with declining exports overseas and with increased international competition, Canadians turned to the American market to sell increasing quantities of agricultural products and industrial materials. The conclusion of the Canada-United States Reciprocity Treaty of 1854 and the beginning of the Civil War in the United States in 1861 provided Canadians with increased opportunities for trading on a continental basis. Commercial interests began to look for greater markets southward rather than eastward and sales to the United States rose rapidly, more than offsetting the loss in overseas trade. But the solution of one problem was the beginning of another — too great an economic dependence on the United States. This became all too clear when the United States abrogated the Reciprocity Treaty in 1866. Moreover, the United States was emerging from the Civil War as one of the world's mighty nations — with the attributes of a young and vigorous nation including the urge for expansion. But Canadians wanted to maintain their political independence and concern was growing that "too close" economic relations might lead to absorption of the North American colonies by the United States.

The fourth was that Canadians began to realize the full implications of national development and political independence — the need to provide a strong economic base and to create an

---

[3] See *Report of the Royal Commission on Dominion-Provincial Relations, Canada: 1867-1939*, Book I, Ottawa, May 3, 1940, p. 20.

adequate government and institutional infra-structure. There was the further need to bring together individual regions with different economic and cultural aspirations into an integrated whole which only a nation could provide, with its network of transportation and communication facilities, its commercial and financial organization, its laws and currency, and the multitude of other government services that facilitate economic growth including the expansion of the domestic and foreign markets as well as opportunities for individual self expression and initiative.

Canadians found that relying on the St. Lawrence waterway and a system of canals, together with rough roads, was an inadequate base to build up secondary industries. For local industries were springing up in Canada in the pre-Confederation period, not so much because it was economic to establish such enterprises, but because it was uneconomic to transport many fabricated products over long distances using inadequate and time-consuming, hence rather costly, means of transportation. The challenge facing Canadians was to find ways and means to break down the barriers of terrain and geography and to make the wilderness both livable and accessible.

Gradually, Canadians became convinced that adequate transportation facilities were an essential link between newly established sources of production and expanding markets, and that without such improvements, Canada's industrial progress and economic development would be long delayed.

CHALLENGE OF CONFEDERATION

There were thus four lessons in basic economics which Canadians were learning in the days leading up to Confederation, representing challenges they would continue to face in the century that was to follow. These lessons and challenges provided a strong impetus to Canadians to industrialize their country, at times involving sacrifices by one generation so that the next generation could do better. These are the lessons:

1. Export trade of primary products is profitable but more vulnerable to changes in market conditions than domestic economic activity.

2. Trade agreements, reciprocity treaties, continental resource allocation and production sharing arrangements are all highly desirable instruments of international co-operation but

they are not substitutes for "old fashioned" nationalism when other countries for good reasons of their own find it necessary to change their economic policies and the terms of international agreements.

3. "Too" great reliance on economic relations with a single country — the United States — may bring many benefits but it also increases Canada's vulnerability. This was an early lesson in the realities of a continental approach to industrial and trade integration and the problems they brought. These problems were as real and topical in 1967 as they were in 1867 though their complexity and dimensions had increased manifold.

4. The development of secondary industries is a prerequisite to national economic development — as a source of expanding employment and real income, as a source of increasing economic strength, and as the basis for a nation to play its proper part in world affairs.

In the early years that followed the founding of Canada, politicians, businessmen, academicians and the public at large became aware of both the opportunities and the responsibilities that rested on the shoulders of their generation to lay the foundation for a strong and viable economy. And notably, there were the first utterings of the need of "planning wisely" long before economic planning became an accepted means for developing a national concensus for social goals and policy action in the 1950's and the 1960's. This can be illustrated by the following quotation taken from the Proceedings of the Conference of the British Association for the Advancement of Science, held in Montreal in 1884:

"We have a vast tract of unsettled territory of unsurpassed fertility, abounding in coals and other minerals. We are now laying the foundations of empire. Our actions to-day must affect the fate of millions. By planning wisely, before society is formed and crystallized, we may arrange its forces so that these antagonisms may be minimized. Our opportunity is grand." [4]

---

[4] W. A. DOUGLAS, "Harmonies and Antagonisms in the Social Forces", in *Canadian Economics, op. cit.,* p. 296.

CHAPTER 3

First Half Century

INDUSTRIAL TAKEOFF — HANDICAPS NOTWITHSTANDING

Economic considerations played an important part in bringing the four North American colonies together to form a new nation, Canada, in 1867. At the time of Confederation Canada's population numbered 3.5 million and the country produced a total of goods and services valued in the order of $400 million. [1]

Most of the people were drawing their livelihood from working in primary industries, mainly agriculture, which provided jobs for about three-quarters of Canada's labour force. About 16 per cent were working in what may be described as rather simple fabricating activities, catering largely to local markets and drawing on native raw materials, mainly lumber. Secondary industries of some significance at the time of Confederation included: shipbuilding, agricultural implements, furniture and the making of matches, flour milling, machinery and tools, woollens, boot and shoe factories, sugar factories, salt works, breweries and distilleries. These industries contributed in total about 20 per cent to the national income of the nation at the time of Confederation. [2]

Canadians had embarked on Confederation full of great hopes and expectations of building a great nation occupying half a continent, with a comprehensive transportation network moulding the country into an integrated economic unit and creating a rapidly expanding domestic market for the new industries that were expected to spring up to meet the requirements of a growing and more prosperous population living increasingly in urban communities.

Economic conditions were in fact favourable in Canada between 1867 and 1873 and work was commenced to build up a national railway system linking the scattered cities and

---

[1] Estimates range between $365 million and $419 million (see Table 1 in Appendix A and Appendix B).
[2] *Canada's Economic Development, 1867-1953, op. cit.*, p. 204.

settlements representing pockets of economic activity in a vast country spanning a continent. But by the end of 1873, the boom broke and a depression followed, worldwide in its ramifications. In the United States, it involved a sharp reduction in railway and building construction. In Great Britain, a severe contraction of credit and a steep decline in foreign trade was experienced. Falling commodity prices and curtailment of international lending brought an abrupt check to economic expansion in new countries. In Canada, the first effect of this general depression was a decline in the demand for lumber. Between 1873 and 1879, exports of forest products fell by one-half. The prices of manufactured goods fell more rapidly than those of agricultural products but by 1876 the country was generally enveloped in a depression which grew gradually worse until 1879. In the latter year, both the price level and the physical volume of exports had fallen by 20 per cent from the peak of 1873. [3]

GREAT DEPRESSION

In general, the three main factors affecting Canadian economic growth and industrialization during the period of the great depression were: (1) a persistent decline in international prices that reduced considerably the proceeds from Canadian exports; (2) a significant drop in international lending which aggravated the existing shortage of capital even further; and (3) a low level of investment in most sectors (with some exceptions, e.g. railway building) as business had little incentive to expand capital facilities in view of uncertain market prospects and unsettled economic conditions.

The manufacturing industries which had progressed during the expansion phase to 1873, shared in the great depression that followed. It lasted 23 years, with some temporary improvement around 1882 and 1883, [4] with a definite economic upturn not taking place until after 1895.

---

[3] *Report of the Royal Commission on Dominion-Provincial Relations, Canada : 1867-1939, op. cit.*, pp. 49 and 50.

[4] Gordon W. BERTRAM, "Historical Statistics on Growth and Structure in Manufacturing in Canada, 1870-1957", in *Canadian Political Science Association Conference on Statistics* 1962 and 1963, Papers edited by J. HENRIPIN and A. ASIMAKOPULOS, University of Toronto Press, 1964, p. 132.

"RECIPROCITY OF TARIFFS"

As the depression continued, the agitation for increased protection of Canadian secondary industries grew. Tariff levels of manufactured products had been comparatively low in Canada between 1867 and 1878. Canada had begun to rely more and more on exports to the United States. The choice that Canadians now faced was either to obtain greater access to that market or to pursue a more nationalistic policy and to develop their industries to cater to the domestic market, protected increasingly from competition of products imported. Canadians were aware that the former policy choice would bring greater long term benefits to their country because they would enjoy the benefits of international specialization and that the latter policy choice would slow down the rate of economic growth and would bring repercussions in the United States.

An election was fought in Canada in 1878 on the issue "Reciprocity of Trade or Reciprocity of Tariffs". This was one of the deciding issues of the Conservative victory in that year. Trade negotiations ensued for the reciprocal removal of tariffs on industrial products between Canada and the United States, but to no avail.

In 1879, the Canadian Government embarked on a policy of vigorous tariff protection designed to foster Canadian industrial development on a broad scale. The policy which was to transform the economy and make a great nation was impressively labelled "The National Policy". [5] This policy continued in existence until 1896 when, with a change to a Liberal Government, the great tariff wall that had been built up, was gradually dismantled.

PROGRESS IN THE MIDST OF ADVERSITY

The industrial development of Canada covering the first 33 years as a nation can be summarized in these terms:

1. Industrial development had an auspicious beginning in the first six years after Confederation and it proceeded again at a rapid pace towards the end of the nineteenth century as the international economic climate improved and domestic employ-

---

[5] *Report of the Royal Commission on Dominion-Provincial Relations, Canada: 1867-1939, op. cit.*, p. 51.

ment and income conditions became more favourable. But during most of the period, Canadian manufacturing industries faced an uphill struggle, shrinking foreign markets, slow growth of the domestic market, little foreign capital to bolster meagre Canadian savings, and insufficient industrial diversification and expansion of scale of operations to enable industry to achieve significant increases in productivity.

2.   Notwithstanding these handicaps, Canadian manufacturers were able to make remarkable progress drawing on their native skill and sheer persistence. Typical of the manner in which Canadians overcame the problem of shortage of capital to speed up the process of industrialization was this comment of a prospering manufacturer: " 'There isn't a manufacturer of us all', declared one of the most successful pioneers in the flourishing agricultural implement industry in 1876, 'who hasn't come up from five dollars.' " [6]

3.   Here is a record of some of the achievements between 1867 and 1900:

(a) Number of persons employed in manufacturing rose from about 170,000 to 443,000, or by 161 per cent.

(b) Gross value of manufacturing rose from approximately $170 million to $556 million, about 3½ times. Since the general price level in 1900 was about the same as that prevailing in 1867 [7] this increase also reflects in approximate terms the growth in the volume of manufacturing production.

(c) Net value of manufacturing output rose from about $85 million to $245 million, representing in 1900 close to one-quarter of the Gross National Product estimated at about $1 billion.

(d) Productivity in terms of output per man-year rose by better than 25 per cent over this period, with an even more significant increase indicated in terms of output per man-hour since hours of work per week in manufacturing had declined by about one hour per day or by more than 10 per cent.

---

[6]   Quoted in "General Economic History 1867-1912", *op. cit.*, p. 123.
[7]   See Table 1 in Appendix A.

(e) Exports of partially and fully manufactured products had risen from about $34 million to close to $100 million or three times what they had been at Confederation.

BROADENING THE INDUSTRIAL BASE

After 1896 and particularly following the turn of the century, manufacturing expanded in most of the important categories: the provision of capital equipment, consumer goods of general consumption and the processing of natural products for export. The program of railway construction, the growth of cities and towns, the equipping of western farms and the extension of community facilities in both east and west gave a great impetus to the production of capital goods. The iron and steel industry particularly made rapid progress. [8]

The period after 1900 has been described as one encompassing the most vigorous industrial growth in the country's history. The ventures of the previous thirty odd years were little more than experiments and beginnings, not major achievements. The era of growing strength and diversification came with the twentieth century. A few industries lagged behind and failed to fulfil their promise. The majority entered on a career of continued and quickened expansion. A steadily enlarging home market — thanks to the thousands of immigrants who moved into the farm lands of the West — combined with a flow of capital from the investors of Europe and the United States maintained expansion on a stable basis, although the evils of a "boom" were too often evident. New mining discoveries brought increasing processing to Canada particularly as a result of important finds of non-ferrous metals and iron ore in Ontario early in the new century.

There was further industrial development drawing on forest resources, with governments taking increasing interest in the conservation of forests and their greater economic use. Wood-pulp and paper production can claim the record among Canadian manufactures for phenomenal growth. In the census of 1871 pulp mills were not mentioned. In 1881 five mills were reported, employing sixty-eight men. Manufacturing

---

[8] *Report of the Royal Commission on Dominion-Provincial Relations, Canada: 1867-1939, op. cit.*, pp. 73 and 74.

then began to grow, but the increase was modest until the twentieth century. Then it quickly passed its older competitors, until at the end of World War I it ranked among the first two or three dominant manufacturing industries in the country.

While no other manufacturing sector showed such impressive development as the pulp and paper industry, many other sectors grew at a rapid rate. The expansion was particularly evident in industries not far removed from the extractive stage, with ample natural resources to give them an advantage over foreign competitors. In these industries the Canadian producer won a dominance at home, and became a prominent exporter to world markets. Old and vigorous industries that had developed as a direct consequence of expansion in agriculture were flour milling and meat slaughtering. Milling kept pace with the expansion of wheat acreage.

The textile industry also made progress though some sectors did better than others, e.g. cotton manufacturing expanded while the production of woollens faced difficulties because of British competition. Other industries that made significant progress during this period included farm implements, rubber, chemicals using domestic mineral products, automobiles, and last but not least an industry that was to give great impetus to further development of Canadian manufacturing in the future — the generation of hydro-electric power which for Canada was destined to play as great a role in the economic development of the country as coal did in an earlier stage of economic development in Great Britain.

The period between 1900 and 1914 when World War I broke out and again after the end of the war until about 1924, witnessed a profound change in the size of the business unit. The process of consolidation was at work and reached its climax in the four years 1909-12, when 58 consolidations embracing 275 firms took place. The principal industries affected were pulp and paper, lumber, machinery, iron and steel, milling, canning, breweries, footwear, bread, jewellery and meat packing.

Foreign capital played an increasing role in aiding the industrial and general economic development of Canada during that period. Capital from Great Britain going largely into industrial and mining developments in Canada during 1900-14 has been estimated at $300 million. During the same period between $600 million and $700 million came from the United States for direct investment largely in Canadian industries. [9]

The following data covering the decade 1900 to 1910 illustrate some of the magnitude of the growth of Canadian manufacturing industries during this period of great broadening and increasing diversification.

1. Persons employed in manufacturing numbering 443,000 rose to 510,000 or by 15 per cent.

2. Gross value of manufacturing production rose from $556 million to $1,152 million, involving a better than doubling in value terms and a two-thirds increase in volume terms.

3. Net value of manufacturing production rose from $245 million to $550 million, equivalent to 26 per cent of the Gross National Product estimated at $2.1 billion for 1910.

4. Productivity in manufacturing in terms of output per man-year rose by better than 40 per cent, the greatest productivity increase achieved in a century of industrial development in Canada.

5. Exports of partially and fully manufactured products rose from approximately $100 million to $136 million or by about one-third, indicating that most of Canada's industrial development was based on serving increasingly the rapidly growing domestic market, with total sales of manufactured products more than doubling over this period.

WORLD WAR I

The outbreak of World War I found Canada in a deepening recession. Unemployment was rising, exports were declining and industrial capacity was increasingly unused. But the threat of the recession becoming a serious depression faded quickly as military requirements for men and materials brought new demands that could only be met by making more effective

---

[9] A. BRADY, "Industrial Development", in *Cambridge History of the British Empire*, Vol. VI, *Canada and Newfoundland*, edited by J. Holland ROSE, A. P. NEWTON, and E. A. BENIANS, Cambridge University Press, 1930, pp. 608-624.

and fuller use of human resources and creating additional industrial and agricultural productive capacity.

The decline in exports from Europe and the high cost of shipping enabled Canadian manufacturers to obtain a larger share of the home market. Although the munition orders which came from overseas were but a temporary factor, they had important long-run effects. The demands imposed and the facilities required to meet them resulted in a considerable increase in technical and mechanical efficiency. The demand for munitions produced also a much needed diversification, particularly in the iron and steel industry which had been highly specialized to meet the requirements of railway building and heavy construction. [10]

The capacity of the steel industry, essential to Canada's broadening industrial base, was nearly doubled, from 1¼ million ingot tons in 1914 to 2¼ million tons of ingot in 1919. In fact, the level reached after World War I was so high that little further change occurred in steel capacity until the outbreak of World War II.

Other manufacturing industries newly created or greatly expanded during World War I were the aircraft and shipbuilding industries. From a modest beginning in 1917 the aircraft industry in the course of two years turned out some 3,000 training aircraft for British and Canadian forces. Shipyards were greatly expanded and produced close to one hundred ships, half the number of steel and the other half of wood, the total tonnage being about 350,000 dead weight tons. Plant facilities and equipment were expanded and managerial and technical knowledge acquired which enabled most industries in the post-World War I period to undertake more diversified, integrated, and efficient operations than they had previously been able to perform. [11]

When World War I came to an end, the Canadian manufacturing industry employed some 586,000 men on a year-round basis, turning out a gross value of production estimated at $3.2 billion. The net value added amounted to about $1.3 billion

---

[10] See *Report of the Royal Commission on Dominion-Provincial Relations, Canada: 1867-1939, op. cit.*, p. 108.
[11] *Canada's Economic Development, 1867-1953, op. cit.*, p. 211.

equivalent to over 25 per cent of the Gross National Product of that year.

The gross value of manufacturing production in 1918 was about 2½ times of what it had been in 1914. But since prices had risen considerably, the increase in real terms was about one-third. But what was even more important than expanding the volume of output was the significant growth in skills and managerial experience that Canadians had been able to acquire as they expanded manufacturing production under the pressure of a major military effort. The other important benefit was the new confidence that was to stand Canadians in good stead as they strove to build a much stronger and more competitive industrial structure in the period that followed the end of World War I.

In a typical Canadian fashion, adversity had been turned into achievement. And as the Royal Commission on Dominion-Provincial Relations put it so aptly: "The Canadian manufacturing industry emerged from the War with a more dominant place in the domestic market, with an enlarged productive capacity, and with much improved and diversified facilities." [12]

---

[12] *Report of the Royal Commission on Dominion-Provincial Relations, Canada: 1867-1939, op. cit.,* p. 108.

CHAPTER 4

Second Half Century

INTERWAR PERIOD

Except for the sharp recession that followed the end of World War I in 1920, the outlook for economic growth and further industrial development appeared to be encouraging. One of the dramatic changes contributing to rapid expansion and further diversification of Canadian manufacturing industries was the realization on the part of American industry that the Canadian market had grown sufficiently to make it economically feasible and financially attractive to set up a number of branch plants in this country to serve this market, and in a number of instances, those foreign markets which could be reached more advantageously from Canadian sources of supply, particularly other Commonwealth countries which accorded Canada preferential tariffs.

Many millions of dollars poured into Canada in the 1920's to build up the motor car industry, the metal processing and fabrication industries, the chemical industries, and the electrical equipment and machinery industries.

Other industries undergoing rapid expansion in Canada, somewhat dependent on foreign capital, were the pulp and paper industries and the non-metallic product industry (largely needed to cater to the building boom of the late 1920's) and the farm implement industry.

Industrial expansion in Canada was so rapid that manufacturing investment in volume terms reached a peak level in 1929 which was not matched by anything that had happened before or that was to happen in the next decade and a half, encompassing the period of World War II and the years of immediate post-war reconstruction following the end of the war. [1]

Close to 100,000 additional jobs opened up in manufacturing industries offering workers wages higher than they

---

[1] *Private and Public Investment in Canada, 1926-1951, op. cit.,* pp. 36 and 150.

could earn in most other sectors of the economy. Total employment in secondary industries reached 666,000 in 1929, a level not reached again until Canada was fully engaged in the major industrial effort required by the exigencies of World War II.

By 1929 Canadian manufacturing industries turned out a great variety of processed materials and fabricated products never produced before. Gross value of production approached the $4 billion mark, greater by about one-quarter in value and over one-half in volume terms as compared with the level shortly after World War I.

But then, late in 1929 came the crash followed by the great depression. Canadian manufacturing industries became one of its casualties. In the short space of four years the industry laid off some 200,000 men. One out of three men, most of them skilled, and with family responsibilities, joined the ranks of the unemployed, the hopeful and the discouraged, lining up in front of soup kitchens or in the offices of welfare agencies, both government and private. Many of the remaining two out of three men who kept their jobs were working part-time and drawing low wages, barely enough to eke out a modest living.

The output of manufacturing declined to $1.9 billion by 1933, representing a drop of one-half in value terms and one-third in volume terms. Many factories closed their doors while others kept on going not knowing how long they could keep on losing money or when their bankers or other creditors would force them into bankruptcy.

The Canadian Government tried desperately to deal with the difficult situation which manufacturing industries were facing, and with them the whole economy and the people. Slowly, commencing with 1934, the economic situation started to improve, little by little, partly as a result of a more favourable external economic environment, as world trade took a turn for the better, and partly because levels of employment, income, and living standards had dropped so low that economic conditions could not get much worse. Business had cut back investment to such reduced levels, structures, and equipment had deteriorated to such an extent that additional capital expenditures were called for if business was to continue to operate. Thus the base was laid for some improvement in economic conditions that was gradually to lead the Canadian economy out of the depression.

While government economic policies were not as effective as their framers had wished — and some of the beneficial results of measures taken by the Federal Government were nullified by economic policies pursued by provincial governments moving in the opposite direction — they did contribute to some stabilization of economic conditions and to a gradual return of confidence on the part of the business community and individuals.

Capital expenditures started to rise, and so did exports. Jobs became more plentiful and wages and salaries began to climb upward. Demand for manufactured products expanded and factory owners were only too happy to oblige and to produce increasing quantities of manufactured goods.

When World War II started, the Canadian manufacturing industry had almost recovered the ground it had lost in the preceding decade though it was still operating significantly below capacity. By 1939, some 658,000 Canadians had factory jobs, and manufacturing output was valued at $3.5 billion.

American participation in Canadian industrial development had only been partially slowed down during the depressed 30's. With the introduction of the British Empire Preferential System in 1932, it became increasingly advantageous for American manufacturers to serve markets within the British Commonwealth (it was the British "Empire" then) from their Canadian subsidiaries. Thus they proceeded to build up those Canadian subsidiaries and establish new ones to serve those markets of the world where trade from British countries was preferred. For it mattered little to American firms whether they made their money in the United States or in their subsidiaries operating in Canada, as long as they made money. And by selling from Canada, American industries continued to be competitive in many markets, overcoming the hurdles of rising tariff walls, so typical of the "beggar-thy-neighbour" trade policies that beset the irrational international community of the 1930's.

World War II

World War II hit the North American continent with unexpected force — Canada being drawn into the conflict long before the United States and with both countries being wholly unprepared militarily, economically and industrially. Pearl Harbor represented a heavy blow to American pride. But it also aroused the wrath of an economic giant who did not know his own strength. Intensive industrial integration followed on a continental scale, with Canada and United States working more closely together than at any time in the history of these two countries.

With Western Europe overrun by Nazi hordes, with the United Kingdom reeling under the destructive onslaught of continuing air raids, and with the U.S.S.R. being pushed further and further towards the east and losing most of her industrial regions to the victorious German armies, North America became the economic and industrial bastion of the free world.

Under the direction of governments, Canadian and American industry developed production sharing arrangements, accompanied by a substantial exchange of research information and technical and managerial know-how.

Canadian and U.S. co-operation and intensive dedication, made it possible for industry to adapt itself readily to the requirements of becoming the arsenal of democracy. Conversion to a full war-time industrial production footing was accomplished in Canada in a comparatively short period of time.

Expansion of productive capacity in manufacturing was particularly striking in such fields as tool making, electrical apparatus, chemicals, steel, aluminum and other non-ferrous metals. New factories were built, shipyards constructed and armament assembly lines installed. Entire new industries were created, for example making roller bearings, magnesium and some synthetic rubber. Many existing industries underwent marked expansion. Some industries with relatively small employment before the war attained such a large wartime employment that the process amounted to the creation of a new industry rather than the expansion of an old one. Examples are aircraft production and shipbuilding. Advances were made in the production of finished goods and equipment, some of which were of a type new to Canadian industry and which had previously been imported, such as optical glass, high octane gasoline, penicillin and sulfa drugs. [2] At the height of the industrial war effort in 1943, about three out of every five persons employed in Canadian manufacturing industries worked on war orders.

Adaptation of manufacturing industries to meet military demands during World War II required still greater diversification and increased skill and technical knowledge, more complex machinery and more closely integrated processes than anything that had previously been known in Canada. Thus simple figures of expansion in terms of capacity and output do not tell the full story of the change which Canadian manufacturing industries underwent in the six-year period. But even in purely statistical terms the growth was remarkable. Between 1939 and the war peak reached between 1942 and 1945, output of steel increased by approximately 120 per cent and of aluminum by about 500 per cent. Entirely new developments included the production of synthetic rubber, commencing with an annual output of 3,000 tons in 1943 and rising to 45,000 tons in 1945.

Fully fabricated war equipment and munitions were also turned out in large volume. From 1939 to 1945 some 816,000 mechanized transport vehicles were produced in addition to over 50,000 armoured fighting vehicles. Canadian shipyards in the same period built over 4,000 naval ships and approximately 400 ocean-going merchant vessels, the latter involving some 3.7 million dead weight tons, in addition to substantial ship conversion and repair work. The aircraft industry produced in the same period over 16,000 military aircraft. The chemical industry turned out some 3 billion pounds of chemicals and one billion pounds of explosives. This tremendous output of munitions and war equipment, valued at about $10 billion, was used only in part by Canadian forces, with the larger proportion, about 70 per cent, being made available to Allied forces. [3]

The creation of this wartime industrial structure absorbed substantial resources of the country. Between September 1939 and August 1945, new business investment in buildings, structures, machinery and equipment, is estimated to have exceeded $4.5 billion, of which some $3.5 billion were either directly

[2] DEPARTMENT OF RECONSTRUCTION AND SUPPLY, *Encouragement to Industrial Expansion in Canada, Operation of Special Depreciation Provisions, November 10, 1944 - March 31, 1949*, Ottawa, 1948, p. 13.
[3] See *Private and Public Investment in Canada, 1926-1951*, op. cit., pp. 36 and 37.

or indirectly associated with the war effort. A substantial portion of this investment program was either financed or encouraged by Government. Up to V-J Day, the Canadian Government spent more than $700 million on industrial plant expansion of which about 75 per cent comprised wholly owned Crown companies and the remainder war equipment and installations added to private industrial plants. In addition, the Canadian Government, through a variety of fiscal measures, encouraged private industry to spend an extra $1 billion on plant expansion serving military purposes.

At the peak of the war effort in the fall of 1943, persons engaged directly or indirectly in war work, mainly in industry, numbered 1.2 million declining to about 600,000 when the war ended on August 14, 1945. [4] During that year manufacturing industries employed over 1.1 million people, about 70 per cent more than had been working in secondary industry in 1939. The gross value of manufacturing output in 1945 amounted to $8.2 billion, about two and one-third in value terms and about one and three-quarters in volume terms of what the industry had produced in 1939, involving a much greater variety and technically more complex fabricated items, comparable in quality in most instances with the best produced in the United States.

The two most remarkable achievements of the Canadian industry during World War II were its ability to: (1) convert fairly quickly from a peacetime to a wartime footing, capable of producing the most complex military hardware and equipment required; and (2) increase productivity even under the stress of great war pressures to such heights that it could provide very large quantities of munitions and supplies to Canada's own armed forces and those of her allies while at the same time providing enough goods for civilian consumption so that Canadians at the end of the war actually enjoyed a higher standard of living than they did at the beginning of the war. [5]

POSTWAR RECONSTRUCTION

When World War II ended, there existed in Canada a widespread concern about the future — the possibility of rising

---

[4]   *Encouragement to Industrial Expansion in Canada, op. cit.,* p. 13.
[5]   *Ibid.,* p. 14.

levels of unemployment and economic adversity of the type experienced after World War I and in the 1930's.

But instead, Canadians achieved the task of converting their wartime industrial structure to one geared to meet rising civilian demand with remarkable alacrity and comparatively little dislocation. Instead of experiencing significant increases in unemployment, the Canadian economy faced substantial demands for most of the goods and services it could produce and the problem was one of inflation rather than one of recession. The conversion to a peacetime footing was fully completed by the end of 1947 and Canadian industry was ready to tackle its next task — to push back new technological and economic frontiers.

New Resources Impetus

Two developments gave a further spurt to manufacturing expansion in Canada from 1950 onward.

First, the intensive search for new supplies of minerals and other natural resources after the end of World War II brought a number of important discoveries. Rapid development followed in crude oil, natural gas, iron ore, non-ferrous metals, and a number of minor metals. New resources development and the resulting need for equipment for exploration and development gave a major impetus to capital goods producing industries.

Further, the greater quantity and variety of indigenous raw materials led to the creation of greater processing capacity and new raw material and power using industries. Foremost among them was the chemical industry, which became increasingly diversified. Major discoveries of oil and natural gas in Alberta made the establishment of such industries in this region feasible despite the distance to the principal markets. Another factor, of course, was the rapid economic expansion of the West, creating new demand for manufactured products including those being produced for the first time. Thus, the handicap of great distance from production to markets which industries in the Prairie Region had hitherto experienced, gradually diminished in importance.

Korean War and Adjustment

Secondly, the outbreak of the war in Korea in mid-1950 led to the establishment of a three-year defence program of some $5 billion. Three industries in particular received great stimulus from the rearmament program: the aircraft industry, which produced for the first time jet aircraft as well as engines for jet aircraft; the electronics industry, which produced a variety of new items, from radar equipment to one-mile infantry pack radio sets which were supplied in increasing quantities to the United States and other NATO members; and the shipbuilding industry, which revived after several years of decline following the end of World War II and drew increasingly on equipment-producing industries to outfit, power, and arm the new naval vessels.

Manufacturing industries that had expanded because of the rearmament program proved adaptable to many civilian uses. The outstanding example is the comparative ease with which a television industry was established. This industry assumed increasing importance toward the end of 1952 as progress was being made toward the establishment of a national television network, later to be supplemented by a number of private television stations across the country. [6] Thus, industrial adjustment was less difficult than it had been after the preceding two periods of heavy ammunition and military equipment production, 1914-18 and 1939-45. [7]

Reconstruction and conversion of secondary industries following the end of World War II had taken 2½ years. This period was followed by a decade of continued economic growth, only temporarily interrupted by two recessions of comparatively short duration and minor in terms of economic dislocation, 1948-49 and 1953-54. By and large the period 1945 to 1957 was one of steady economic progress accompanied by high levels of employment, income and industrial development.

In fact, Canada's manufacturing industries continued to expand more rapidly than the economy as a whole, both in

---

[6] From a modest beginning of $0.5 million spent on television advertising expenditures in 1952, such spending rose to an amount in excess of $100 million in 1967.   For an assessment of the growth of the television industry in Canada, see O. J. FIRESTONE, *Broadcast Advertising in Canada, Past and Future Growth*, Ottawa, University of Ottawa Press, 1966, particularly Chapters 3 and 6.
[7] *Canada's Economic Development, 1867-1953*, op. cit., pp. 215-217.

terms of its contribution to national income and in terms of employment as the following data indicate: [8]

| | EMPLOYMENT | | GROSS DOMESTIC PRODUCT AT FACTOR COST | |
	Total [9] Thous.	Manufacturing Thous.	Total $ Mill.	Manufacturing $ Mill.
1945 [10]	5,183	1,118	10,804	2,960
1957 [10]	5,891	1,359	28,455	7,904
Per Cent Increase	13.6	21.6	163.4	167.0

SLOWDOWN IN ECONOMIC GROWTH

The next four years, 1957 to 1961, were a period of slow growth with Canada's labour force expanding more rapidly than employment opportunities and this country experiencing higher levels of unemployment than at any time since the depressed 1930's. What aggravated a difficult economic situation even further, were large balance of payments deficits, greater than anything Canada had ever seen before, leading to an exchange crisis followed by devaluation of the Canadian dollar in mid-1962.

Growing unemployment and substantial increases in imports affected adversely Canada's manufacturing industry. Some plants closed down and others went on part-week production schedules. Those industries that continued to operate on a regular basis cut back their expansion plans and growth of the manufacturing sector as a whole slowed down to a crawl. In fact employment in secondary industries declined between 1957 and 1961 by 6 per cent while the general employment level rose by almost as much. Still Canada had on an average 466,000 persons unemployed in 1961, equivalent to 7.1 per cent of the labour force. Gross Domestic Product in manufacturing rose by 8 per cent over the same period below the rate of increase in total Gross Domestic Product, 17 per cent (see below):

---

[8] Based on DOMINION BUREAU OF STATISTICS, *National Accounts, Income and Expenditure, 1962* and earlier issues, and *id., Labour Force,* supplement to the March 1965 issue.
[9] Covers civilian employment and persons in the armed forces.
[10] Excludes Newfoundland in 1945 and includes Newfoundland in 1957.

| | EMPLOYMENT | | GROSS DOMESTIC PRODUCT AT FACTOR COST [11] | |
	Total [12] *Thous.*	*Index of Manufacturing Employment* [13]	*Total $ Mill.*	*Manufacturing $ Mill.*
1957	5,731	115.8	28,455	7,904
1961	6,055	108.9	33,351	8,501
Per Cent Change	5.7	—6.0	17.2	7.6

STRONG EXPANSION AGAIN

After reaching a low point in the downswing phase of the business cycle in February, 1961, [14] the Canadian economy resumed its upward course again. Strong expansionist forces came into play, largely the result of heavy capital spending by business and rising export trade, supported by increased consumer and government demand for goods and services. Rapid economic growth followed bringing to Canada the longest expansion phase in peacetime history, six years in a row with further growth indicated for the years following Canada's first centenary celebration. [15]

Accompanying this rapid growth in the economy as a whole, and in fact contributing substantially to it, was the significant increase in manufacturing activity. Employment in secondary industries rose between 1961 and 1967 by about one-third and gross value of production by approximately one-half. During this six-year period, manufacturing industries had reestablished their role as a dynamic factor in Canadian economic growth.

---

[11] DOMINION BUREAU OF STATISTICS, *National Accounts, Income and Expenditure, 1964,* and earlier issues, Ottawa, 1965.

[12] Covers civilian employment. The data are from DOMINION BUREAU OF STATISTICS, *Labour Force,* supplement to the March 1966 issue.

[13] The index of manufacturing employment is used because changes in classification adopted by the Dominion Bureau of Statistics in 1960 make the absolute level of manufacturing employment not comparable over the period 1957 to 1961. The base of the index is 1949 = 100. The data are from DOMINION BUREAU OF STATISTICS, *Employment and Payrolls,* Ottawa, 1961.

[14] The period 1957 to 1961 includes two recessionary downswings, 1957-58 and 1960-61.

[15] The rate of growth of the Gross National Product in real terms slowed down as the period of expansion proceeded apace, 6½ per cent in 1962 over 1961, as compared with about 2½ per cent in 1967 over 1966 (see Table 1, Appendix A).

CHAPTER 5

International Orientation and Competition

DEGREE OF MANUFACTURING

With the consolidation of the gains made during World War I and with the broadening of its base and greater diversification, Canadian manufacturing industries had come of age in the 1920's. No more did they feel dependent primarily on meeting local and regional needs, or required to rely on the forced pace of providing supplies serving military efforts. Manufacturers began to look increasingly to international markets to sell their products. Their efforts were rewarded and such industries as the pulp and paper industry and farm implement manufacturers became leading exporters of fully manufactured products.

As a result, Canadian industries which up to World War I had relied on exporting less than 10 per cent of the value of their output, in most years of the nineteen twenties, about doubled this proportion. In 1920, some 17 per cent and in 1930 about 15 per cent of total Canadian manufacturing production was exported, notwithstanding in the latter year the beginning of the "great depression" and a falling of exports.

During the 1920's, fully and chiefly manufactured products comprised between 40 per cent and 50 per cent of total exports, as against between 30 per cent and 40 per cent in earlier decades, with this important difference: that now fully or chiefly manufactured products exported involved a much greater degree of processing and fabrication than had been the case during the first half of century of Canada's industrialization.

During the 1930's, the proportion of Canadian manufactured products exported dropped substantially, as foreign markets shrank even more substantially than the domestic market. Even by 1939 when the threat of war early in the year and actual hostilities in the autumn gave new impetus to Canadian industry in selling more of its products abroad, fully or chiefly manufactured items comprised only about 11½ per cent of the value of total domestic production, equivalent to 43 per cent of total exports.

World War II, of course, pushed the exports of manu-factured products to new peak levels, as Canadian industry supplied large quantities of munitions and military and civilian supplies and equipment to its Allies and other friendly trading nations. This heavy flow subsided as the war came to a close. Still, even in 1945, the proportion of manufactured products to the total value of domestic production was 22 per cent and that of commodity exports, 55 per cent.

INCREASING COMPETITION

But the pattern changed considerably after World War II. Initially Canada continued to export large quantities of manu-factured products, helping the war devastated countries of Europe in their post-war reconstruction and supplying other countries with capital goods and production materials in short supply on a world-wide basis. Within the short space of five years most of the nations had recovered from the ravages of the war. They resumed again their position as important industrial and trading nations, particularly countries in Western Europe and Japan. Hence, Canadian secondary industries which had not felt strong international competition for over a decade had to adjust themselves to a new international trading climate. International division of labour, low cost of production, high quality, early delivery dates, adequate financing and proper servicing became the basis of building up international trade in manufactured products.

While Canada was facing growing difficulties in the changing international economic environment, good fortune offered new opportunities for Canadian industry to penetrate world markets. Important resource discoveries, crude oil and natural gas, iron ore, non-ferrous metals and non-metallic minerals, accompanied by a strong push forward in developing Canada's pulp and paper industry, all contributed to raising materially Canada's exports to world markets. Sales of wheat and flour overseas expanded by leaps and bounds and com-munist countries became Canada's best customers for cereals. Canadian exports to the United States including both raw and processed materials rose rapidly, partly because of the growing dependence of the U.S. economy on basic materials from abroad, and partly because of a deliberate effort of making more effect-ive use of natural sources available in North America on a continental scale, e.g. the increasing flow of Canadian crude oil to the Pacific and North Western United States, as part of a national oil policy.

The domestic market for manufactured products during most of the post-war period grew rapidly, at least until 1957, slowing down somewhat between 1957 and 1961, only to resume its vigorous upward trend again and continuing unabated — though at varying rates — to 1967.

CHANGING POSITION IN WORLD MARKETS

With the world clamouring more for Canada's natural resource materials and for food stuffs, and with the international tariff system continuing to encourage the importation of materials in raw or processed form rather than in fabricated form, Canadian manufacturing industries had to face a situation which they had not experienced for half a century.

During the late 1940's and the 1950's, Canadian manufacturing industries had again found it necessary to rely on the Canadian market for more than 90 per cent of their production, with exports of fully manufactured products comprising less than 10 per cent of total output, dropping in some years to as low as 7 per cent. The proportion of manufactured products to total commodity exports which had been up to 50 per cent during the 1920's, and around 55 per cent at the end of World War II, dropped to a range between 35 per cent and 40 per cent in the period up to 1960.

As the thoughts of Canadians turned to their first centenary, Canadian manufacturing industries in the 1960's began to realize that they had been losing ground in world markets, as far as the exportation of fully manufactured products was concerned. Not that this was anything new, for Canadian manufacturers had already encountered increasing international competition during the preceding decade. But what was new, was the realization that unless industry could put its house in order, increase productivity, lower costs and acquire expanding markets both at home and abroad, it was destined to stagnate and to fall behind the development and progress made by manufacturing industries in most other industrialized countries in the world. Further, successive conservative and liberal governments made it clear to Canadian industry that it could not rely on government to bail industry out by obtaining increased protection on a significant scale. Canada had embarked with other nations on efforts towards dismantling trade barriers on a gradual but ever widening scale, with the objective of encouraging increased international division of labour. In this changing international environment and policy climate, Canadian industry had to adjust itself and compete effectively with the industries of other countries or bear the consequences of declining sales and business losses.

RESPONSE TO POSTWAR CHALLENGES

The 1950's and the early 1960's were characterized by Canadian industry continuing to lose ground in international trade, particularly serious since world demand for industrial products expanded by leaps and bounds, with many of Canada's foreign competitors gaining increasing access to global markets for manufactured products, both in absolute terms and in terms of the share of the market.

Here was Canada, a country that could claim to be among the eight leading industrialized nations of the world, in terms of absolute value of its manufacturing operations, and among the first four nations on the basis of value of manufacturing output per capita, losing ground steadily as an industrialized nation in comparison with other countries.

Was it due to Canadian industry being content to cater mainly to the domestic market where competition was less fierce ? Was it due to the Canadian dollar being overvalued making it difficult for Canadian manufacturers to hold their own in international markets ? Was it due to a failure of Canadian trade negotiators to obtain adequate trade concessions from the main markets of the world on a quid-pro-quo basis ? Was it due to Canadian manufacturing industry not keeping pace with the technological, scientific and managerial progress, and new design developments made abroad ? Was it due to a lack of incentives on the part of Canadian producers to increase their output, as much as their main competitors abroad did, forcing them to fight for expanded sales opportunities both in the domestic and foreign markets ?

DEVALUATION OF CANADIAN DOLLAR

Probably all these factors contributed to the changing role of Canadian manufacturing industries in international trade though some of the factors assumed greater weight than others. For example, when Canada devalued the dollar from a premium level over the American dollar to 92½ cents (U.S.) in mid-1962, significant improvements in the competitive position of Canada's secondary industries ensued, with the downward trend gradually being reversed and exports of fully manufactured products rising again, both in absolute and in relative terms.

WORLD TRENDS

The problems confronting Canadian manufacturing industry have been assessed by the Economic Council of Canada in these terms:

> The postwar reductions in trade barriers, together with other underlying economic forces, have particularly encouraged a much more rapid growth of world trade in manufactured products and processed materials. [1]

But Canada did not quite keep pace with world trends.

To illustrate:

	PER CENT INCREASE IN WORLD EXPORTS, 1955-61
Primary Products	26
Processed Materials	47
Manufactured Products	66

Two other developments marked the international trade pattern of the 1950's and 1960's:

> First, there have been much more rapid rates of increase in such product groups as machinery, transportation equipment, chemicals and plastics, and much less rapid rates of increase in such other groups as textiles and clothing and primary products. Second, the expansion of world trade has become increasingly concentrated among the industrially advanced countries, and there has been a relative decline in the importance of trade between the industrially advanced and the economically less developed countries...

---

[1] ECONOMIC COUNCIL OF CANADA, *Economic Goals for Canada to 1970,* First Annual Review, Ottawa, Queen's Printer, December 1964, p. 81.

Canada has been adversely affected by the shift in the structure of international trade. [. . .] Countries which export mainly manufactured products have had an improvement in their so-called terms of trade during this period, while countries such as Canada, which export mainly primary products and industrial materials, have experienced a deterioration in their terms of trade. This deterioration in Canada's terms of trade, which represents a reversal of the trend of the previous two decades, may also partly reflect the reduction in the exchange value of the Canadian dollar. Thus, for Canada, a larger volume of exports was required in 1963 than in 1953 to finance a given volume of imports. [2]

As the figures below show, West Germany, the United Kingdom and the United States were the main gainers; Canada, Australia and Argentina were among the main losers. [3]

	RATIO OF EXPORT PRICES TO IMPORT PRICES, 1963 (1953 = 100)
West Germany	120
United Kingdom	116
United States	112
Japan	102
Canada	92
Argentina	83
Australia	74

One of the main reasons for this development has been the more rapid growth of the industrial production on a worldwide scale as compared with the rate of expansion of consumption of raw materials, with some notable exceptions such as pulp wood and fertilizer.

These developments help to explain why Canada's share in world trade has not been expanding. In fact, in recent years it has been below that of a decade ago. This decline has occurred despite the fact that Canada has increased its share of the world market for primary materials. But this sector of world trade has been growing relatively slowly. In the increasingly important sectors of processed materials and

---

[2] *Ibid.*, pp. 82 and 83.
[3] *Ibid.*, p. 83.

manufactured products, Canada's share of world trade has tended to decline. [4]

To illustrate: [5]

| | CANADIAN EXPORTS AS PER CENT OF WORLD EXPORTS | | | |
	1955	1957	1960	1961
Primary Products	3.7	4.3	4.3	4.6
Processed Materials	13.7	11.4	10.7	10.5
Manufactured Products	1.3	1.5	1.3	1.4
All Products	4.7	4.6	4.4	4.4

The key element in explaining the setbacks experienced by Canadian manufacturing industries in world trade — and also affecting their competitive position in the domestic market as Canada gradually reduced tariffs on manufactured products in the post war period — was a continuing inability of these industries to raise their productivity at a rate comparable to that of other industrialized nations.   Thus Canadian industries fell behind the progress made by industries in other countries. As the data below show, of nine industrialized countries in Western Europe and North America, seven had greater productivity increases in manufacturing industries than Canada over the period 1950 to 1960.   Only the United Kingdom had fallen behind Canada.

But British industries were able to achieve a decided improvement in the 1955 to 1960 period while Canadian industries continued to slip.   In that five-year period, productivity increases in Canadian manufacturing industries were one-fifth those of France and Western Germany, and one-third those of the United States and the United Kingdom.   Thus Canada had the doubtful distinction of being far behind other major industrialized nations in raising productivity in manufacturing.   Obviously, such a situation could not continue without change for any length of time, without disastrous effects on Canadian economic growth and standards of living (see below). [6]

---

[4] *Ibid.,* p. 84.
[5] *Ibid.,* p. 85.
[6] GRAHAM BANNOCK, "Productivity in Manufacturing, Prewar to 1960", in *Productivity Measurement Review*, Paris, Organisation for the Economic Co-operation and Development, November 1962, No. 31, p. 11.

	AVERAGE ANNUAL GROWTH IN OUTPUT PER MAN-HOUR IN MANUFACTURING — PER CENT		
	1950-1960	1950-1955	1955-1960
1. France	5.9	5.4	6.5
2. Western Germany	5.6	5.4	5.9
3. Austria	5.3	5.7	12.8
4. Netherlands	4.3	4.7	3.8
5. Belgium	3.6	—	—
6. Sweden	3.2	2.7	4.2
7. United States	3.2	3.2	3.2
8. Canada	3.0	4.7	1.2
9. United Kingdom	2.6	2.1	3.1

RAISING PRODUCTIVITY

Faced with the challenge to meet increasing international competition, Canadian manufacturing industries responded by embarking on the largest capital investment program in their history and by endeavouring to increase significantly the productivity of their operations. Between 1962 and 1966, Canadian manufacturing industries invested close to $10 billion in expanding and improving their productive capacity, over 50 per cent more than they had spent in the preceding five-year period.

Results began to show in terms of increases in productivity. In 1965, industrial output rose by 7 per cent in volume terms over 1964. With employment in manufacturing up approximately 3 per cent, this indicated a possible rise in productivity, as reflected in increases in output per man year of the order of 4 per cent, a better record of achievement in a single year than the industry had been able to realize during the preceding decade. [7]

Gradually, Canada started to export greater quantities of fully manufactured products and the proportion to total domestic output turned upward again.

New and more sophisticated statistical measurements became available. Instead of providing statistics of Canadian exports of "fully and chiefly manufactured" products, of "partially manufactured" products and of "raw materials," as it had done for about half a century, the Dominion Bureau of Statistics

---

[7] But this improvement was temporary in nature, with productivity increases lessening in 1966 and 1967.

switched to a new classification distinguishing between crude materials, fabricated products and end products. The main change from the old classification was to narrow down considerably the definition of "fully or chiefly manufactured" products, now called "end products". By moving such items as flour, newsprint, steel rolling mill products and almost all chemical and allied products to the partially manufactured group and by renaming the latter as the "fabricated" product group. Such items as man-made fibres and asbestos milled products were moved from the partially manufactured group and all kinds of scrap materials from the fully manufactured class to raw materials, with this group renamed "crude" materials.

The effect of this new classification which came closer to a grouping facilitating the assessment of a country's industrial progress in terms of changes in the structure of manufacturing production and marketing, was to reduce the old grouping of "fully and chiefly manufactured" products by two-thirds and increasing the "partially manufactured" grouping by about three-quarters and the "raw material" grouping by approximately 8 per cent.

On the basis of these new groupings, evidence became available indicating that as the nation approached its first centennial, Canadian manufacturing industries were on the march again in international markets. They were able to increase sales significantly abroad of fully manufactured products, both in relative and in absolute terms, as the following figures indicate:

	TOTAL MERCHANDISE EXPORTS $ Bill.	VALUE OF END PRODUCTS EXPORTED AS PER CENT OF	
		Total Exports	Total Manufacturing Production
1960	5.3	11.6	2.6
1963	6.8	15.4	3.6
1964	8.1	17.6	4.5

GOVERNMENT ENCOURAGEMENT

In this effort of increasing exports of highly fabricated products, Canadian manufacturing industries had the full support of the Federal Government. Measures taken by the Canadian Government included proposals strongly advocating removals or reduction of tariffs on fully manufactured products among the major trading nations of the world, substantial financial assistance particularly in the area of export financing, and significant fiscal incentives to expand and improve production facilities and to increase exports of processed material and fabricated products, accompanied by vigorous trade promotional efforts.

Canada supported strongly the United States in what became known as the "Kennedy Round" of Trade Negotiations. The key objectives of Canada's trade policy in these negotiations were explained by the Minister of Finance in these terms:

> These negotiations will be more concerned with manufactured products and we must keep clearly in mind that the expansion of efficient secondary industries is necessary to provide adequate employment opportunities for Canada's growing labour force. For this reason we shall be looking for those particular tariff reductions abroad which will open up new export markets for the products of our secondary industries. This will help them to achieve better economies of scale, which are vital to the attainment of cost efficiency. [8]

ENCOURAGEMENT OF BUSINESS

The problems that Canadian manufacturing industries were facing in the post-World War II period to share adequately in the growing markets of the world for industrial products including capital equipment urgently needed by many nations, drove home one lesson — among many.

To be successful in international competition a firm had to be big enough (1) to have the benefits of large scale operations reflected in high productivity and low per unit costs, (2) to have the management, sales and service organization, and research and technical know-how required to manufacture the scientifically most advanced products and to distribute them on a worldwide basis; and (3) either to have the financial resources or at least have access to them to be able to handle even the largest orders becoming available to the most competitive producer.

Large scale of operations became a much more important objective of industrial management than ever before. For it became increasingly clear that the chances of a business firm

---

[8] *Budget Address*, by the Honourable Walter GORDON, Minister of Finance, *House of Commons Debates*, Ottawa, March 16, 1964, p. 973.

for success in this increasingly competitive environment were greatly enhanced if the corporation was large, with adequate resources and competent management. Large firms were likely to make more money than smaller or medium-sized firms in most manufacturing sectors. They would be able to pay higher wages and salaries to their work force and they would be in a position to reward management more effectively, thus attracting the best men in the country. They could offer investors a higher return for the risk they may have taken, thus attracting more capital on more favourable terms over the longer period.

Of some 20,000 manufacturing corporations in Canada, over 70 per cent were making money in 1962 and somewhat less than 30 per cent were losing money. [9] Most of these would be small enterprises and some of medium size. Very few really large corporations in manufacturing have been losing money since the end of World War II except on occasion when they went through a brief period of adjustment, adaptation and further integration.

Definition of what constitutes a small manufacturing company will vary depending on the type of the industry, size of the market, capital resources and technical know-how available, etc. The Canadian Government, in introducing legislation in Parliament to require reporting under the proposed Corporations and Labour Unions Returns Act [10], exempted small business corporations from reporting under this Act. The Act applied only to what were considered medium-sized and large companies, defined as firms whose gross revenues during a reporting period exceeded $500,000 or whose assets exceeded $250,000. [11]

In the first report under that statute covering the year 1962, close to 6,000 manufacturing corporations reported, indicating that about 14,000 manufacturing corporations in Canada involved small operations.

---

[9] There were 13,788 manufacturing firms reporting a profit and 5,878 reporting a loss, involving a total of 19,666 corporations in 1962 (see DEPARTMENT OF NATIONAL REVENUE, *Income Tax Statistics*, 1964, Ottawa, Queen's Printer, 1965, p. 53).

[10] *Statutes of Canada*, Chapter 26, 10-11 Elizabeth II, passed by Parliament in April 1962.

[11] Besides small corporations, a limited number of other business enterprises were exempted from reporting under the Act because such firms were already providing similar information under other statutory authority, e.g. insurance loan and trust companies, companies operating under the Small Loans Act and the Radio Act, etc.

Of the 6,000 corporations, close to 600 were large manufacturing enterprises defined as companies with assets of $5 million and over. [12] Hence, the structure of the Canadian manufacturing industry as far as size is concerned, is briefly as follows: seven of ten firms involve small enterprises and three are either medium-sized or large corporations. Of the latter group, nine out of ten are medium-sized and one out of ten is a large manufacturing concern. Or to put it differently: out of thirty Canadian manufacturing corporations, twenty-one would be small, eight would be medium-sized and one would be large.

Most of the money lost in Canada in operating a manufacturing business would be by small companies. Something like nine out of twenty-one small companies would be losing money while most of the medium-sized and the larger manufacturing concerns would be making money.

The approximately 14,000 small manufacturing companies are estimated to have assets of the order of $8 billion. Medium size companies of which there are some 5,400 have assets of about $5 billion while the close to 600 large corporations have assets approaching $20 billion, for a total for the industry as a whole of some $33 billion. [13]

Large manufacturing corporations make a good deal more money in absolute terms and in relation to capital invested than do medium or small enterprises. Large corporations comprising about 3 per cent of the total in number, have assets of close to $20 billion or about three-fifths of the total. Their profits amounted to about $2 billion.

Medium-sized companies comprising 27 per cent of all manufacturing firms have assets of about $5 billion, equivalent to one-sixth of total assets in the manufacturing industries. Their profits amounted to $383 million in 1962, the year to which these tabulations apply.

---

[12] *Corporations and Labour Unions Returns Act, Report for 1962,* Ottawa, Queen's Printer, June 1965, pp. 83-86.
[13] Estimates are based on *Income Tax Statistics, 1964, op. cit.,* p. 53, and *Corporation and Labour Unions Returns Act, Report 1962, op. cit.,* pp. 83-86. The data from these two sources are not fully comparable and therefore the above quantitative assessment should be considered only as a general indication of the order of magnitude and not as full measurement.

The figures below illustrate that it pays to be associated with large manufacturing operations in Canada: [14]

CORPORATIONS WITH ASSETS	ASSETS $ Mill.	PROFITS $ Mill.	PROFITS AS PER CENT OF ASSETS
Under 500,000 [15]	799	54	6.8
$500,000 - $999,999	961	60	6.2
$1,000,000 - $4,999,999	3,271	269	8.2
$5,000,000 and over	19,441	1,926	9.9

The above figures reflect the situation as it existed in 1962. This was a year of comparatively moderate profits for business generally because the Canadian economy was just recovering from the recession of 1960-61. Since then the profitability of Canadian manufacturing industries has improved a great deal further, with total profits of this sector rising by 28 per cent between 1962 and 1966, and with further advances indicated in some manufacturing industries [16] notwithstanding a general profit squeeze and a slowdown in the rate of economic growth as Canada celebrated her 100th anniversary in 1967.

[14] *Corporations and Labour Unions Returns Act, Report 1962, op. cit.,* pp. 83-86.
[15] Covers only corporations required to report under the Corporations and Labour Unions Returns Act.
[16] Examples include industries manufacturing transportation equipment, paper and paper products and petroleum products (see DOMINION BUREAU OF STATISTICS, *Corporation Profits Third Quarter 1967,* Ottawa, January 1968, p. 8).

CHAPTER 6

Foreign Control and Ownership

LIBERAL POLICIES

For three-quarters of the first century as an independent nation, Canada pursued liberal policies [1] welcoming the inflow of foreign capital and its participation in the industrial and general economic development of the country. In most areas of economic activity, Canada did not impose restrictions on the inflow and outflow of foreign capital. Funds could go into any secondary industry or natural resource sector in which foreign investors wished to invest. [2] Such capital was treated equally with domestic capital, a privilege accorded to foreign investors, unmatched in any other industrially developed country in the world.

Foreign capital was attracted by the opportunity to obtain a higher return for funds invested in Canada, the ease of transferability of dividends earned and capital repatriated, and the liberal character of fiscal policies pursued by both conservative and liberal governments alike, as far as the treatment of foreign investment was concerned. Large and increasing amounts of foreign capital moved into Canada, most of it since the end of World War I, going into industrial and resources development.

NET INTERNATIONAL INDEBTEDNESS

Even though Canada invested abroad what were for this country significant amounts, Canada's external net international

---

[1] "No systematic overall policy has emerged, however, and Canadian policy remains one of the most liberal in the world" (*Foreign Ownership and the Structure of Canadian Industry*, Report of the Task Force on the Structure of Canadian Industry, Ottawa, Queen's Printer, 1968, p. 384).

[2] In the more recent period, some limitations were imposed on foreign capital going into certain "sensitive" Canadian economic sectors, such as the Canadian chartered banks, life insurance companies, and radio and television business and newspapers. The above report includes a survey of government measures taken during the period 1957-1967 affecting foreign investment in Canada (*ibid.*, pp. 384-392).

indebtedness increased by leaps and bounds over the last several decades, as the following figures indicate: [3]

	GROSS LIABILITIES TO OTHER COUNTRIES $ Bill.	GROSS EXTERNAL ASSETS $ Bill.	NET INDEBTEDNESS $ Bill.
1926	6.4	1.3	5.1
1939	7.4	1.9	5.5
1955	15.1	7.1	8.0
1960	25.6	9.0	16.6
1963	30.4	11.1	19.3
1964	32.8	12.7	20.1

EXTENT OF CONTROL

The result was that foreign investors took overwhelming control over Canadian secondary industries and natural resources development, as the following data illustrate: [4]

	PERCENT OF FOREIGN CONTROL		
	Manufacturing	Petroleum and Natural Gas	Other Mining and Smelting
1948	43	40	
1954	51	69	51
1957	56	76	61
1959	57	75	61
1961	59	72	59
1962	60	74	58
1963	60	74	59

The overwhelming proportion of this control was exercised by U.S. corporations and investors (see below):

	PERCENT OF FOREIGN CONTROL — 1963		
	Manufacturing	Petroleum and Natural Gas	Other Mining and Smelting
United States	46	62	52
Other Countries	14	12	7
All Countries	60	74	59

---

[3] DOMINION BUREAU OF STATISTICS, *The Canadian Balance of International Payments, 1963, 1964 and 1965, and International Investment Position,* Ottawa, 1967, p. 63.

[4] *Ibid.,* p. 80.

Certain industries within the manufacturing sector are subject to a very high degree of foreign control, with ownership predominantly in the hands of United States residents. This is indicated by the following data for 1963 showing total percentages of capital controlled by foreigners in specific manufacturing industries, with United States percentages shown in brackets. [5]

> Automobiles and parts, 97 per cent (97 per cent)
> Rubber, 97 per cent (90 per cent)
> Chemicals, 78 per cent (54 per cent)
> Electrical equipment, 77 per cent (66 per cent)

> In the last few years, Canadian purchases of foreign equity securities have been substantial, averaging $27 million a year from 1961 to 1964, rising to $92 million in 1963 and $245 million in 1966, and standing at $66 million in the first six months of 1967. Over the same period, there has been a substantial net repatriation of Canadian stock owned abroad: $117 million average for 1961-64, $242 million in 1965, $83 million in 1966 and $53 million in the first six months of 1967. While this repatriation reduced ownership, its nature does not appear to have been such as to reduce foreign control to a corresponding extent. [6]

RISKS AND REWARDS

The claim has been made that foreign investors, particularly American industries, have moved into those sectors of economic pursuit in Canada that bring the greatest rewards for risks taken, the implication being that Canadian investors have to be content to place their savings in safe and conventional forms, or in industries that are less profitable than those that are owned and/or controlled by foreign investors.

New evidence has become available with the publication of the first report under the Corporations and Labour Unions Returns Act suggesting that this claim is not borne out, as far as investment in Canadian manufacturing industries is concerned.

The 1962 Report provides details for nineteen sectors of manufacturing activity in Canada. Of these, eleven industry

---

[5] *Foreign Ownership and the Structure of Canadian Industry*, *op. cit.*, p. 11.
[6] *Ibid.*, p. 13.

groups showed greater foreign ownership [7] and eight groups showed greater Canadian ownership. [8]

Of the eleven industry groups with greater foreign ownership, corporations that were more than 50 per cent non-resident owned in five sectors showed profit ratios to assets in excess of 10 per cent, the transportation equipment industry (mainly motor cars), 15 per cent, the machinery industry, 13 per cent, the non-metallic products industry, 12 pert cent, miscellaneous manufacturing, 12 per cent, and the chemical industry, 11 per cent. [9]

Of the eight industry groups with greater Canadian ownership, [10] three sectors showed profit ratios to assets in excess of 10 per cent, the beverage industry, 18 per cent, the printing and publishing industry, 12 per cent, and the paper industry, 11 per cent. [11]

While there are distinct differences in the profitability between industries, foreign owned and Canadian owned, in total the differences are offset to some extent, with investors investing largely in Canadian owned companies doing about as well as foreign investors investing in largely non-resident owned manufacturing corporations, as the following figures show: [12]

---

[7] On the basis of assets held by companies with 50 per cent or more non-resident ownership. The eleven groups include: tobacco industries, rubber industries, primary metals, metal fabricating, machinery industry, transportation equipment, electrical products, non-metallic products, petroleum and coal products, chemical industries and miscellaneous industries (special compilation based on *Corporations and Labour Unions Returns Act, Report for 1962, op., cit.,* pp. 52-68).

[8] The eight groups include the following industries: food manufacturing, beverage industries, leather industries, textile industries, wood products, furniture and fixture industries, paper industries, and the printing and publishing industry (*ibid.*).

[9] These rates cover only corporations in those industries that were 50 per cent or more non-resident owned, not all firms in the industry.

[10] These rates are only for corporations less than 50 per cent owned by non-residents, not all firms in the industry.

[11] The above ratios are based on a separate industrial grouping within each sector distinguishing between firms with more *or* less than 50 per cent of non-resident ownership.

[12] *Ibid.*

	ASSETS $ Mill.	PROFITS $ Mill.	PROFITS AS PER CENT OF ASSETS
Non-Resident Ownership, 50 Per Cent or More	13,842	1,313	9.5
Non-Resident Ownership, Less than 50 Per Cent	10,630	996	9.4
Total	24,472	2,309	9.4

CANADIAN DILEMMA

The inflow of foreign capital has brought many benefits to domestic industry and to Canadians generally. American industries in particular, in sending capital to Canada, were not only desirous of obtaining an adequate return on their investment but they were also interested in acquiring a long term stake in the economic growth of the host country — whether this included access to raw materials, access to energy sources, or access to markets. American investors thus took the long term point of view in placing judiciously their direct investments in Canada, particularly in the field of natural resources development and manufacturing industries.

They were primarily interested in the continuing success of their subsidiaries operating in Canada and not in quick profits. They re-invested large amounts of their earnings in the country and they sent additional capital to Canada as and when this was required to finance further expansion and integration of operations. With this capital came American management, American skill, and American know-how, as well as, in a number of instances, assurances of markets either in the United States or overseas.

Canadians were able to expand their manufacturing industries more rapidly than they could have done had they to rely on their own savings and their own initiative. And further, Canadians were able to increase the productivity of their manufacturing operations, in many instances either up to the level of performance achieved in the United States or close to it — sometimes even exceeding it — because they were able to draw freely on American scientific and technological progress and managerial experience. This applies to some extent also to foreign investment coming from overseas though its impact and non-financial contributions to Canadian industrial development were in the last half century less than the contributions made by American investors.

While the benefits brought to Canadian industrial development from foreign investment were fairly readily observable, the disadvantages were less apparent, though in the views of some just as real. While some complaints were being voiced about American controlled industries in Canada not behaving as "good" Canadian corporate citizens — there were fewer complaints about foreign control from other countries — what concrete evidence was presented to substantiate such claims was hotly debated.

The public's uneasiness about growing foreign control over Canadian industry and natural resources development became more pronounced, particularly in the decade commencing with the mid-1950's, when figures released indicated that foreign investors had achieved majority control over most of Canada's key economic sectors, particularly manufacturing and mining. It represented a concern not so much about the lack or the inadequacy of opportunities for Canadians to participate in foreign controlled businesses operating in Canada — though this was one factor — but rather an innate aversion against economic control that could lead to political control and interference in Canadian national affairs.

POLITICAL ATTITUDES

Politicians were slow to sense this growing public uneasiness about increasing foreign control of Canadian industry and resources. Canadian-American economic and political relations had, by and large, remained friendly for many years, and there appeared little that the U.S. Government could do to help Canadians in the dilemma they were facing.

For as long as Canadian laws freely permitted the inflow of U.S. capital and American private investors chose to direct a large portion of the capital available for investment abroad to Canada, the matter of limiting inflow of foreign capital, the manner of prescribing its participation in Canadian industrial and resources development, and ways and means of encouraging Canadian investors to acquire a greater stake in that development, was largely a domestic matter for Canadians to resolve.

Gradually, both major political parties in Canada recognized this basic truth. Principles and policies were evolved which in their broad outlines had striking similarities.

To quote the Right Honourable John Diefenbaker when he was Prime Minister of Canada, leading an overwhelming conservative majority in Parliament:

> We have had to import capital on a large scale. [. . .] This continued inflow of capital into Canada has desirable and undesirable features. We like the higher and accelerated rate of growth and development it makes possible. We do not like to have a large proportion of many of our major industries owned or controlled outside Canada . . .
>
> We have made it clear that we expect foreign concerns operating in Canada, or Canadian subsidiaries of foreign companies, to carry on operations as Canadian businesses. We expect them to make available a fair portion of their equity securities for purchase by Canadians; to include Canadians on their Boards of Directors; to make proper disclosure of their Canadian operations; to employ competent Canadians in senior management and technical positions; to conduct a fair share of their research in Canada; to purchase their requirements within Canada if those are available on competitive terms; and not to be denied by those in control a fair opportunity to sell their Canadian products in export markets. [13]

Three years later, the Honourable Walter Gordon, Minister of Finance in a Liberal minority government, had this to say about Canadians relying too greatly on the savings of other nations to finance part of their economic development which had brought Canada large balance of payments deficits:

> There is a clearly recognized danger that if deficits continue at this rate, they will lead to a growing measure of control of our economy passing abroad. There is a danger that in allowing these deficits to continue we are sacrificing our birthright, the birthright which our forefathers laboured so hard to hand on to us. [14]

The Minister then proceeded to present to Parliament a number of fiscal measures designed to encourage foreign controlled companies to offer Canadians at least a 25 per cent

---

[13] *Address* by the Right Honourable John. G. Diefenbaker, to the Canadian Chamber of Commerce in Great Britain, London, England, May 2, 1960, p. 5.
[14] *Budget Address* by the Honourable Walter Gordon, Minister of Finance, *House of Commons Debates*, Ottawa, June 13, 1963, p. 998.

equity interest in their firms. While some of the fiscal proposals were altered, as the debate about their merits and demerits continued both within and outside Parliament, the actions taken by the Canadian Government were symptomatic of its desire to search for ways and means to lead Canadians out of the dilemma of too great reliance on foreign savings, with its consequent growing non-resident economic control over manufacturing industries and natural resources development.

UNITED STATES ACTION

While the Canadian Government was searching for a solution, an unforeseen development was to offer some possible assistance from an unexpected source. The U.S. balance of payments had been deteriorating for several years. When mild measures of exhortation to American industry and investors were not fully effective, the U.S. Government presented a set of guide-lines with the specific objective, among other things, to reduce the capital outflow for direct investment abroad. Canada which had been receiving the largest share of U.S. capital going to a single country, was likely to be more significantly affected than most other nations by this new guide-line policy imposed by the U.S. Government as a temporary measure to safeguard its balance of payments position.

Faced with the possibility of a reduction of capital inflow from the U.S., Canadians protested to Washington. One point particularly at issue was that Canadian subsidiaries were affected by U.S. directives given to American parent companies through the control which these companies exercised.

At a conference of the Joint United States-Canadian Committee on Trade and Economic Affairs, Canada obtained a clarification of what was regarded in this country as an important matter of principle. United States authorities re-emphasized the view that "United States subsidiaries abroad should behave as good citizens of the country where they are located". This was a diplomatic way of saying that the American Government had no intention of interfering in Canadian domestic economic affairs, thus allaying public fears in Canada.

GUIDE-LINES

This announcement was followed shortly thereafter by the tabling in the House of Commons on March 31st, 1966, of a statement of guide-lines set out by the Canadian Government to cover "principles of good corporate behaviour for subsidiaries" of foreign countries operating in Canada. This twelve-point program put forward by then Liberal Minister of Trade and Commerce, the Honourable Robert H. Winters, encompassed all the essential points presented six years earlier by the Conservative Prime Minister, with some changes in wording and emphasis. [15]

Of these twelve points, two are singled out here for brief reference, to indicate the uphill struggle any Canadian Government faces to come to grips with the problems in the light of the strongly entrenched control of Canadian industry by foreign interests.

Point 9 of the guide-lines called for "a Canadian outlook within management" including the "promotion of qualified personnel and inclusion of a major proportion of Canadian citizens on its Board of Directors".

Point 10 called for providing "opportunity for equity participation in the Canadian enterprise by the Canadian public". [16]

The first Report under the Corporations and Labour Unions Returns Act throws some interesting light on the dimensions of the problems to which the two guide-lines referred to above apply.

There were in Canada 217 large corporations operating in the manufacturing and mining fields, each with assets of $25 million and over. Their total assets amounted to $19.3 billion; 138 companies with assets of $12.8 billion were 50 per cent or more non-resident owned while the remaining 79 companies with assets of $6.5 billion were less than 50 per cent non-resident owned. [17]

The 138 major corporations, all predominantly foreign owned and controlled, indicated the following participation of Canadian citizens in the holding of senior executive positions and as members of Boards of Directors. [18]

---

[15] *House of Commons Debates,* Ottawa, March 31, 1966, pp. 3643, 3713 and 3714.
[16] *Ibid.,* p. 3714.
[17] *Corporations and Labour Unions Returns Act, Report for 1962, op. cit.,* p. 34.
[18] *Ibid.,* pp. 35 and 36.

	Total Number	Canadian Citizens Number	Canadian Citizens as Per Cent of Total Number
Presidents	138	62	44
Boards of Directors	1,332	598	46

Many of the Canadian citizens who were members of Boards of Directors of foreign controlled companies were nominal members of these boards and they included frequently the Canadian lawyer and accountant representing the interests of foreign subsidiaries and their parent companies in Canada. Hence, the data illustrate that Canadians have a long way to go to obtain a major say in the management of the big industrial corporations which largely shape Canada's economic destiny.

What opportunities do Canadians have to participate in the equity of the 217 giant industrial corporations in Canada? During the period 1958 to 1962, 18 of these 217 large corporations "offered voting shares to the public. These 18 corporations consisted of nine corporations owned largely by Canadian residents; the degree of non-resident ownership in these corporations ranged from 3 to 17 per cent. The other nine corporations were largely owned by non-residents, with one corporation being 57 per cent owned by non-residents, one 68 per cent and the remainder between 80 and 95 per cent non-resident owned. These 18 corporations offered shares to the public that would represent approximately 15 per cent of the equity at the end of 1962. This amount would be slightly over two per cent of the equity of the 217 corporations with assets over $25 million." [19]

Two per cent is a long way from the 25 per cent which the former Minister of Finance described as a desirable goal of Canadian participation in Canadian industrial and resources development, controlled by foreign investors.

---

[19]   *Ibid.*, p. 37.

CHAPTER 7

Role of Government

CANADIAN PHILOSOPHY OF INDUSTRIAL DEVELOPMENT

Have Canadians pursued their struggle to industrialize their country in a haphazard and improvised fashion with little direction or definite purpose, or have they evolved a philosophy of industrial development based on sheer necessity to build up an economically and politically independent country? The traces of the philosophy of industrial development are faint, but the broad outline is recognizable.

All through Canada's first century as a nation, governments have taken a firm hand to encourage the growth of secondary industries in this country to foster their productivity and viability, to spur them on to greater competitiveness both at home and abroad, to spread their benefits and to distribute them regionally so as to achieve a more balanced economic development of the country as a whole.

EFFECT ON THE BALANCE OF PAYMENTS

In June 1967, the Honourable Robert H. Winters, the Minister of Trade and Commerce, released a report surveying the economic impact of foreign-owned companies operating in Canada. The report was based on a canvas of 266 major corporations each with assets exceeding $5 million and whose voting shares were more than 50 per cent held by non-resident corporations.

> The companies covered in this report had sales in 1964 amounting to $13,562 million, increasing to $15,132 million in 1965. This volume of business is approximately 20 per cent of the business carried on by all non-financial, non-government corporations in Canada. The importance of these corporations is somewhat greater in the mining and manufacturing industries, where their activities accounted for about one third of the total sales in the two years 1964 and 1965. [1]

---

[1] *Foreign-Owned Subsidiaries in Canada* (A Report on Operations and Financing based on Information supplied by the larger Subsidiary Companies), Ottawa, Queen's Printer, 1967, p. 5.

The majority of the companies covered were manufacturing firms. For the first time, the survey, among other features, threw light on the extent to which foreign-controlled companies contribute to Canada's balance of payments deficit. In 1965, for example, the 266 firms were responsible for a balance of payments deficit of $486 million or 45 per cent of Canada's total balance of payments deficit of $1,083 million. [2] The $486 million were a net deficit being made up of a deficit with the United States of $860 million and a surplus with other foreign countries of $374 million. The make-up of the net deficit in 1965 was as follows: [3]

	$ Mill.
Export sales	2,746
Merchandise imported	2,568
Capital equipment imported	115
Total import trade	2,683
Balance on merchandise trade	63
Other current receipts	55
Dividends paid	352
Other current payments	251
Total current payments	603
Balance on non merchandise transactions	−549
Total receipts	2,801
Total payments	3,296
Current account balance	−486

In undertaking this survey, the Minister of Trade and Commerce restated the Government's position by saying:

> The Canadian Government is desirous that subsidiaries be free to develop their full potential within the Canadian community. In this regard it is most important that subsidiaries should not have restrictive limitations placed upon their sound development by their parent organizations. [4]

The Minister asked firms to keep his Department advised of what they were doing in following the guide-lines which he had set out in Parliament and which he had communicated to them.

---

[2] *The Canadian Balance of International Payments, 1963, 1964 and 1965 and International Investment Position, op. cit.,* p. 11.
[3] *Foreign-Owned Subsidiaries in Canada, op. cit.,* p. 11.
[4] *Ibid.,* p. 40.

A TASK FORCE OF EIGHT ECONOMISTS

While the Minister of Trade and Commerce was exhorting foreign-controlled companies to cooperate with the Canadian authorities on a voluntary basis, the Honourable Walter L. Gordon, former Minister of Finance, and more latterly the President of the Privy Council, felt that appeals to reason may be insufficient to achieve satisfactory progress in the direction of Canadianizing foreign-controlled firms, at a rate acceptable to the public. He therefore arranged, with Government approval, for a task force of eight Canadian economists to investigate and report on "Foreign Ownership and the Structure of Canadian Industry". This task force, headed by Prof. Melville H. Watkins, of the University of Toronto, reported to the Canadian Government on January 12, 1968, with the report tabled in Parliament on February 15, 1968.

While pointing out the many benefits that Canadians have enjoyed from the inflow of foreign capital, the task force emphasized in particular two adverse effects:

1. Foreign investment discouraged the adequate development of Canadian technical and managerial skills. To quote:

> There has been a hesitancy in perceiving and implementing changes in the Canadian environment, the recruitment and education of management being a case in point. While the ease with which foreign capital could be imported *via* portfolio and direct investment, skilled manpower *via* immigration, and technology and entrepreneurship *via* direct investment has expanded the size and complexity of the economic base and increased opportunities for Canadians, it has, at the same time, diminished the pressures for Canada to develop these skills amongst Canadians to their fullest extent. [5]

2. Foreign decision-making has hampered the effective formulation of Canadian economic policies in a number of instances:

> The tendency inherent in direct investment to shift decision-making power in the private sector outside Canada has, on occasion, posed serious problems for those responsible for formulating Canadian policy. [6]

---

[5] *Foreign Ownership and the Structure of Canadian Industry,* op. cit., p. 20.
[6] *Ibid.,* p. 21.

The task force concluded its report by offering six major proposals: [7]

1. The establishment of a special agency "to *coordinate* policies with respect to multi-national enterprise".

2. To obtain additional information regarding the operations of foreign subsidiaries in Canada to meet three distinct purposes: "public disclosure, economic analysis, and governmental surveillance of firms."

3. To deal more effectively with problems arising out of "imperfections of competition" and in particular "to maintain a stronger Canadian public presence to countervail foreign private economic power and foreign government power as applied through the latter".

4. To pursue more effective industrial policies to facilitate "rationalizing Canadian industries" and "to improve the quality of Canadian factors of production", as well as "to limit any tendencies under free trade for the locus of private decision-making to shift outside Canada and for overall Canadian employment to suffer in the short-run and the long-run".

5. To take positive steps "to block the intrusion into Canada of United States law and policy applicable to American-owned subsidiaries".

6. To make available greater incentives "to encourage large corporations, including foreign-owned subsidiaries, to offer their shares to Canadians, thereby increasing the supply of Canadian equities, facilitating disclosure, and providing levers for public regulation and for dealing with extra-territoriality".

While the Government made it clear in a note on the cover page of the report that the study reflected the opinions of the authors, the evidence presented and the proposals made were another step of Canadians moving in the direction of a more critical assessment of whether it made good sense over the long run to have more and more of their industries and natural resources owned and controlled by citizens of other countries, particularly of the United States.

All through that first century Canadians have been trying to steer an effective course to achieve continued economic

---

[7]   *Ibid.*, pp. 395-415.

growth of a type and a rate that would bring the greatest benefits to the nation as a whole and to its citizens. In this process they became preoccupied with the argument whether greater economic benefits were to be derived from pursuing liberal trade policies and concentrating mainly on the development of their natural resources and such secondary industries as were competitive in world markets, or whether they should encourage the growth of the whole range of manufacturing industries to become a "fully" industrialized nation.

Even before Confederation, and continuing thereafter for a hundred years, the argument centered around whether Canadians should remain a nation of "hewers of wood and drawers of water" or whether their true destiny was to be found in expanding manufacturing industries and pursuing a course of nationalism, whatever the cost.

When the Minister of Finance introduced his proposals for substantial tariff increases in Parliament in 1879, he said:

> The time has arrived when we are to decide whether
> we will simply be hewers of wood and drawers of water; [. . .].
> The time has certainly arrived when we must consider whether
> we will allow matters to remain as they are, with the result
> of being an unimportant and uninteresting portion of Her
> Majesty's Dominions, or will rise to the position, which
> I believe Providence has destined us to occupy. [8]

This argument has continued all through the century, though latterly along more sophisticated lines, under the veil of pious endorsement of liberal trade principles, though not necessarily engendering less heat.

What those engaging in this "eternal" debate are apparently overlooking is that shaping the pattern and direction of Canadian economic development is not just a matter of choice made by sectors representing self-interest, by armchair strategists or by improvising politicians — but a matter of economic circumstances and social forces that vary over time and are subject to strong domestic and international influences, both economic and political.

The whole pattern of Canada's economic development over the last century provides ample evidence that the choice

---

[8] *Budget Address* by the Honourable Samuel L. Tilley, Minister of Finance, *House of Commons Debates*, Ottawa, March 14, 1879, p. 429.

Canadians had to make was not one of black or white, whether to remain "hewers of wood and drawers of water" or not. What Canadians had to decide was the degree to which they could balance the expansion of secondary industries with the growth of primary industries, and in the twentieth century, with a significant expansion of tertiary industries (the service sector). It was through this balancing of expansion in one sector with the growth in another sector, through the balancing of development of one region with improvements in another region, with the balancing of increases in income levels of the majority of the population with the support of income levels of those less well-endowed, that Canadians were able to make their greatest economic and social progress.

Canadians have always been a self-relying and energetic people, and for most of the century have preferred "less" government intervention to "more" government intervention. On the subject of industrial development there has been comparatively less public controversy about government participation than on any other major economic, social, or political issue facing the nation. As a result, governments have formulated a variety of economic policies and taken numerous steps to foster and achieve continuing industrialization of the Canadian economy, usually with a considerable amount of public support.

GOVERNMENT ASSISTANCE TO INDUSTRIAL DEVELOPMENT

The very act of Confederation in 1867 brought into focus the ambitions of a fledgling nation: to create a stronger, more integrated and more unified economic base on which to build a confident and prosperous nation by developing the vast natural resources of half a continent and by speeding up the process of industrialization.

All through Sir John A. MacDonald's National Policy in the making between 1879 and 1887, through the period of liberal trade policies of Sir Wilfrid Laurier in the early twentieth century, through the great tariff raising contest in the R. B. Bennett era of 1930 to 1932 when increases in the general level of duty on the bulk of imports approximated 50 per cent — exceeding in broad terms the increases of even the National policy, 25 per cent to 30 per cent for most items — to the post-World War II period when successive Liberal and

Conservative Governments subscribed to the principle of Canada joining other countries in the gradual freeing of international trade, politicians have striven to encourage, strengthen, and broaden Canada's industrial development.

Some of these measures became fully effective only after considerable delay such as the great industrial impetus given to Canadian economic development after the turn of the century, some two decades following the introduction of the National Policy in 1879.

Other policies proved to be successful shortly after their implementation such as for example the building up of a huge industrial war machine during World War II and its reasonably smooth and greatly effective conversion to peacetime industrial uses in the years 1945 to 1947.

Still other policies did not go beyond declarations of hope and exhortation to business to act in the national interest, sometimes accompanied by ineffective government action. An example would be the efforts to increase the financial stake of Canadians in foreign controlled industries operating in Canada.

Both the Federal Government and the provincial governments have stepped up their policies to encourage industrial development in Canada in the post-World War II period.

C. D. HOWE: A GREAT NATION BUILDER

The outstanding architect of putting Canadian industry on a sound footing, and a great nation builder in an economic sense, was an engineer turned politician, an American by birth, who made Canada his home and who devoted all his adult life to making this country strong. His name: the Right Honourable Clarence Decatur Howe, Minister of the Crown in the Federal Government from 1935 to 1957. During this period he held eight portfolios, all concerned with major aspects of Canada's economic development: Railways and Canals, and Marine, and Transport before the war, Munitions and Supply during the war, Reconstruction, Reconstruction and Supply, Trade and Commerce, and Defence Production after the war.

His economic achievements are legendary and his direct contributions to building up Canadian industry more numerous than those of any Cabinet Minister before him and since his departure from the political scene. C. D. Howe was once asked:

> "Has the Canadian Government a long-term industrial development program ?" He replied in the affirmative, saying: "Our program, though, may be less distinct and publicized than that of some other countries. We do not tie our program of industrialization to a particular period of time like some of the four or five year plans which have become so fashionable to-day. Our program is a continuing one because we consider further industrialization of the Canadian economy as one of the important factors contributing to a continuing high level of employment and income, with which a rising standard of living for the Canadian people is intimately associated. To this end we are devoting all the means at our disposal. [9]

C. D. Howe was the first Minister of the Crown who laid down some of the basic principles that could usefully guide government in developing policies to encourage Canada's long term industrial development. Briefly these included:

1. Canada is a free enterprise economy and the initiative for industrial expansion rests with private individuals and firms.

2. The Government will endeavour, through its policies, to create a climate within which private initiative thrives and industrial expansion is encouraged.

3. The Government will take the initiative and do what it can to co-ordinate the efforts of governmental, business and other interested groups in achieving full and effective utilization of industrial expansion in the interests of all citizens in the country.

4. If industrial expansion and economic development is hampered by the lack of initiative, the Government, where the national interest demands, will take appropriate action. [10]

In essence, C. D. Howe's philosophy reflected a great deal of the pragmatism that has been so typical of Canadian economic policy formulated during the last century: let private enterprise do the best job it can in building up industry and let it reap the appropriate rewards for risk and initiative.

Let government help private business in any way it can to do a better job itself. But if individual initiative fails or is

---

[9] The Right Honourable C. D. Howe, Minister of Trade and Commerce, "Industrial Development in Canada", in *Public Affairs,* December 1948, Halifax, The Institute of Public Affairs, Dalhousie University, p. 213.
[10] *Ibid.*

unwilling to proceed with industrial development, clearly called for as being in the national interest, then government intervention must take place, preferably indirectly, but if necessary, directly.

When Canadians needed a synthetic rubber industry during World War II, C. D. Howe approached a number of companies to build up such an industry. He offered financial and other government assistance but there were no takers. The Canadian Government established the Polymer Corporation in 1942. This company has become in the postwar period one of the most successful business corporations in Canada, operating as a Crown company, producing synthetic rubber and a wide range of chemicals. Drawing on substantial research achievements and a high rate of productivity, this company competes successfully in world markets and produces profits which are the envy of many a large private corporation in Canada.

FEDERAL MEASURES

Some of the measures taken by the Federal Government to encourage Canada's industrial development in the postwar period include: the setting up of the Industrial Development Bank to provide credit to industries, particularly small enterprises, not obtainable from commercial sources, providing fiscal incentives such as tax concessions and accelerated capital cost allowances to establish new industries and to modernize and expand existing industries, offering export credit insurance and financing to increase sales abroad of products manufactured in Canada (including some services), and assistance to encourage more industrial research and improved design, subsidies for specific manufacturing sectors and tariff concessions for infant industries.

A new government department was established in 1963, the Department of Industry, specifically charged with the responsibility to foster the establishment, growth, efficiency and improvement of manufacturing industries by programs: (1) to assist the adaptation of manufacturing industries to changing conditions in domestic and export markets and to changes in the techniques of production; (2) to assist manufacturing industries that require special measures to develop an unrealized potential or to cope with exceptional problems of adjustment; and (3) to promote the development and use of modern industrial technology in Canada and improve the effectiveness of participation by the Government of Canada in industrial research. In 1968, the Canadian Government announced that it was amalgamating the Department of Industry with the Department of Trade and Commerce.

Other measures taken by the Federal Government were designed to help certain specific high productivity industries to become even more efficient through a substantial expansion of the markets they were serving. The outstanding examples included the special arrangements worked out with the U.S. Government and the automobile industry for Canadian firms to share access on an equal basis with American firms, to the whole North American market for automobiles and production parts. Other far reaching measures proposed by the Canadian Government included the establishment of a Canada Development Corporation whose functions were outlined by the Minister of Finance to include:

> Financing the initial development, or expansion of large scale industrial projects in Canada, and to provide financing, including refinancing, for large Canadian enterprises which might otherwise be led to seek funds outside Canada, with a consequent loss of ownership and control to non-residents. The Corporation would be expected to invest in projects and enterprises which are likely to contribute to the sound economic development of Canada and to be profitable in the long run. [11]

New Role of Provincial Governments

While the Federal Government has persistently pursued policies towards promoting Canadian industrial development over the last century, at times encouragingly effective and at times frustratingly ineffective, provincial governments have come more into their own as far as industrial development is concerned in the last half century, and particularly since the end of World War II.

---

[11] *Budget Address* by the Honourable Walter Gordon, Minister of Finance, *House of Commons Debates,* Ottawa, April 26, 1965, p. 434. By the end of 1968, the proposal to establish the Canadian Development Corporation was still pending in the House of Commons.

Three factors have contributed to the increasing importance of provincial governments in the field of industrial development in Canada:

1. Many government measures relate to problems facing specific industries located for the most part in Canada's major urban centers and thus, under Section 92 of the British North America Act, under the "property and civil rights" clause, are the direct concern of provincial governments.

2. Industry has relied increasingly on services which provincial governments can provide and have been willing to offer, the training of labour, the building of plants, the construction of adequate transportation facilities, the opening and expansion of regional and local markets.

3. The fiscal strength of provincial governments in the post-World War II period improved greatly, partly the result of Canada's great prosperity and partly the result of popular demands for increased decentralization of government functions and regional and local autonomy, though provinces persevered in their claims that the fiscal resources available to them were insufficient to meet the expanding demands for capital projects and services required by the public.

Measures taken by provincial governments in the more recent period include a wide range of incentives and assistance to Canadian manufacturing industries, through direct means such as the building of industrial estates and through indirect means such as industrial development loans. Other actions taken include the provision of low cost energy sources and industrial research of particular use to industries located in these provinces.

CHAPTER 8

Whither Canadian Industry?

BLESSINGS AND TOIL

What did industrial development mean to Canadians during the first century of their nationhood?

It represented to Canada as to other young nations, a highly desirable objective: to speed up the process of economic progress, to pass quickly through the stages of economic growth, and to become a "developed" nation, both as a symbol of material welfare and of political independence.

What Canadians had to learn early in their economic history and throughout the century was that industrial development brought not only blessings but also required sacrifices and hard toil — with one generation doing the toiling in the hope that the next generation would get the benefits. But the next generation would find itself in a similar situation and the full fruits of industrialization remained more of a promise for the future than a realization for the present.

This is not to deny that industrial development did not bring many benefits to Canadians during the first century. It did — more jobs, higher real incomes, improved and more variegated standards of living, a sense of national achievement and an ability to play a greater role in international affairs.

BALANCED GROWTH

These results were achieved not because of industrial progress alone but because Canadians were able to travel along a reasonably balanced economic growth path over the last century — of blending industrial progress with improvements in the food and raw material producing industries, and rapid expansion of the service sector which provided an adequate private and public infrastructure serving both the industrial and the resources development of the country, as well as making possible an improvement in the quality of living, so essential if economic progress is to be equated with human advancement. [1]

A Canadian Minister of the Crown who did more than any other single person in Canada to speed up the process of industrialization of this country, was once asked: What is the secret of Canada's success to achieve such a high degree of industrial advancement that this country is able to provide for its people a standard of living second only to that of the United States, a country ten times the size of Canada in terms of population and fifteen times in terms of national income? The Minister replied:

> The high degree of industrialization achieved has been the result of many factors — the availability of a multitude of natural resources, both at home and in the adjoining United States, the skill and co-operation of the Canadian worker, the vision and organizing enterprise of management, the willingness and confidence of the North American financial community to invest in Canadian development, and our ability to borrow American technology and technical personnel to complement our own efforts. [2]

In emphasizing the contributions which the Canadian worker and Canadian management had made to the industrial development of this country, the Minister was not unmindful of the fact that Canada was a North American nation and as such owed a great deal of its progress to its ability of drawing on the experience, resources and capital of the United States.

CONTINENTAL APPROACH

The record of the last century, and particularly since the end of World War II, contains ample evidence of growing American participation in Canada's economic development, freely invited by Canadians though not always looked on with favour.

---

[1] Balanced economic growth in Canada was achieved without major dislocations in the primary industry sectors: "By the middle of the twentieth century Canada had become an industrial nation. [...] Industrial development took place without adverse repercussions upon the older sectors of Canadian economic activity. Canada moved away from her former specialization in primary production and achieved a condition which might reasonably be called one of balanced growth" (*Canadian Economic History, op. cit.,* p. 522).
[2] "Industrial Development in Canada", *op. cit.,* p. 207.

This flow has not been one-sided for an increasing flow of Canadian capital has gone to the United States seeking profitable investment opportunities, some of it in direct investment and a good deal of it in securities of the great American corporations. And more than capital, a large number of Canadians have been moving to the United States, many of them highly trained, with this flow ebbing and expanding depending on economic circumstances and other factors. One of the main reasons included greater opportunities for material rewards, education and research. Many of these men have made great contributions in the United States — in industry, the universities, the professions and other fields of economic endeavour.

Hence, the fact that both Canadians and Americans live on the same continent has brought about a closer relationship between people, industry and governments, unmatched in scope and understanding by any other two countries of such disparate size.

Notwithstanding this close and in fact growing interrelationship at many levels of industrial "togetherness", Canadians have pursued a course of manufacturing development that bears, as one scholar explained more than half a century ago, "a stamp of its own". [3]

What makes Canada's industrial development different in some respect from the American, is not its outward symbols. For Canadian managers toil just as hard as their American colleagues to make a success out of their industrial enterprises. Investors are just as keen to obtain an adequate return for their risk and loan capital. And Canadian workers are just as interested in earning higher wages as are Americans, knowing only too well that increases in real earnings over the long term have to be earned through greater productivity.

No — it is not what one can readily see that distinguishes Canadian from American industrial development. What makes it so different is the broader objectives it serves.

To Americans, industrial development serves primarily economic aims. It raises national productivity, it diversifies the economy and it contributes to an improvement in the standard of living of the American people. It increases the ability of

---

[3] "Industrial Development: Introduction", *op. cit.,* p. 6.

the United States to play an effective role in efforts to maintain world peace and to aid less well endowed nations.

NATIONAL SURVIVAL

To Canadians, industrial development means all these things — though the dimensions of the task and the resultant benefits are correspondingly smaller. But to Canadians industrial development means many more things. It also means:

- — a source of strength
- — a source of confidence
- — a source of reassurance
- — a source of unity.

And strength, confidence, reassurance and unity are what Canadians need if they are to progress and prosper as a vibrant nation. Hence, industrial development is even more vital for political reasons. If Canadians want to remain an independent and viable North American nation, living as they do next to two giant neighbours — the U.S.A. and the U.S.S.R. — then they must build up their economic and industrial strength on a continuing and internationally competitive basis. In this uncertain world, balanced economic growth and sustained industrial development are essential to Canada's national survival.

CHAPITRE 9

Sommaire

1. *Bienfaits de l'industrialisation.* — La première partie
de cet ouvrage retrace l'histoire d'un siècle de l'essor économique
au Canada: comment le progrès industriel a contribué à la
croissance économique du pays et a permis aux Canadiens de
vivre mieux et plus confortablement; comment ces bienfaits se
sont étendus à tout le pays et même à l'étranger; comment
l'industrialisation fut réalisée — à quelles difficultés les Canadiens eurent à faire face et comment ils en ont triomphé; quels
furent leurs succès et leurs revers, leurs espoirs et leurs aspirations; quel rôle jouèrent les individus et les gouvernements, la
main-d'œuvre et la direction des entreprises.

2. *Les réalisations.* — De 1867 à 1967, la population du
Canada a sextuplé; les emplois sont devenus sept fois plus
nombreux; le produit national brut, 150 fois plus élevé en terme
de dollars, soit 30 fois quant à sa valeur réelle; les exportations
de marchandises, 200 fois — 40 fois quant à leur valeur réelle.
Dans l'industrie, la valeur brute des produits manufacturés s'est
accrue près de 250 fois, soit 50 fois quant à leur valeur réelle;
le nombre des emplois a été plus que décuplé; la production de
chaque ouvrier, dans un an, a quintuplé; le nombre d'heures de
travail par semaine a été réduit de deux cinquièmes; le salaire
hebdomadaire moyen de l'ouvrier est devenu 21 fois plus élevé,
soit un pouvoir d'achat quatre fois plus grand.

3. *Emplois (embauchage) et revenu.* — L'industrie est le
secteur le plus important de l'économie canadienne quant au
nombre d'emplois et au revenu: un emploi sur quatre, et un
dollar sur trois de revenu proviennent de l'industrie. L'industrie
manufacturière a dépassé l'agriculture après la Première Grande
Guerre quant au revenu des salariés; après la Deuxième Grande
Guerre, elle l'a dépassée également quant au nombre d'emplois
procurés et est ainsi devenu le secteur le plus important dans le
développement économique du Canada.

4. *Marché domestique et étranger.* — Les industries canadiennes vendent la plus grande partie de leurs produits sur le
marché canadien: environ 90%. Leurs exportations de produits

entièrement manufacturés représentent moins de 10% de leur production totale, descendant parfois jusqu'à 7%. Les produits manufacturés, qui avaient atteint 50% des exportations totales durant les années 1920-1929 et jusqu'à 55% à la fin de la Deuxième Grande Guerre, descendirent à un niveau de 35 à 40% durant la période suivante s'étendant jusqu'à 1960.

5. *Tendances mondiales.* — Durant la période de 1956 à 1961, les exportations mondiales de produits totalement manufacturés se sont accrues plus rapidement que celles des produits transformés ou celles des matières brutes: le taux de croissance a été de 66% pour les premières, de 47% pour les secondes et de 26% pour les dernières. Les exportations canadiennes n'ont pas suivi cette tendance mondiale: les exportations de matières brutes, qui représentaient 3,7% des exportations mondiales en 1955, se sont élevées à 4,6% en 1961; celles des produits transformés sont passées de 13,7% à 10,5%, tandis que celles des produits manufacturés ont peu varié: 1,3% en 1955 et 1,4% en 1961.

6. *Écart dans le rendement.* — L'écart croissant dans l'amélioration du rendement est la principale raison pour laquelle les Canadiens ne marchent pas de pair avec les autres nations industrialisées, dans le commerce mondial des produits manufacturés ou transformés. Des neuf grandes nations industrialisées d'Europe et d'Amérique du Nord, sept réalisèrent un accroissement de rendement plus considérable que celui du Canada durant la période s'étendant de 1950 à 1960, ainsi que le montre le pourcentage de la croissance annuelle du rendement horaire de chaque ouvrier: France, 5,9%; Allemagne de l'Ouest, 5,6%; Autriche, 5,3%; les Pays-Bas, 4,3%; Belgique, 3,6%; Suède, 3,2%; États-Unis, 3,2%; Canada, 3,0%; Royaume-Uni, 3,6%.

7. *L'Économie de la « Grandeur ».* — Des quelque 20.000 corporations industrielles canadiennes, plus de 70% réalisèrent des profits en 1962; et un peu moins de 30% subirent des pertes. Sur trente corporations industrielles canadiennes, vingt et une sont considérées comme petites; huit, de moyenne importance, et une est considérable; le capital de cette dernière doit s'élever à $5 millions ou plus. Les chiffres suivants, pour l'année 1962, indiquent que le pourcentage des profits, comparé au capital, croît à mesure que la firme grossit: les firmes ayant un capital

entre $500.000 et $999.000 ont réalisé un profit de 6,2% ; celles dont le capital se chiffre entre $1.000.000 et $4.999.000, un profit de 8,2% ; celles dont le capital est de $5.000.000 ou plus, un profit de 9,9%.

8. *Mainmise étrangère.* — Environ 60% des industries canadiennes sont contrôlées par des industries étrangères, 46% par des citoyens des États-Unis; 14% par des citoyens d'autres pays; les Canadiens ne contrôlent que 40% de leurs industries secondaires. Dans certains secteurs de l'industrie, la mainmise étrangère est encore plus sensible; par exemple, dans l'industrie de l'automobile, 97% ; dans celle du caoutchouc, 97% ; dans celle des produits chimiques, 78% ; dans celle des appareils électriques, 77%. Bien que les Canadiens aient réussi à rapatrier, durant les années 1960, un montant considérable de valeurs canadiennes, réduisant ainsi quelque peu la mainmise étrangère, la tendance se maintient plutôt à la hausse qu'à la baisse de cette mainmise étrangère.

9. *Rôle du gouvernement.* — Les Canadiens ont toujours été indépendants et énergiques, et durant la plus grande partie du siècle ils ont préféré que le gouvernement intervienne le moins possible dans les affaires. Cependant, on rencontre moins de controverse sur la participation du gouvernement dans le domaine de l'essor industriel, que dans tout autre secteur important, soit économique, soit social, soit politique. En conséquence, les gouvernements ont formulé toute une gamme de lignes de conduite dans le domaine économique et ont adopté plusieurs mesures pour promouvoir et réaliser l'industrialisation de l'économie canadienne, généralement, avec l'appui du public.

10. *Politiques publiques.* — Durant toute la période d'élaboration de la « Politique nationale » de Sir John A. Macdonald, entre 1879 et 1887, durant la période libre-échangiste de Sir Wilfrid Laurier, au début du XXe siècle, durant la période de la course à l'augmentation des barrières tarifaires, sous le régime de R. B. Bennett (1930-1932), durant laquelle le niveau général de la douane sur l'ensemble des importations s'élevait à environ 50% — dépassant même, en chiffres ronds, de 25 à 30% sur la plupart des items, l'augmentation résultant de la « Politique nationale », — jusqu'à la période de l'après-guerre alors que les gouvernements successifs, libéraux et conservateurs, ont admis le principe que le Canada doit se joindre aux autres pays afin

de libéraliser graduellement le commerce international, les politiciens ont travaillé à encourager, à fortifier et à accroître le développement industriel. Quelques-unes de ces mesures n'ont atteint leur pleine efficacité qu'après un long délai; par exemple, le grand essor industriel survenu au début du siècle, quelque deux décennies après l'adoption de la Politique nationale en 1879. D'autres mesures ont connu un plein succès peu de temps après leur mise en œuvre; par exemple, l'organisation de l'industrie de guerre durant la Deuxième Grande Guerre, et sa transformation en industrie de temps de paix, transformation qui s'est effectuée sans trop de heurts et d'une façon très efficace, entre 1945 et 1947. D'autres lignes de conduite encore, quelquefois accompagnées de mesures gouvernementales qui n'eurent pas de suite, ne dépassèrent pas le stade des grandes déclarations proclamant l'espoir dans l'avenir et exhortant le monde des affaires à agir dans l'intérêt national. Comme exemple, on pourrait citer les efforts pour augmenter les intérêts financiers des Canadiens dans les industries canadiennes contrôlées par des étrangers. Les gouvernements fédéral et provinciaux ont pris des mesures pour encourager le progrès des industries au Canada après la Deuxième Grande Guerre.

11. *C. D. Howe.* — Celui qui a contribué le plus à donner à l'industrie canadienne des bases solides, qui fut un des grands fondateurs de la nation dans le domaine économique, était un ingénieur devenu politicien, un Américain de naissance, qui vint habiter le Canada et consacra toute sa vie à faire de son pays d'adoption un pays fort. Il se nommait le très Honorable Clarence Decatur Howe, ministre de la Couronne dans le gouvernement fédéral de 1935 à 1957. Durant cette période, il détint huit portefeuilles, tous touchant des secteurs du domaine économique. C. D. Howe fut le premier ministre de la Couronne à mettre en avant les principes de base des lignes de conduite gouvernementales concernant le développement industriel. Entre autres: « 1° L'économie du Canada est fondée sur la libre entreprise, et l'initiative dans le domaine de l'expansion industrielle appartient aux individus et aux firmes privées. 2° Le gouvernement va s'efforcer, par ses lignes de conduite, de créer un climat favorable à l'initiative privée et à l'expansion industrielle. 3° Le gouvernement devra prendre l'initiative et concentrer ses énergies à coordonner les efforts des organismes gouvernementaux, du monde des affaires et des autres groupes intéressés à

l'utilisation pleine et efficace de l'expansion industrielle pour le plus grand bien de tous les citoyens du pays. 4° Si l'expansion industrielle et le développement économique sont compromis par le manque d'initiative privée, le gouvernement prendra des mesures appropriées lorsque l'intérêt national l'exigera. »

12. *Essor et survie nationale.* — L'essor industriel est nécessaire au progrès économique du Canada et à la survie nationale. En effet, il permet au pays d'augmenter sa productivité (rendement), de diversifier son économie et contribue à élever le standard de vie de ses citoyens. Il permet également au Canada d'augmenter sa participation aux affaires, au commerce, aux opérations bancaires et aux plans d'aide sur le plan international et de contribuer ainsi au maintien de la paix. Le développement industriel est aussi important pour des raisons politiques. Si les Canadiens désirent demeurer un peuple nord-américain indépendant, capable de survivre au milieu de ses deux voisins géants, les États-Unis et l'U.R.S.S., ils doivent construire leur force économique et industrielle sur une base durable et concurrentielle sur le plan international. Dans ce monde incertain, un progrès économique équilibré et un essor industriel soutenu sont nécessaires à la survie du Canada comme nation indépendante.

PART II

Education and Economic Development

Desiderantes Meliorem Patriam [1]

---

[1] "They desire a better country" is the motto of the Order of Canada, awarded for outstanding service, and increasingly, serving the nation well requires education, more education and still more education.

CHAPTER 10

Concepts of Economic Growth, Development and Progress

On July 1, 1967, Canada celebrated the anniversary of her first century of nationhood, thus completing the second phase in her 362 years of political history of settling the northern half of North America, with the first phase comprising the colonial period from 1605 to 1867.

In economic terms, Canada's development followed broadly the five stages delineated by W. W. Rostow in his attempt to generalize about the sweep of economic history; [2] it moved through the changes in industrial structure as suggested by Colin Clark in his search for the basic causes of economic progress; [3] and it embarked on a process of economic growth, more or less continuously widening and broadening the scope of the industrial and resources base of the country and its economic relations with other nations, bringing in its wake significant increases in productivity and standards of living, as observed by Simon Kuznets in his comprehensive comparative studies of economic growth on an international scale. [4]

Part II of this book assesses the relationship of education and economic growth and development in aggregate, in structural and micro-economic terms on the basis of one hundred years of Canadian experience. It sets out the concepts of economic growth, development and progress, examines the role of education in the developmental process and analyzes quantitative evidence relating to the interrelationship between economic and educational advancement as well as the benefits accruing to individuals and to society as a whole.

---

[2] W. W. ROSTOW, *The Stages of Economic Growth*, London, Cambridge University Press, 1960. The reader may wish to note the reference to "broadly" above as a reminder that a case can be made for a number of economic developments over the last century not fitting Rostow's stages approach and that in fact efforts to delineate stages oversimplify the full meaning of Canadian economic development in its great diversity, its regional variations and its historical context.

[3] Colin CLARK, *The Conditions of Economic Progress*, 2nd edition, London, Macmillan and Company Limited, 1951.

[4] Simon KUZNETS, *Modern Economic Growth, Rate, Structure and Spread*, New Haven and London, Yale University Press, 1966.

To commence with a brief explanation of the concepts of economic growth, economic development and economic progress.

Some economists use the concepts of economic growth, economic development and economic progress interchangeably. Some use certain criteria as common to two or three of the concepts while others assign specific meaning to each of these concepts. Some economists quantify these concepts by using macro-economic indicators while others claim that many elements defy adequate measurement including changes in qualitative and welfare aspects.

An understanding of the dynamic role of education in the economy can be facilitated if its implications are assessed separately in relation to economic growth, economic development and economic progress.

VARIETY OF MEANING OF ECONOMIC GROWTH

Economic growth in its broadest context may be described as a process involving the expansion of a nation's real output over the longer term, bringing with it improvements in the standard of living of the population and increasing the capacity to produce an expanded volume and a greater range of goods and services so as to maximize consumer satisfaction, as well as to create the social framework and economic climate conducive to further expansion and development. [5]

---

[5] While some economists exclude changes in structure in the concept of economic growth, others include them. They refer not only to industrial change and disposition of the nation's output, but also to changes in the structure of consumption. One of the leading proponents of this point of view submits: "Economic growth of nations as sustained increase in per capita or per worker product [is] most often accompanied by an increase in population and usually by sweeping structural changes. In modern times these were changes in the industrial structure within which product was turned out and resources employed — away from agricultural toward nonagricultural activities, the process of industrialization; in the distribution of population between the countryside and the cities, the process of urbanization; in the relative economic position of groups within the nation distinguished by employment status, attachment to various industries, level of per capita income, and the like; in the distribution of product by use — among household consumption, capital formation, and government consumption, and within each of these major categories by further subdivision; in the allocation of product by its origin within the nation's boundaries and elsewhere; and so on. And of course, nations do not live alone but in association with others, so that the growth of one affects others and is in turn affected by them. Hence, in addition to the aggregative and structural, there are the international aspects of economic growth" (see *Modern Economic Growth : Rate Structure, and Spread, op. cit.,* p. 1).

In a narrow sense, it can be said that economic growth takes place when a nation's output expands. It is usually measured in terms of an increase in the Gross National Product in real terms. Such economic growth may take place because the factors of production, land, labour and capital, are expanding and sufficient demand for the resulting goods and services is engendered to warrant an increase in the nation's output. [6]

ESSENTIAL FEATURES OF ECONOMIC DEVELOPMENT

Economic growth can take place without productivity rising, that is a unit of output being produced with a lesser input, without significant technological advances and without changes in the industrial and social structure. For if the factors of production are expanding, society is capable of creating a greater output of goods and services if demand for these also expands. But most nations are not satisfied with this type of economic growth. They aim also at continuously increasing productivity and they endeavour to achieve this objective through the adoption of technological advances, the application of entrepreneurial initiative, the accumulation and effective use of physical capital and human resources, changes in industrial structure and the build-up of social investment, as well as the pursuit of appropriate economic policies conducive to economic advancement. When economic growth takes this form it is usually described as economic development and it is measured in terms of changes in Gross National Product in real terms per person working, or in terms of output produced per man-hour.

In a broad sense, economic development involves continuing economic expansion [7] of an adequate rate [8] achieved through

---

[6] There are many other definitions of economic growth. Some economists emphasize the importance of improving the quality of performance and increasing leisure. To illustrate: "The best measure of growth is real GNP, modified by data on leisure, population size, distribution, quality, and noneconomic factors" (see Paul A. SAMUELSON and Anthony SCOTT, *Economics, An Introductory Analysis,* Toronto, McGraw-Hill Company of Canada Limited, 1966, p. 851).

[7] Some economists stress the continuity of the development process. For example: "Development — that is, increase in productivity — may go on forever" (see Everett E. HAGEN, *The Economics of Development,* Homewood, Illinois, Richard D. Irwin, Inc., 1968, p. 5).

[8] The meaning of what constitutes an "adequate rate" would differ, depending on national economic circumstances, policy objectives and academic interpretation. Broadly speaking, an economy can be said to expand at an adequate rate if it maximizes both *potential* and *actual* Gross National Product. Potential Gross National Product can be maxi-

a substantive broadening of the industrial base of the country concerned, the advancement of technological and managerial know-how, the raising of the quality of human capital and the creation of an adequate infrastructure covering both public facilities and private institutions. [9]

Putting it briefly, the essential features of economic development are changes in the state of technology and the extent to which such changes are incorporated in the production and distribution process, leading to productivity improvements with consequent beneficial effects on the economy as a whole in both national and international terms. For economic development to take place, it must be not only growth-inducing but also growth-sustaining.

INTERRELATIONSHIP BETWEEN ECONOMIC GROWTH AND ECONOMIC DEVELOPMENT

Economic growth can occur without economic development as a nation expands its real output by a variety of means such as increases in the labour force, either by natural increase, net migration or changes in labour force participation rates, a greater number of hours worked per week, moon-lighting, etc.

When economic development takes place, economic growth must occur because one of the prime motivating and contributing factors to economic expansion results from the massive introduction of innovations, technological progress, and changes in

---

mized by expanding the factors of production and devising ways and means of combining them in the most effective manner. Actual Gross National Product can be maximized by making full or near full use of the expanding productive potential of the nation.

    [9] In defining economic development, most authors emphasize changes in industrial structure and the continuity of introducing innovations. To illustrate: The development of an economy involves "the infusion and the incorporation of science and technology into its methods of production, accompanied or followed by major changes in the pattern of its industry, with a consequent rising and more variegated standard of living. Used in this sense, development is most pronounced in an economy's history in the stages when it begins to absorb a technology based on science, to enter an 'industrial' revolution. In Rostow's excellent delineation of stages in the process, the economy reaches maturity when it has absorbed and is applying a large proportion of the latent available science and technology. But development can continue in lesser degree throughout its subsequent history after reaching maturity. It may even experience further sharp changes as new major discoveries and inventions occur, when entrepreneurs convert these into innovations" (see T. M. BROWN, *Canadian Economic Growth*, Study prepared for the Royal Commission on Health Services, Ottawa, Queen's Printer, 1965, pp. 4 and 5).

industrial structure which in turn yield higher productivity and higher average real income per person working. [10]

DEFINITION OF ECONOMIC PROGRESS

When economic growth occurs without economic development, little or no economic progress may be made if economic progress is defined as an increase in the share of the nation's output available to each citizen. In this sense, economic progress can be measured in terms of changes in Gross National Product in real terms per capita. This means that potentially the average person may have access to a greater amount of output (i.e. income), but whether in fact he obtains a greater piece of the bigger pie, will depend on how the pie is divided.

But even if each individual were to get a greater piece of the larger pie, to judge whether economic progress has taken place, will also depend on what that pie consists of. For Gross National Product may increase because government spends more money on defence and military pursuits. In that case, Gross National Product per capita in real terms may be up. But as a result of a shift in the disposition of Gross National Product, the consumer may be less well off.

There is also a situation where the economy may be devoting a larger proportion than usual to capital formation and the proportion of the nation's output devoted to consumer spending may decline. In that case, the consumer may be said to be *potentially* better off, for he can expect that at some future date the large investment expenditures made will pay off in terms of rising real incomes and access to a greater volume of consumer goods and services. But in terms of the welfare benefits obtained by the consumer in the year in which the large capital expend-

---

[10] The overlapping aspects of the two concepts have been stressed by a number of economists. For example: "Economic growth means more output, and economic development implies both more output and changes in the technical and institutional arrangements by which it is produced. Growth may well imply not only more output, but also more inputs and more efficiency, i.e., an increase in output per unit of input. Development goes beyond these to imply changes in the structure of outputs and in the allocation of inputs by sectors. [...] Growth and development go together, of course, at least up to a point where the economy loses its capacity to adapt to changed circumstances" (see Charles P. KINDLEBERGER, *Economic Development*, Second Edition, New York, McGraw-Hill Inc., 1965, pp. 3 and 15).

itures are made, he may not be better off, even though Gross National Product in real terms per capita may be up. [11]

One way to overcome the problem of measuring economic progress in terms of changes in real Gross National Product per capita is to use changes in the volume of personal expenditures on consumer goods and services per capita. While this measurement indicates the progress the average individual in society makes through obtaining access to an increased volume of consumer goods and services, it still falls short because it limits the assessment to a quantity of output obtainable.

Allowance is still lacking for (1) changes in the quality of goods and services becoming available — though presumably some of the changes would be reflected in the increase of the price level — (2) changes in consumer satisfaction obtained from the greater access to more and better material comforts, and changes in individual attitudes towards work — which facilitates (3) the earning of income and the making of consumer purchases — and leisure — which increase non-material satisfaction and thus present an antidote to the materialistic instincts of North American society dating back to the pioneering days and are still strong a century later.

INTERRELATIONSHIP BETWEEN ECONOMIC DEVELOPMENT AND ECONOMIC PROGRESS

Some economists consider economic progress and economic development as two sides of the same coin and they use the two terms synonymously. [12] They develop the theme further by saying that economic progress is not only concerned with the

---

[11] "Practically everyone wants a higher standard of living, in the sense of 'command over more goods, services, and leisure.' We can also observe that practically everyone is willing to make *some* sacrifice in order to have a higher standard of living. Welfare economics tries to balance the satisfaction of these wants with the sacrifices 'at the margin'; each individual is supposed to equalize the marginal rates of substitution among goods and services, between goods and services and leisure, and between income now and income later" (see Benjamin HIGGINS, *Economic Development, Principles, Problems, and Policies*, Revised Edition, New York, W. W. Norton & Company, Inc., 1968, p. 365).

[12] "Economic progress consists in an improvement in the efficiency of the use of means to attain ends. [...] Economic progress, therefore, means the discovery and application of better ways of doing things to satisfy our wants." When applying this concept of economic progress to the formulation of government policy, Boulding speaks of economic development (see Kenneth E. BOULDING, *Principles of Economic Policy*, London, Staples Press, 1963, pp. 22, 23 and 405).

ability of a person or of a nation to satisfy more effectively an expanding array of diverse wants, but it is also related to the changing character of such wants. [13] This distinction achieves particular meaning in conjunction with the claim that modern advertising efforts have been increasingly used to affect individual preferences and to distort the consumer spending pattern.[14]

For economic progress to take place, individual welfare has to increase; if not for all, so for the majority of the population. Hence, measurement of economic progress also involves an assessment of changes in income distribution. Variations in income distribution may be the result of market forces and individual initiative and/or the result of fiscal policies affecting income distribution including a progressive income tax system and a broadly based social security and primary industry support programme. [15]

When a nation's capacity to produce is raised, this potential can be used either to create more goods and services and improve their quality and the satisfaction they yield to the individual and to society as a whole, or to reduce the number of hours worked, hence potentially increasing leisure time, [16] or

---

[13] "Economic progress", says Boulding, "enables us to get what we want more easily than before, but it says nothing about the propriety of what we want. It we want the wrong things, then economic progress may enable us to damn ourselves all the more quickly. [...] Indeed, economic progress makes a critique of wants all the more necessary, for the better we are able to satisfy our wants the more important it is that our wants should be 'good' wants". This reasoning, according to Boulding, applies with equal force to the manner in which economic progress affects the wants of individuals and of society as a whole (*ibid.*, p. 23).

[14] J. K. GALBRAITH, *The New Industrial State*, Boston, Houghton Mifflin Company, 1967, pp. 211 ff. (See discussion of "Revised Sequence".)

[15] If the majority of the population does not benefit from rising incomes, with efforts being made to compensate those not participating in material improvements through social justice measures, then an increase in real Gross National Product per capita, considered from a welfare point of view, reflects an increase in *potential* welfare and not *actual* welfare, if the latter is defined as an improvement of living conditions of the population as a whole (see Barry N. SIEGEL, *Aggregate Economics and Public Policy*, Revised Edition, Homewood, Ill., Richard D. Irwin, Inc., 1965, p. 285).

[16] Lest the claim be made that allowance for leisure as a factor in assessing economic growth, economic development and economic progress is the brainchild of modern economists, the reader is referred to the writing of Leon Walras (1834-1910) who appears to be one of the first economists to take account of leisure in his work on national income (Leon WALRAS, *Elements of Pure Economics*, Homewood, Ill., Richard D. Irwin, Inc., 1954, pp. 215 and 379).

to achieve both. As a result, economic progress will occur not only when Gross National Product per capita rises, but also when the average number of hours worked per week declines and/or the number of days taken as holidays increases.

Historically, developed nations have endeavoured to achieve both objectives: to increase output per capita and leisure time. Increasingly, less developed countries have also adopted such achievements as a long term objective of national policy.

To the extent then that economic growth, economic development and economic progress include efforts to maximize consumer welfare, with an appropriate blend of policies designed to enhance the quality of living of the present generation, while at the same time aiming to strengthen the economy's capacity to safeguard progress of future generations, one primary task of growth theory is to explain the working of the economic system and its ability towards achieving continuing improvement in consumer satisfaction with a lessening of effort and sacrifice on the part of the working force. [17]

ECONOMIC GROWTH AND LABOUR-FORCE QUALITY

A key factor in economic growth, development and progress is the labour-force — the people who make efforts to produce goods and services, and who have the skill, initiative and enterprise to wrest resources from a reluctant nature and inimical elements, and convert raw materials into final products for consumption and investment.

Without denying the importance of the other factors of production, capital (which in a modern sense includes both physical capital as well as the willingness of the entrepreneur to risk capital and thus covers also entrepreneurial initiative) and land (which includes natural resources availability and potential, both underground and above ground), the human

---

[17] Higgins stipulates as "the overall goal of economic development [...] raising per capita productivity as much as possible over some long-run 'perspective planning' period, and spreading the consequent improvements of welfare among all major groups and regions; in the process, due weight should be given to people's wishes regarding the choice between goods and services or leisure, between more income now and more income later, and between a higher per capita income and larger families, expressed as collective choices made by the smallest group whose decisions can be effective in promoting development" (see *Economic Development, Principles, Problems, and Policies, op. cit.*, pp. 368 and 369).

element has always been a major determinant of economic and social progress. [18]

The labour force in turn, if appropriately trained and productively employed, can be a most effective element in furthering economic development and economic growth. This will particularly be the case if labour is employed with other factors of production in a most favourable and efficient manner, and if its quality is enhanced, combined with the spirit of adventure and determination to do well in both material and non-material terms. [19]

Among the many factors that may contribute to raising the quality of the labour force and influencing its attitudes toward economic progress and social change, one element is singled out for examination in this part of the book, and that is education, as it relates to Canada's economic development over the last century.

---

[18] "Natural resources [...] may play an important role in the structure and *pattern* of economic development, but the most important *dynamic* elements in growth must be sought elsewhere. [...] Our most valuable capital is our human capital, and the skills and the education and the knowledge which our people possess" (see Arthur J. R. SMITH, "The Economics of Human Productivity", Address to the 15th Annual Conference of The Alberta Council of Personnel Associations, Edmonton, Alberta, May 9, 1968, pp. 9 and 10).

[19] Dr. Smith, the Chairman of the Economic Council of Canada emphasized the difficulties which Canada has been facing during the last decade in raising national productivity: "Why [...] did the large investment boom in the mid-1950's not produce any significant 'pay-off' in terms of growth in productivity and living standards in Canada over the latter part of the 1950's and into the early 1960's ? Why, for example, is there a much lower *level* of productivity and average living standards in Canada than in the United States when the volume of capital per employed person is not appreciably different in the two countries ? And again, why is it that various other countries, without comparable levels of growth in investment, have achieved a significantly better performance in the growth of productivity and per capita income than we have in Canada over the post-war period ?" Lest Canadians pay inadequate attention to the development of human resources relying as in the past more on the benefits to be derived from bountiful natural resources, Dr. Smith warned: "In today's world [...] the countries achieving the fastest productivity advances are not large countries with rich bases of natural resources" (*ibid.*, p. 9).

CHAPTER 11

The "Stages" Framework

DELINEATION OF STAGES

W. W. Rostow, in offering his generalization of "stages-of-growth", explained that this method of analysis of economic development was designed "to dramatize not merely the uniformities in the sequence of modernization but also — and equally — the uniqueness of each nation's experience." [1] At the same time, Rostow acknowledged that this approach was "an arbitrary and limited way of looking at the sequence of modern history." [2] This limitation is particularly applicable to a country like Canada, with her great dependence on exports, heavy and fluctuating inflows of immigrants and capital, and regional economic and cultural diversity.

Rostow distinguishes five stages : the traditional society, the preconditions for take-off, the take-off, the drive to maturity, and the age of high mass-consumption. Rostow mentions three terminal dates for Canada, the take-off period, 1896-1914, [3] and achievement of "technical maturity" in 1950. [4] From these dates, the five stages applied to Canada can be delineated as follows :

1. The traditional society, 1605-1867.

2. The preconditions for take-off, 1867-1896.

3. The take-off, 1896-1914.

4. The drive to maturity, 1914-1950.

5. The age of high mass-consumption, 1950-1967 (and continuing).

Some changes in terminal dates could be suggested. The period of the traditional society could be taken to have ended in 1825, when the North American Colonies embarked on a

---

1   *The Stages of Economic Growth, op. cit.,* p. 1.
2   *Ibid.*
3   *Ibid.,* p. 38.
4   *Ibid.,* p. 59.

period of expansion which lasted four decades, some interruptions in the growth process notwithstanding. [5]

Or the first stage could be taken to have ended in 1848 when the first responsible government was formed in Canada which at that time comprised Lower Canada (Quebec) and Upper Canada (Ontario), with the new ministry taking increasingly independent action to deal with domestic economic problems, particularly those arising out of a depression which followed "Sir Robert Peel's last and most revolutionary budget" of 1846 and which "turned England into a virtually free trade country", bringing calamity to Canadian trade overseas, particularly timber and wheat. [6] These two commodities were the most important items in Canada's trade balance with England and they had enjoyed for many years the benefits of British preferences.

The choice of an earlier year than 1867 as the terminal date of the traditional society stage is supported by the large commercial expansion experienced by the British North American Colonies in the four decades prior to Confederation, as both domestic and international trade increased, using the St. Lawrence waterway. Construction of a comprehensive system of canals contributed to domestic economic growth and facilitated exports and immigration. Industrial development and land settlement proceeded at an increasing pace.

Against this, economic progress during the period 1825-1866 was intermittent, and the country lacked both the will and the commonness of interest that are so essential to continuing economic, social and cultural advancement within a cohesive national framework.

---

[5] "The new economic expansion took place [. . .] especially in the years from 1825 to 1831. Trade was good, and numerous enterprises such as the Welland and Rideau Canals were undertaken, the Lachine Canal being already in working order. New roads were opened up and older ones improved. The operations of the Canada Company and other private land enterprises were bringing to Canada many of its best settlers. Numerous local industries were begun or expanded in various parts of the Maritime Provinces, and in Upper Canada in particular" (see Adam SHORTT, "The Financial Development of British North America" in J. Holland ROSE, A. P. NEWTON, and E. A. BENIANS, Eds. *The Cambridge History of the British Empire*, Vol. VI, London, Cambridge University Press, 1930, p. 369).
[6] A. R. M. LOWER, *Colony to Nation*, New Edition, Toronto, Longmans, Green & Company, 1947, p. 272.

British colonial administrators and local politicians made many well intended attempts to get the people of the regions that were to become a united Canada in 1867 to strengthen and diversify their economy on a continuing basis and to subordinate their traditional and clannish loyalties to the greater good of building a North American nation.

But this was not to be. Prejudice that fed on linguistic and religious differences was rampant. Political strife, and commercial and financial jealousies prevailed. Many economic policies pursued by the British and the Americans adversely affected the North American colonies. All these factors combined to make it difficult during the four decades preceding Confederation for Canadians to create the infrastructure, the productive capability and the managerial and political establishment necessary to pursue an independent and persistent course of continuing economic growth and development.

Hence, the period 1825-1866 was largely one of breaking down the barriers to economic progress by removing one by one the shackles of the traditional society to the extent they existed — for there were large parts of the region and many inhabitants to which the concept of traditionalism was not applicable — and replacing them with the rudiments of a viable society, capable and willing to embark on the exciting adventure of nation-building and to respond to the formidable challenge to better the lot of its people in a harsh northern country.

Some other minor changes in delineating economic stages could be suggested. For example, the commencement of the take-off period could be moved from 1896 to 1895, the starting point of an upswing phase and the period could end with 1913, a prosperous year, rather than with 1914, a recession year, notwithstanding the commencement of World War I. The year Canada moved into the stage of high mass-consumption, accompanied by technological maturity could be changed from 1950 to 1947, the year this country completed successfully the conversion from a complex war-time industrial structure to an effectively working economic system serving peaceful and increasingly internationally oriented economic objectives.

But such changes are not sufficiently substantial to materially affect the pattern of economic development as visualized by Rostow. Thus the analysis that follows is presented within

the stages framework as developed by Rostow using his delineation of terminal dates for Canada, bearing in mind the
controversy that exists about the applicability of the Rostow's
stages concept to a country like Canada, which from the
beginning was commercially oriented and whose economic
development depended largely on the growth of export staples,
and only in more recent periods on the expansion of secondary
and tertiary industries.

Some broad economic aggregates are used to measure the
varying rates of progress made during the stages, including
population, labour force, employment and Gross National Product in constant dollars, totals per capita and per person working.
It bears emphasis that such an assessment of trends and economic achievements is of necessity limited. It is designed
primarily to provide in broad strokes the general background
of Canadian economic development to facilitate perceiving
the contribution of education to economic development in
perspective.

There is the further point that in following the terminal
dates suggested by Rostow, single years are used for the purpose
of comparison. Such analysis introduces a cyclical bias since
the reference dates do not always reflect similar phases in the
business cycle. While by and large the distortions over the
longer term are not of major significance, the phasing based
on single years rather than on quinquennial averages or annual
averages of overlapping decades such as Kuznets has used, [7]
has the effect that some rates of growth may be moderately
under or overstated for particular periods. To minimize such
possibilities, the analysis is supplemented by quinquennial averages of rates of growth of some of the economic indicators.

TRADITIONAL SOCIETY

The traditional society covers a stage of limited horizons
in a country's economic history, with "a ceiling [...] on the
level of attainable output per head. [...] This ceiling resulted

---

[7] *Income and Wealth of the United States, Trends and Structure*,
two papers by Simon KUZNETS and Raymond GOLDSMITH, ed. by Simon
Kuznets, Income and Wealth Series II, International Association for
Research in Income and Wealth, Cambridge, Bowes & Bowes, Publishers
Ltd., 1952, and *Modern Economic Growth: Rate, Structure, and Spread*,
op. cit.

from the fact that the potentialities which flow from modern science and technology were either not available or not regularly and systematically applied." [8]

For Canada, the "traditional society" is a story of 262 years of colonial period, 1605-1867, from the time when the French explorer Pierre du Gua de Monts founded a colony at Port Royal in 1605 (in what was later to become the Province of Nova Scotia) and Samuel de Champlain at Quebec in 1608. [9]

British settlements followed on the Atlantic coast and "the Governor and Company of Adventurers of England trade into Hudson's Bay" established posts at the mouth of the rivers flowing into Hudson Bay and James Bay in the years following 1670. The animosity of the British and French in their struggle for European supremacy was paralleled by rivalry in North America, inherent in the clash of interest between the great competing gateway to the continental interior, namely the Hudson River, the St. Lawrence and Hudson Bay. For a century fighting among the settlements, interrupted by uneasy peace of short duration, hampered the economic development of the region. Then, after one last battle in 1760, the Fleur de Lis came down in Quebec and the whole of North America became British.

The southern half of the continent embarked on a course of independence, with the breakaway of the thirteen colonies from Britain in 1776, spreading westwards and southwards to become the United States. The settled areas of the northern half of North America remained a group of British colonies, run from Westminster in London. Long distance management became increasingly unpopular among the settlers and increasingly costly to the colonial power.

When the Civil War ended in the United States in 1865, interest in that country to expand northward mounted. Unification of the northern part of the continent into an independent nation, Canada, appeared to be the political answer to the growing indifference of Britain and the expansionist policies of the United States, and the economic answer to the colonists

---

8 *The Stages of Economic Growth, op. cit.,* p. 4.
9 These settlements followed two previous attempts that ended in failure, Sieur de Roberval's settlement on the St. Lawrence in 1542 and 1543, and the Marquis de la Roche's effort to take a French colonizing expedition to Canada in 1584.

who wanted to develop their country's bountiful resources in the hope that a larger domestic market, ultimately extending over the breadth of the continent, would provide a sound foundation for economic progress and prosperity.

During most of this early period of Canada's "traditional society", the settlers struggling to wrest a livelihood from a harsh nature in a northern country, relying to a large extent on trade abroad and foreign capital to create a viable economic base, sometimes helped and sometimes hindered by a well-disposed but distant and not always fully knowledgeable colonial administration, had little direct contact with the post-Newtonian world. Rostow described the latter as the time "when men came widely to believe that the external world was subject to a few knowable laws, and was systematically capable of productive manipulation." [10]

But in the latter phase of this period, as foreign commerce expanded and became multi-country in its orientation, and settlement continued to expand, these northern settlers asked the question more frequently: Would independence, unity and nationhood not enable them to do a better job themselves in developing their country's resources and improving their standard of living than to continue in a stage of dependence on the mother country for entrepreneurial initiative, introduction of innovations and financial underwriting to pay for the expansion of the social infrastructure, essential to spur on economic progress?

There was the further question that concerned Canadians: How to assure that the British North American west would be tributary to the St. Lawrence gateway and not be lost to the American sphere of economic influence.

Discontent with both the political and economic implications of the "traditional society" and its confining hierarchical social structure — the strong bonds of family units and clan connections — as well as changes in attitude towards the British and the Americans, led to the founding of Canada as an independent nation in 1867 thus laying the foundation for Rostow's second state : the preconditions for take-off.

---

[10]   *Ibid.*

PRECONDITIONS FOR TAKE-OFF

In this second stage, society undergoes a transformation, for as Rostow puts it, "it takes time to transform a traditional society in the ways necessary for it to exploit the fruits of modern science". [11] In this period, the basic pattern of the production and social structure develops including a significant expansion of transportation and communication facilities, and business, institutional and government services, representing an essential part of the structural framework and economic climate conducive to further economic growth.

As Rostow explained : "Education, for some at least, broadens and changes to suit the needs of modern economic activity. New types of enterprising men come forward — in the private economy, in government, or both — willing to mobilize savings and to take risks in pursuit of profit or modernization. Banks and other institutions for mobilizing capital appear." [12]

But perhaps even more important than economic achievements and new social attitudes, political factors play a decisive role, involving, as Rostow remarked, "the building of an effective centralized national state." [13]

Many of these characteristics of the transitional phase to the take-off are evident in the Canadian economy during the period 1867-1896. The northern half of the North American continent, united into one nation saw the Federal Government give strong leadership in both political and economic terms, with a social infra-structure being created including transportation and communication services linking the country from the Atlantic to the Pacific Ocean. Broad national economic policies were evolved, designed to facilitate the industrialization of the country (by the introduction of high tariffs, called "The National Policy"), to expand the domestic market (by immigration), and to encourage the inflow of foreign capital (partly to finance railway building, with a larger part coming from Britain and a smaller part coming from Continental Europe and the United States, and partly to participate in new industrial undertakings and resources development, including forestry

---

[11] *Ibid.*, p. 6.
[12] *Ibid.*, pp. 6 and 7.
[13] *Ibid.*, p. 7.

and mining, a trend that was to accelerate markedly in the twentieth century).

During 6 years after Confederation, the new Canada prospered. But by 1873 the boom broke and during the next 23 years, Canada experienced a protracted period of stagnation that in extent and duration [14] even overshadowed the Great Depression of the 1930's. One of the main contributing factors was that of unfavourable economic conditions abroad and the substantial decline in world prices of Canada's major export commodities. Still, sufficient progress was made in building up the domestic economy to offset some of the adverse international economic effects, the latter including also a substantial outward movement of Canadians to the United States in search for greater economic opportunities in a more developed and larger country.

Here is a brief record of Canadian economic development during the preconditions for take-off stage, 1867-1896 (see Summary Table 1 and Table 1 in Appendix A) :

1. Population rose from 3,463,000 to 5,074,000, or by 46.5 per cent or 1.4 percent annually. [15]

2. Labour force rose from 1,104,000 to 1,780,000, or by 61.2 per cent or 1.6 per cent annually.

3. Employment rose from 1,060,000 to 1,704,000, or by 60.9 per cent or 1.6 per cent annually.

4. Gross National Product in constant dollars [16] rose from $1.5 billion to about $4 billion or by 157.8 per cent in total, 76.1 per cent per capita and 60.8 per cent per person working. These increases are equivalent to annual rates of growth of 3.3 per cent, 2.0 per cent and 1.6 per cent respectively.

The rate of economic progress is somewhat greater if the comparison is made on the basis of annual averages for five-year

[14] There were some temporary improvements in economic activity during this period, particularly in 1882 and 1883, but a definite upturn did not occur until after 1895.

[15] Annual compound rates are used in presenting the growth of the economy in the stages analysis.

[16] In 1957 dollars. In current dollars, Canada's Gross National Product in 1867 was probably of the order of $400 million to $420 million and in 1896 between $950 million and $975 million. For difficulties in converting the constant dollar series into current dollar estimates and the reasons why the current dollar figures of Gross National Product for the 19th century, as shown in Table I of Appendix A are on the low side, see Appendix B.

periods. Such estimates are available [17] for the period 1870-
1874 to 1890-1894 indicating annual average rates of increases
of 3.7 per cent for total Gross National Product in constant
dollars and 2.4 per cent for Gross National Product per capita. [18]
This compares with 3.3 per cent and 2.0 per cent increases using
the single years indicated above.

TAKE-OFF

Rostow describes the "take-off" as a period "when the old
blocks and resistances to steady growth are finally overcome.
The forces making for economic progress, which yielded limited
bursts and enclaves of modern activity, expand and come to
dominate the society. Growth becomes its normal condition." [19]
He further observes :

> During the take-off new industries expand rapidly, yield-
> ing profits a large proportion of which are reinvested in new
> plant; and these new industries in turn, stimulate, through
> their rapidly expanding requirement for factory workers, the
> services to support them, and for other manufactured goods,
> a further expansion in urban areas and in other modern indus-
> trial plants. [. . .] New techniques spread in agriculture as
> well as industry, as agriculture is commercialized, and increas-
> ing numbers of farmers are prepared to accept the new
> methods and the deep changes they bring to ways of life. [20]

In Canada, the take-off period, according to Rostow, en-
compasses the years 1896 to 1914. During this stage, Canada
experienced the largest influx of immigrants in her history, the
widespread settlement of western farmlands and the commencement of agricultural operations on a mass scale spearheaded by
the development of wheat as a great export staple, relying increasingly on mechanized and scientifically based farming methods,
strong impetus to urbanization, particularly in eastern Canada,
infusion of substantial amounts of foreign capital and large
expansion of commercial, financial and government services.

---

[17]   O. J. FIRESTONE, Canada's Economic Development, 1867-1953,
With Special Reference to Changes in the Country's National Product and
National Wealth, Paper delivered at the Third Conference of the International Association for Research in Income and Wealth, Castelgondolfo,
Italy, 1-6 September 1953, published with a Preface by Simon KUZNETS,
Income and Wealth Series VII, London, Bowes & Bowes, 1958, p. 68.
[18]   In 1935-1939 dollars.
[19]   The Stages of Economic Growth, op. cit., p. 7.
[20]   Ibid., p. 8.

Expanding foreign markets for Canada's raw materials and agricultural products, with wheat exports assuming major significance, both in terms of increasing quantities and higher prices, as well as a reduction of per unit transportation costs with bulk movements and sales, added a new dimension to the economic base of the country.

Significant resources developments followed, particularly as a result of important discoveries of non-ferrous metals and iron-ore. Secondary industries began to expand by leaps and bounds drawing on foreign technology, managerial know-how and financial resources. Manufacturing industries expanded after 1896, and particularly following the turn of the century in most of the important categories : the provision of capital equipment, goods for general consumption and the processing of natural products for export. The programme of railway construction, the growth of cities and towns, the equipping of western farms and the extension of community facilities in both east and west gave a great impetus to the production of capital goods. The iron and steel industry particularly, made rapid progress.

Here are some of the indicators of Canada's economic progress during the take-off stage, 1896-1914 :

1. Population rose from 5,074,000 to 7,879,000, or by 55.4 per cent or 2.4 per cent annually.

2. Labour force rose from 1,780,000 to 3,090,000, or by 73.6 per cent or 3.1 per cent annually.

3. Employment rose from 1,704,000 to 2,900,000, or by 70.0 per cent or 3.0 per cent annually.

4. Gross National Product in constant dollars [21] rose from about $4 billion to some $7.7 billion or by 93.1 per cent in total, 25.1 per cent per capita and 14.3 per cent per person working. These increases are equivalent to annual rates of growth of 3.7 per cent, 1.3 per cent and 0.7 per cent respectively.

The question arises why the annual rate of increase in total Gross National Product in the period of take-off, 1896-1914, of 3.7 per cent was only moderately above the rate of increase in

---

[21]   In 1957 dollars.

the preceding stage, 1867-1896, of 3.3 per cent and why Gross National Product per capita and per person working were significantly below those of the previous period (see Summary Table 1).

Apart from the crudeness of the estimates, [22] the use of quinquennial averages suggests a somewhat greater improvement than is indicated on the basis of single year comparisons. For total Gross National Product, comparing 1890-1894 with 1910-1914, the annual average rate of increase is 4.0 per cent and in the case of Gross National Product per capita, the rate is 1.8 per cent. The corresponding single year rates of increases are 3.7 per cent and 1.3 per cent respectively. [23]

Thus, with the elimination of cyclical influences, the slight decline in the annual rates of change in Gross National Product in total indicated when making the comparison of the third stage with the second stage on the basis of single years, turns into a moderate increase on the basis of comparing quinquennial annual averages. But in terms of Gross National Product per capita, there still remains a differential suggesting a greater rate of growth in the period of the preconditions for take-off as compared with the take-off period. What are some of the reasons ?

One factor has been mentioned previously, the particularly rapid expansion of population, due to heavy immigration. Canada's population grew during the period 1896-1914 at an annual average rate of 2.4 per cent, and this compares with 1.4 per cent for the period 1867-1896 and 1.8 per cent for the period 1867-1967.

Other factors were the heavy concentration on building up a production and social infra-structure involving the devotion of a large proportion of the nation's resources to capital formation, with the result that productivity increases were delayed to a time when the newly developed industries had got into their stride and penetrated their markets, and as housing and other community facilities which were essential to accommodate the millions of people coming to Canada's shores during this period, had been built up. Gross capital formation during the investment boom reached in 1910 the proportion of 26.5 per cent of

---

[22]   See Appendix B.
[23]   *Canada's Economic Development, 1867-1953, op. cit.,* p. 68.

Gross National Product, as compared with 15.5 per cent in 1890, [24] the highest ratio on record in the country's history.

In general, some of the indicators of economic growth available for the period 1896-1914 support Rostow's suggestion that Canada moved into the take-off stage during these years while other indicators, particularly the rate of increase in Gross National Product, raise some questions.

DRIVE TO MATURITY

The stage of the drive to maturity, according to Rostow, covers the period 1914 to 1950. It includes two world wars, a decade of rapid economic expansion, particularly in the latter part of the 1920's, the great depression of the 1930's and a period of economic reconstruction and consolidation after World War II, laying the foundation for a new phase of rapid expansion, associated with natural resources development, scientific and technological advances and growing participation in international economic affairs and emphasis on multilateral trade.

Over these 36 years, the Canadian economy showed all the general characteristics of a country going through Rostow's drive to maturity stage which he described in the following terms :

> After take-off there follows a long interval of sustained if fluctuating progress, as the now regularly growing economy drives to extend modern technology over the whole front of its economic activity. Some 10-20% of the national income is steadily invested, permitting output regularly to outstrip the increase in population. The make-up of the economy changes unceasingly as technique improves, new industries accelerate, older industries level off. The economy finds its place in the international economy. [...] Some sixty years after take-off beginnings (say, forty years after the end of take-off) what may be called maturity is generally attained. The economy, focused during the take-off around a relatively narrow complex of industry and technology, has extended its range into more refined and technologically often more complex processes. [25]

Canada from the time Europeans came to her shores had been an economy geared to international trade. But what happened during the 1914-1950 period, was that Canada under-

---

[24] *Ibid.*, p. 72.
[25] *The Stages of Economic Growth, op. cit.*, p. 9.

went profound changes in industrial structure, referred to later, with the most significant gains made in terms of development of her secondary industries.

The first boost to Canadian fabricating industries came during World War I, when a number of new industries were established in this country including the aircraft industry and shipbuilding, the latter expanding at such a rate as to be tantamount to the creation of the new industry, while such a basic sector as the steel industry about doubled its output.

After a short, though sharp, recession following the end of World War I, the Canadian economy resumed its upward path of expansion. A major factor in the industrial development in the 1920's was the many millions of dollars of American capital, with a large part being invested in new manufacturing industries in Canada, including motor-cars, metal-processing and fabrication, chemical industries, electrical equipment and machinery industries.

> There was a virtual doubling in the value of United States investments in Canada between 1918 and 1926, and a further rise of almost one half in the succeeding four years. [. . .] New technologies were imported as well as capital, accelerating the process of industrialization and urbanization. [26]

Other industries that expanded at a significant rate were the great resource industries which in turn were supported by and contributed to the development of hydro-electric power; similarly, such industries as pulp and paper, farm implements and non-metallic products, the latter catering largely to the building boom of the 1920's, grew rapidly. The expansion was so rapid that manufacturing investment in volume terms reached a peak level in 1929 that was not matched by anything that had happened before or that was to happen in the next decade and a half, including the period of the Second World War and the years of reconstruction following it.

While Canada's long-term industrial progress was temporarily delayed during the depressed thirties, some sectors slowed down only briefly and then continued on their upward path of expansion including the chemical and non-ferrous metal indus-

---

[26] DOMINION BUREAU OF STATISTICS, *Canada, One Hundred, 1867-1967*, Ottawa Queen's Printer, 1967, p. 322.

tries, particularly gold, and some heavy equipment industries, in part the result of increasing American participation in Canadian industrial development, as the introduction of the British Empire Preference System in 1932 made it appear advantageous for American firms to serve the markets of the United Kingdom and other Commonwealth countries through their Canadian subsidiaries.

After 1933, the year of the bottom of the depression, Canadian exports slowly began their upward climb, partly as a result of increased sales of raw materials to Europe, particularly non-ferrous metals, and partly as a result of improved trade relations with the United States after conclusion of new trade agreements in 1935 and 1938. With an improvement of Canadian sales abroad, particularly the great export staples, the domestic economy responded, with the expansion that followed, only briefly interrupted by a recession in 1938.

When World War II broke out in 1939, Canada had an expanded industrial capacity. Even though in scientific terms Canada was a sophisticated country, she lacked the latest advances in technology in certain areas and the diversified industrial structure, typical of a country that reaches the stage of "technological maturity". [27] This deficiency was changed rapidly under the stresses of the global conflict and as a result of close cooperation with the United States, leading in fact to industrial integration on a continental scale to a greater extent than had been the case at any time in the history of the two countries. [28]

In the brief compass of two years, following the conclusion of World War II, Canada achieved a remarkable consolidation of the scientific, technological and managerial advances she had made during the period of the preceding military conflict. By 1947, Canada had not only completed the conversion of her economy to full peace-time uses, but she was also able to provide

---

[27] *The Stages of Economic Growth, op. cit.*, p. 59.
[28] Industrial expansion and new science orientation were particularly striking in such sectors as the electronics industry, the aircraft and shipbuilding industries, the chemical and synthetic material products industries, etc.

substantial economic assistance to war-devastated countries of Europe and elsewhere. [29]

While Canada experienced a brief recession in 1948, significant discoveries of new resources, particularly oil and natural gas in the Prairie Provinces in the latter part of the 1940's and into the 1950's set the stage for further industrial diversification, accompanied by a major expansion of service industries, leading to a new stage of economic development.

By 1950, Canada had reached "maturity" which Rostow defines

> as the stage in which an economy demonstrates the capacity to move beyond the original industries which powered its take-off and to absorb and to apply efficiently over a very wide range of its resources — if not the whole range — the most advanced fruits of [then] modern technology. This is the stage in which an economy demonstrates that it has the technological and entrepreneurial skills to produce not everything, but anything that it chooses to produce. [30]

During the drive to maturity stage, 1914-1950, the Canadian economy expanded as follows :

1. Population rose from 7,879,000 to 13,712,000, or by 74.0 per cent in total or 1.5 per cent annually.

2. Labour force rose from 3,090,000 to 5,216,000, or by 68.8 per cent in total or 1.5 per cent annually.

3. Employment rose from 2,900,000 to 5,029,000, or by 73.4 per cent in total or 1.5 per cent annually.

4. Gross National Product in constant dollars [31] rose from $7.7 billion to $23.1 billion, or by 200.5 per cent in total, 72.7 per cent per capita, and 73.2 per cent per person working. These increases are equivalent to annual rates of growth of 3.0 per cent, 1.5 per cent and 1.5 per cent respectively.

Some of the cyclical influences in comparing economic progress between 1914, a year of recession, and 1950, a year

---

[29] On a per capita basis, Canada's assistance programme in the early post-war period was greater than that of any other country. Total post-war loans and assistance amounted to $1.8 billion including a loan of $1,250 million to Britain.

[30] *The Stages of Economic Growth, op. cit.*, p. 10.

[31] In 1957 dollars.

of economic expansion, can be removed by reference to annual average rates of increases covering a number of years. Such information is available for the period 1910-1914 to 1950-1953. [32] Over this period, Canada's Gross National Product in constant dollars [33] rose by 3.1 per cent in total per annum and 1.4 per cent on a per capita basis. [34]

Hence the rates of increases on the basis of five-year averages, suggest similar rates of growth, as are indicated in the rates of expansion based on single years, 3.0 per cent for Gross National Product in total and 1.5 per cent for Gross National Product per capita.

AGE OF HIGH MASS-CONSUMPTION

While Rostow assigns 1950 as the date at which Canada appears to have reached "technological maturity" and thus signifies the beginning of the stage of high mass-consumption, he observes in another passage of his book that Canada, together with Australia had entered the stage of high mass-consumption before she reached maturity and he refers to the 1920's when Canada embarked on a programme to provide the public with a great volume and variety of consumer durable goods. [35]

Rostow makes the further point that "the technological definition of maturity must [. . .] be an approximation, when applied to a whole national society." [36] He cites as an example that "contemporary mature Canada contains the still-lagging province of Quebec." [37] It is quite true that at the time that Rostow carried on his investigations, the province of Quebec and the four Atlantic Provinces were lagging behind the economic development of the country as a whole. But in the more recent period, the situation has changed materially, with Quebec becoming one of the dynamic growth areas of Canada [38] cul-

---

[32]   Four year average.
[33]   in 1935-1939 dollars.
[34]   *Canada's Economic Development, 1867-1953, op. cit.,* p. 68.
[35]   *The Stages of Economic Growth, op. cit.,* footnote to chart preceding p. 1 and p. 69.
[36]   *Ibid.,* p. 67.
[37]   *Ibid.*
[38]   Between 1950 and 1966, private and public investment in the Province of Quebec increased by 313 per cent, in Ontario, Canada's most populous and industrialized province by 260 per cent, and for Canada as a whole by 292 per cent (see DOMINION BUREAU OF STATISTICS and Department of Trade and Commerce, Private and *Public Investment in Canada, Outlook 1967,* Ottawa, 1967, and earlier issues).

minating in Montreal's Expo 67 with its theme "Man and his World" and with a total of some 50 million visitors, hailed as the most successful culturally and scientifically oriented international exhibition. [39]

Hence in accepting 1950 as the year in which Canada, according to Rostow, reached technological maturity, the period 1950-1967 (and continuing) can be described as one in which Canadians were enjoying the fruits of industrial progress including the benefits of higher standards of living attainable in the age of high mass-consumption.

Rostow describes this stage as a period when "the leading sectors shift towards durable consumers' goods and services." [40] During this period the structure of the working force changes in increasing "not only the proportion of urban to total population, but also the proportion of the population working in offices or in skilled factory jobs." [41] Rostow concludes :

> In addition to these economic changes, the society ceased to accept the further extension of modern technology as an overriding objective. It is in this post-maturity stage, for example that through the political process, Western societies have chosen to allocate increased resources to social welfare and security. The emergence of the welfare state is one manifestation of a society's moving beyond technical maturity; but it is also at this stage that resources tend increasingly to be directed to the production of consumers' durables and to the diffusion of services on a mass basis if consumers' sovereignty reigns. [42]

Three sets of data illustrate Canada's economic achievements typical of the characteristics of the high mass-consumption stage, as described by Rostow.

Consumer expenditures per capita rose from $877 in 1950 to $1,749 in 1966, or by 99.4 per cent in current dollar terms and 41.5 per cent in constant dollar terms. [43]

Passenger cars registered per thousand population increased from 139 in 1950 to about 290 in 1966, or by 110 per cent.

---

[39]   For a discussion of "The Industrialization of Quebec", see André RAYNAULD, *The Canadian Economic System*, The Macmillan Company of Canada Limited, Toronto, 1967, Chapter 3, pp. 64 ff.
[40]   *The Stages of Economic Growth, op. cit.*, p. 10.
[41]   *Ibid.*
[42]   *Ibid.*, p. 11.
[43]   In 1957 dollars.

A substantial expansion of government social security pro-grammes have put a floor under consumer spending to a greater extent than ever before. To illustrate: Government transfer payments to persons, largely social security payments by the Federal, provincial and municipal governments rose from $1 billion in 1950, or 5.7 per cent of the Gross National Product, to about $6.2 billion, or 10.0 per cent of the Gross National Product in 1967.

During this period of high mass-consumption, Canadians reached the second highest living standard in the world, follow-ing the United States. While in overall terms, the years 1950 to 1967 brought Canadians great economic, industrial and social progress, the economic system itself underwent a significant transformation.

Examples include the much greater emphasis on the ex-pansion of science-oriented industries and the service sector, on the improvement of human capital, and attempts to strengthen the weaker segments of the economy. The latter entailed helping low income groups through expanding welfare and retraining programmes, and assisting slow growth regions, localities and industries through specialized measures including fiscal con-cessions, loans, grants, etc.

Economic progress from 1950 to 1957 was rapid, only briefly interrupted by a short recession in 1954. Major factors con-tributing were the major discoveries and development of mineral and ore resources, an investment boom and inflows of large amounts of foreign capital participating in and in fact speeding up the process of growth of the Canadian economy.

There followed a period of slow growth, 1957-1961, with unemployment reaching the highest levels since the 1930's and a balance of payments crisis that led to a devaluation of the Canadian dollar in mid-1962 from a premium level over the American dollar to 92½ cents. The period of slow growth ended in February 1961 and since that time the Canadian economy has experienced the longest phase of economic expansion in its history, continuing in 1967, though within this period the rate of economic expansion has differed somewhat from year to year.

In overall terms, the record of achievements during this period of industrial maturity and high mass-consumption, 1950-1967 has been more substantial and more variegated than anything that Canada has experienced before. This blissful stage made it possible for Canada to devote a considerably greater proportion of her resources to improving human capital, and in particular to spending on education, as explained in Chapter 17.

To summarize the economic progress from 1950 to 1967:

1. Population rose from 13,712,000 to 20,405,000, or by 48.8 per cent in total or 2.4 per cent annually.

2. Labour force rose from 5,216,000 to 7,800,000, or by 49.5 per cent in total or 2.4 per cent annually.

3. Employment rose from 5,029,000 to 7,485,000, or by 48.8 per cent in total or 2.4 per cent annually.

4. Gross National Product in constant dollars [44] rose from $23.1 billion to about $49.0 billion, or by 112.0 per cent in total, 42.5 per cent per capita and 42.4 per cent per person working. These increases are equivalent to annual rates of growth of 4.5 per cent, 2.1 per cent and 2.1 per cent respectively.

The rates of growth are somewhat different if the comparison is made on the basis of five-year averages, showing a more moderate increase in the annual rate in total Gross National Product per capita. The latter, in part, is due to a somewhat slower rate of population growth on the basis of five-year averages as compared with single-year increases.

The following rates of growth per year are indicated comparing the average 1950-1954 (which includes the recession year of 1954) with the average of 1963-1967 (which covers five years of economic expansion): [45] Gross National Product in real terms rose by 4.3 per cent and Gross National Product per capita by 1.9 per cent This compares with single-year increases of 4.5 per cent and 2.1 per cent respectively. [46]

---

[44] In 1957 dollars.

[45] Based on Table 1 in Appendix A.

[46] It bears emphasis that even in the period of industrial maturity great variations in productivity improvements may occur from year to year. For example, output per person employed in commercial non-agricultural industries rose by 3 per cent per annum between 1961 and 1964, by 2.5 per cent in 1965 and by 1.8 per cent in 1966. In the last two years, the Canadian economy operated at a virtually full employment level and this blissful state of economic affairs was accompanied by a significant slackening in the increase of output per person employed (see "Aggregate Productivity Trends, Canada, 1946-66", DOMINION BUREAU OF STATISTICS, *Daily Bulletin*, Ottawa, July 20, 1967, p. 3).

This chapter has emphasized the many factors that characterize Canadian economic growth over the last century and the great diversity of variables, both economic and non-economic, which make it particularly difficult to fit the pattern of economic development of this country into a neat framework of stages analysis.

Put in a general way, some elements listed by Rostow as being characteristic of a "traditional society" can be observed in Canada's economic development before 1867. But there are other characteristics which do not fit the pattern, suggesting that the colonial period of Canada's economic development was more one of a pre-industrial society operating on the margin of a large international commercial system, led by Britain in the eighteenth and nineteenth centuries.

The economic development of Canada in the years after 1867 fit more closely the characteristics as set out by Rostow, particularly the period leading to the industrial take-off and the take-off itself, as well as some of the main economic and social consequences flowing therefrom.

For the purpose of examining the relationship between education and economic development, the stages approach is incidental. Somewhat similar results appear to be indicated if the analysis is conducted on the basis of intermittent changes, say rates of growth or ratio determination at decade or two decade intervals, provided of course that appropriate allowance is made for cyclical factors and random disturbances such as the two World Wars.

CHAPTER 12

A Century of Economic Development

EXTENT OF PROGRESS

The results of Canada's economic development over the last century can now be summarized :

1. Population rose from 3,463,000 to 20,405,000, or by 489 per cent in total or 1.8 per cent annually.

2. Labour force rose from 1,104,000 to 7,800,000, or by 607 per cent in total or 2.0 per cent annually.

3. Employment rose from 1,060,000 to 7,485,000, or by 606 per cent in total or 2.0 per cent annually.

4. Gross National Product in constant dollars [1] rose from $1.5 billion to about $49.0 billion or by 3,093 per cent in total, 442 per cent per capita, and 352 per cent per person working. These increases are equivalent to annual rates of growth of 3.5 per cent, 1.7 per cent and 1.5 per cent respectively (see Summary Table 1).

The rapid rate of economic growth, as well as the quality and the depth of that development in the stage of industrial maturity propelled Canada to the level of one of the eight leading industrialized and trading nations of the world, with a Gross National Product per capita second only to the United States. According to estimates by Simon Kuznets, Canada, with a population comprising 0.6 per cent of the world's total, contributed 2.4 per cent to the world's output. [2]

The estimates relate to 1958. This was a year of slow growth for Canada, with many other countries experiencing a more rapid rate of expansion. The situation was reversed in the 1961-1967 period when Canada's total output rose at a substantial rate, surpassed only by a few countries of which Japan is a notable example. Hence Canada's contribution to the world's output in 1967 is likely to be greater than the 2.4 per

---

[1] In 1957 dollars.
[2] *Modern Economic Growth, op. cit.,* p. 360.

cent indicated for 1958. But even if the contribution is not materially larger than the 2.4 ratio, it suggests that Canada's role in world production is four times its contribution in terms of world population. By comparison, the contribution of the whole of northern and western Europe to world output is less than three times that of its population and that of the U.S.S.R. less than twice. [3]

SNOWBALL EFFECT

The question arises : Has Canada's economic development been gradual over the last century ?   Or has the progress been subject to a snowball effect as the economy moved through the five stages from the "traditional society" to industrial maturity ? The answer is that the greatest advances have been made in approximately the last two decades as the Canadian economy was able to meet most of the production and social challenges that resulted from scientific and technological advances and newly developed ideas and objectives.

Mastery over nature and making effective use of expanding knowledge, together with the will and capacity to tackle economic problems more effectively and more scientifically, have made it possible for Canada to raise both the quantity and the quality of the input (and that particularly applies to human resources) and the quantity and the quality of output (the greater range of more sophisticated goods and services produced by the nation).

While the quality changes in the input factors are difficult to measure, the results of such improvements in quality are reflected in the ability of the economy to increase its national productivity. The latter is represented by the capacity of the nation producing a given unit of output with a lesser input, or for a given input to produce a greater output. Data on productivity over the longer term are scanty and estimates that can be prepared represent nothing but a crude yardstick of change. Still they are indicative of trends and they show in the Canadian case, as in the case of a number of other developed nations, that the greatest economic and social advances were made in the stage of industrial maturity.

---

[3]   The percentages are as follows: northern and western Europe, Gross National Product 13.6 per cent and population 4.9 per cent; U.S.S.R., Gross National Product 12.0 per cent and population 7.2 per cent.

PRODUCTIVITY IMPROVEMENTS

In terms of Gross National Product per person working, the most rapid rate of growth, 2.1 per cent per annum, was achieved in Rostow's stage five and this compares with 1.6 per cent during stage two, 0.7 per cent during stage three and 1.5 per cent during stage four, with an overall annual average rate of growth over the last century of 1.5 per cent (see Summary Table 1). [4]

The data reflecting output per man-year understate the real improvement in productivity if measured in terms of changes in output per man-hour since the number of hours worked per week declined considerably during this period. Partial data available for the manufacturing sector and supporting descriptive information suggest that the average work week may have declined in length from some sixty hours in 1867 to about forty hours in 1967, or by approximately one-third. Hence, the Canadian economy appears to have experienced improvements in productivity, measured in terms of output per man-hour of some 2 per cent per annum over the last century.

That the improvement in the annual rate of increase in output per man-hour is about one-third greater than the improvement in the rate of expansion in output per man-year is supported by data covering a more recent period, published by the Dominion Bureau of Statistics. [5]

Inadequate quantitative evidence is available to state specifically to what extent the improvement in productivity of

---

[4] While Gross National Product data covering totals per capita and per person working have certain uses, their limitation in stages or long-term period analysis should be borne in mind. Such enquiry, to become meaningful must go beyond the aggregate character of the estimates, involving in particular sector, industry, regional and manpower analyses, a task that goes beyond the scope of this study.

[5] Output per man-hour in Canadian commercial non-agricultural industries rose at an annual trend rate of change of 3 per cent between 1947 and 1963, as compared with 2.3 per cent for output per person employed (see DOMINION BUREAU OF STATISTICS, *Indexes of Output per Person Employed and per Man-hour in Canada Commercial Non-agricultural Industries 1947-63*, Ottawa, 1965, p. 15). Kuznets has produced estimates showing the following rates of real growth for Canada on a decade basis: 1870-1913, total product, 45.1 per cent, population, 19.1 per cent, product per capita, 21.8 per cent, and product per man-hour, 22.7 per cent. For the period 1913-1960, the estimates are: 34.9 per cent, 18.6 per cent, 13.7 per cent, and 24.5 per cent respectively (see *Modern Economic Growth, op. cit.*, p. 353).

Canada's economy over the last century was due to greater labour efficiency and the availability of more capital per worker. But some data relating to the effect of education and expanded knowledge on economic growth examined in Chapter 21 suggest that the improvements in the human factor had been a major source contributing to economic progress. What information is available appears to support in a general way the conclusions arrived at by Simon Kuznets in his study of international comparison of long-term factors of economic growth :

> The scanty available data suggest that increase in inputs per head of man-hour and material capital combined accounted for less than a fifth of the secular rise in production per capita, and for a decreasing fraction in recent decades. Modern economic growth is distinguished by the fact that the rate of rise in per capita product was due primarily to improvements in *quality*, not quantity of inputs — essentially to greater efficiency or output per simple unit of input, traceable to increases in useful knowledge and better institutional arrangements for its utilization. [6]

The Canadian economy experienced the most rapid advances during the period of technological maturity, 1950-1967, not only in terms of rates of increases in productivity, but also in terms of expansion of the total national output as the labour force expanded at a rapid rate and employment opportunities grew correspondingly. During this period, Gross National Product in constant dollars rose at an annual rate of 4.5 per cent as compared with 3.3 per cent during 1867-1896, 3.7 per cent during 1896-1914, 3 per cent during 1914-1950, [7] and 3.5 per cent over the century 1867-1967 (see Summary Table 1).

In effect then, Canada was able in the most recent stage of economic expansion to achieve an annual rate of growth in terms of the real Gross National Product of about one third greater than in the preceding eight decades. The data suggest that the potential rewards that a nation can reap in terms of higher productivity and advancement in the standard of living are greatest in the age of technological maturity, provided that

---

[6] *Ibid.*, p. 491.
[7] The fact that national output rose at a slower annual average rate during the 1914-1950 period than during the preceding approximately half century, is indicative in part of the impact of depression and war on the rate of economic growth. It took the Canadian economy more than a decade to make up for the substantial losses in unused economic capacity experienced during the great depression of the 1930's and to make up for the deferment of consumption and peace-time investment necessitated by the exigencies of World War II.

SUMMARY TABLE 1. — PERCENT CHANGES OF POPULATION, LABOUR FORCE, EMPLOYMENT AND GROSS NATIONAL PRODUCT IN CONSTANT DOLLARS,[1] TOTALS FOR FIVE PERIODS AND ANNUAL RATES,[2] CANADA, 1867-1967.

ITEM	1867-1896		1896-1914		1914-1950		1950-1967		1867-1967	
	TOTAL	ANNUAL RATE	TOTAL	ANNUAL RATE	TOTAL	ANNUAL RATE	TOTAL	ANNUAL RATE	TOTAL	ANNUAL RATE
Population	46.5	1.4	55.4	2.4	74.0	1.5	48.8	2.4	489.2	1.8
Labour Force	61.2	1.6	73.6	3.1	68.8	1.5	49.5	2.4	606.5	2.0
Employment	60.9	1.6	70.0	3.0	73.4	1.5	48.8	2.3	606.1	2.0
Gross National Product										
Total	157.8	3.3	93.1	3.7	200.5	3.0	112.0	4.5	3,092.6	3.5
Per Capita	76.1	2.0	25.1	1.3	72.7	1.5	42.5	2.1	442.2	1.7
Per Person Employed	60.4	1.6	14.3	0.7	73.2	1.5	42.4	2.1	352.1	1.5

Source: Based on Table 1 in Appendix A.
[1] In 1957 dollars.
[2] Compound rates.

effective and full use is made of the growing economic capacity. To achieve the latter objective requires in turn a proper blend of expansion at an appropriate rate of both the physical capital and the human resources of the nation. At the same time there is need of creating an infra-structure which facilitates, and an economic climate which encourages individual initiative and enterprise as well as social responsibility.

It is precisely this growing economic capacity and the greater understanding of leaders in government, industry, labour, agriculture, and the professions of how to make more effective use of the nation's growing potential for individual as well as social advancement that make it possible for a country to devote a greater proportion of its resources to human improvements whether these cover health, education or cultural advancement.

As the data in Chapter 17 show, it is only in the period of industrial maturity and high mass-consumption that Canada has been able to make giant strides forward in telescoping educational progress and in providing the younger generation with new and exciting opportunities for learning and the accumulation and advancement of knowledge, to an extent unknown to the present or previous generations.

The Canadian case of a century of economic development and the concomitant growth of the education sector raises the basic question. What comes first ? Economic development or education ? Or can both be developed at similar rates as the growth of the education sector leads to better-trained men and they in turn help in speeding up the growth process. This question and the economic rewards that learning brings are dealt with in Chapters 17 and 18. Before proceeding with the quantitative assessment there is need to consider whether structural changes so essential to economic development may be affected by education, and what in fact are the main economic implications of education.

CHAPTER 13

Structural Changes

STRUCTURAL CHANGES DEFINED

The preceding analysis has been concerned with an assessment of Canadian economic growth over the last century in aggregate terms. While useful in that it provides a broad perspective of the overall sweep of Canadian economic development as a background to aid in assessing the economic implications of education on this process, it represents of necessity only a bird's eye view of progress made, and even this view covers only a limited horizon.

Given the limitations of the scope of this study, only a few fundamental structural changes that have taken place in Canada over the last century can be referred to, in part because they help to assess the growth process, and in part because they have significant implications in explaining variations over time in the output of the education industry.

Structural changes in their broadest context refer to any significant variation over a longer period of time [1] of the factors that contribute to input (and that includes the basic sources of productive capability, e.g. population which is a source of labour, and resources discoveries, which, when utilized, provide the raw materials for product creation, as well as the different industries that produce goods and services to meet final demand) and to output (and that includes the manner in which product is used whether for investment or for consumption, with the latter in turn subject to structural classification, encompassing numerous sub-sectors of personal expenditures of consumer goods and services to which individuals will attach different priorities).

In a narrower sense, structural changes refer to changes in relative importance of the major industrial sectors that contribute to creating national output and in the process to providing opportunities for gainful employment and the earning

---

[1] Long-term economic analysis is used mainly to eliminate cyclical, random and catastrophic effects, e.g. the effects of two world wars.

of income. Colin Clark has emphasized more the narrower concepts of changes in industrial structure while Simon Kuznets has extended the concepts of structural change to a broad range of areas including in addition to economic changes, also to variations in social and political structure. [2]

No attempt has been made in this study to examine such structural changes as demographic factors, urban-rural distribution of the population, and the composition of the labour force, all of which have an important bearing on the economic growth pattern of Canada and the educational requirements of the country, [3] or the many non-economic structural variations which Simon Kuznets and other economists have examined in recent years. Instead, brief reference is made only to two types of structural changes.

The first is changes in industrial structure covering agriculture, manufacturing and services. Such structural changes have had a significant impact in transforming the Canadian economy from that of a pre-industrial nation to a technologically mature society over the last century. Industrial maturity was reached after eight decades of industrial immaturity.

From the point of view of education, changes in industrial structure brought much greater pressures on the content and quality of the output of the education industry, on the orientation and objectives of the educators and the educated, and on the training and vision of teachers and scientists on whose shoulders the main burden rested to create new knowledge [4] and to communicate it to new generations of Canadians.

The second is changes in the structure of final demand for product, distinguishing between private consumption, government consumption and capital formation, both domestic and foreign. Such structural changes have affected education in a number of ways.

As educational expenditures rise, they add to government consumption. But the decision of what resources a nation will

---

[2] *Modern Economic Growth, op. cit.*, particularly Chapters 3 and 8.
[3] A brief quantitative assessment of the effects of education on the structure of the labour force is included in Chapter 18.
[4] Canada also benefited greatly from drawing on the results of research and development of knowledge in other countries, particularly the United Kingdom and the United States.

devote to government consumption is not guided by the forces of the market. Different considerations of priority affect the composition of the government product. These may be affected, among other things, by changes in the public's attitude on the role of government in economic affairs and the personality factor in political life, as the quality of government leadership varies over time. For public education has to be paid for out of taxes and government leaders have to decide how much they wish to tax the population and how to spend the money. The latter factor may in part explain the timidity which several generations of politicians have demonstrated in Canada in coming to grips with the educational problems of this country.

As to capital formation, a large share, and over time a greatly varying proportion of total output devoted to it, have been financed in Canada from foreign sources. And with foreign capital came technological and managerial know-how contributing to a speed-up in the rate of industrial development and providing many new opportunities for employment of people with advanced education and training. At the same time, with the emphasis growing on science-oriented industries, particularly in the stage of technological maturity, strong pressures were exerted on the education industry to turn out the type of young people best adapted to the new age.

As to private consumption, education plays the ambiguous role of being considered by some economists as consumption, by some as investment, and by others as part of both. Increasingly, professional opinion has steered in the direction of considering education, or a large part of it, as investment in human capital and as one of the key variables of balanced economic development and effective resource allocation. [5] This subject is discussed further in Chapter 14. Here, one main point should be noted :

As incomes rise, consumers find that the range of choice of how to spend their money has greatly expanded. With out-

---

[5] "The formation of capital by education is obviously relevant in planning for economic development when the objective is that of achieving an efficient allocation of investment resources in accordance with the priorities set by the relative rates of return on alternative investment opportunities" (see Theodore W. SCHULTZ, "The Rate of Return in Allocating Investment Resources to Education", in *The Journal of Human Resources*, Vol. II, No. 3, Summer 1967, p. 293).

lays for the necessities of life representing a declining proportion of personal disposable income, more money is left to spend on items other than the essentials of living. Greater private and national affluence makes it possible to spend more money on education, both in absolute and in relative terms.

To turn now to a discussion of the main types of structural changes and to some of the general effects of education on structural change, and vice versa.

CHANGES IN INDUSTRIAL STRUCTURE

During the first half of the century, Canadians relied on agriculture and other primary industries for their livelihood to a greater extent than on any other sector of economic activity. Following the end of World War I, manufacturing became a major source of national income. If the industrialization of the Canadian economy is measured in terms of the proportion of income earned, then it can be said that this country became industrialized in the 1920's when about one quarter of all income earned originated in manufacturing. In terms of employment, however, agriculture remained a more important sector than manufacturing, with about one-third of the total number of persons employed in 1920 working on farms and about 18 per cent in secondary industries (see Summary Table 2).

The situation changed after World War II when Canada became a fully industrialized nation, with manufacturing providing a major source of both employment and income, and agriculture becoming considerably less important, following a very large movement of workers from the farms to the cities in search of industrial employment which could be fairly readily found during most of the last two decades. By 1966, manufacturing contributed to about 26 per cent of total income and 6 per cent respectively for agriculture (see Summary Table 2).

SUMMARY TABLE 2. — CHANGES IN INDUSTRIAL STRUCTURE, AGRICULTURE, MANUFACTURING AND SERVICES, OUTPUT AND EMPLOYMENT, CANADA, 1870-1966.

YEAR	PERCENT OF TOTAL GROSS DOMESTIC PRODUCT [1]			PERCENT OF TOTAL EMPLOYMENT [2]		
	Agriculture	Manufacturing	Services	Agriculture	Manufacturing	Services
1870	33.3	19.0	20.9	50.0	13.1	17.0
1890	27.0	23.5	28.1	45.8	16.2	24.2
1910	22.8	22.7	27.8	34.3	19.9	33.4
1920	19.4	24.2	29.7	32.8	17.5	36.9
1945	10.7	27.4	53.3[3]	24.4[4]	26.5	40.7
1950[5]	10.4	28.7	48.9	21.1[4]	26.1	42.4
1965	5.0	25.8	57.2	9.5[4]	23.1	57.2
1966	5.9	25.8	56.9	8.3[4]	24.0	56.9

Source: Gross Domestic Product data from 1945 to 1966 are from DOMINION BUREAU OF STATISTICS, National Accounts, Income and Expenditure, 1966, Ottawa, 1967, and earlier issues; data on employment are from Labour Force Surveys, Monthly Bulletins, July 1966, and earlier issues; other estimates are from O. J. FIRESTONE, Canada's Economic Development, 1867-1963, London, Bowes & Bowes, 1958, pp. 185 and 189.

[1] Covers value added by industry as a percent of Gross National Product at market prices for the period 1870-1920, and Gross Domestic Product at factory costs for the period 1945-1966. The data are not fully comparable, but they are indicative of trends.
[2] The data relate to the year following, i.e., 1871 instead of 1870, 1891 instead of 1890, etc., to 1920. For the period 1870-1920, the data cover the number of gainfully occupied persons, as of the beginning of April for 1871 and 1891, and as of the beginning of June for 1911 and 1921. The data for 1945 relate to November, 1950 to June, and for 1965 and 1966 to the average for the 3-month period April to June. The estimates cover persons employed full-time and part-time, and percentages are on the basis of the total civilian labour-force. As in the case of Gross Domestic Product, the data for the period 1870-1920 are not fully comparable with the data for 1945-1966, but they are indicative of trends.
[3] Includes government military spending which inflates the proportion for that year.
[4] If annual averages are used, the share of agriculture in total employment is about one percentage point less than is indicated in mid-year estimates (see The Labour Force, Supplement to March 1965 Report, Dominion Bureau of Statistics, April 1966, p. 5).
[5] Includes Newfoundland commencing in 1950.

Kuznets has provided a somewhat broader classification of the three sectors. He combined with agriculture such related industries as fisheries, forestry and trapping. He included in industry, manufacturing, mining, construction, power and light utilities, transportation and communication; and he used a narrower definition of services by including in this sector trade, finance, real estate, personal, business, domestic, professional and governmental services. [6] He then split changes in industrial structure approximately half-way over the last century, with the following results : [7]

SHARES IN NATIONAL PRODUCT — PERCENT

	Agriculture	Industry	Services
Gross National Product			
1870-1920	50-26	26-35	24-39
Gross Domestic Product			
1926/28-1961/63	19-7	47-48	34-35

Kuznets' data indicate similar long-term trends to those observed previously: that agriculture declined significantly in relative importance and that industry expanded rapidly during the first half of the century but occupied a more stable position in the second half of the century. Similarly, there has been a substantial increase in the relative importance of the service sector in the first half of the century continuing into the second half. However, Kuznets' data indicate that the rate of growth of the service sector has slowed down in the more recent period in terms of structural change while the data shown in Summary Table 2 suggest, on the basis of the grouping of service industries which differs from the grouping employed by Kuznets, that the service sector still continues to expand in relative terms.

CHANGES IN STRUCTURE OF OUTPUT

The tabulation below shows the varying proportions of private consumption, government consumption, gross domestic capital formation, both home and foreign financed [8] in Gross National Product over close to a century of Canadian economic development. [9]

[6] *Modern Economic Growth, op. cit.*, p. 86.
[7] *Ibid.*, p. 91.
[8] The term "gross domestic capital formation" refers to investment in durable physical assets in a given year covering both home and foreign financed capital expenditures. The term "gross national capital formation" refers to that portion of gross domestic capital formation that has been financed from Canadian savings.
[9] *Modern Economic Growth, op. cit.*, p. 238.

SHARES IN GROSS NATIONAL PRODUCT — PERCENT

	Private con- sumption	Govern- ment con- sumption	Gross domestic capital formation	Capital imports (—)	Gross national capital formation
1870 and 1890	86.5	5.6	15.2	—7.3	7.9
1890, 1900, 1910	82.1	7.4	18.5	—8.0	10.5
1920, 1929	71.5	10.5	22.9	—5.0	17.9
1926-1930	73.0	7.5	21.5	—2.0	19.5
1950-1959	63.5	14.1	25.0	—2.6	22.4

Three points are noteworthy. One is the continuing decline in private consumption from 86.5 per cent in the early period to 63.5 per cent in the more recent past.

The second point is the continuing growth of government consumption, only temporarily interrupted during the inter-war period, with governments assuming a much greater role in the nation's economic and social affairs in the last two decades.

The third point is that capital formation has become a much more important economic sector, almost twice the relative role it played at the beginning of the century, indicating that as society moves from a stage of preconditions of take-off, through take-off to a period of technological maturity, it requires large and in fact increasing capital expenditures to introduce most of the innovations and scientific advances into the economic system.

CHANGES IN STRUCTURE OF CONSUMER SPENDING

The growing affluence of the Canadian population is, among other things, reflected in its ability to spend more money on things other than the necessities of life. In other words, the modern consumer has at his disposal considerably more discretionary income both in absolute and in relative terms than his forefathers had one, or two, or three generations ago.

More discretionary income in turn makes it possible for the consumer to spend money on things he values highly, having more money left after paying for the essentials of living. This trend of rising discretionary income over the long term, coupled with greater absolute levels of earnings in real terms has been one contributing factor to make it possible for Canadian parents to underwrite more costly and lengthier periods of education and training of their children. This has involved not only higher out-of-pocket costs on the part of the parents, but has also meant increased foregone earnings during the learning process (after the age of sixteen).

Further, to the extent that parents are taxpayers, they have been required to pay higher taxes so as to enable government authorities to spend increasing amounts on public services including education, training and research. The latter type of activity has become particularly important in the stage of technological maturity as Canada could not rely to the same extent as in earlier periods on the research efforts of other countries. [10]

Information that would make it possible to prepare reasonable estimates of discretionary income is woefully inadequate. But broad trends can be observed by classifying consumer expenditures on goods and services in three categories of essential living, food, clothing and shelter, and bulking all other expenditures in one grouping.

This is not to say that a number of items in the "other" category are not essential. Many of them are, and further the concept of what is essential and what is not, changes over time, as the state of affluency rises and as personal preferences and priorities vary. Allowing for the inadequacies of the data, Summary Table 3 shows that the role of "essential" expenditures declined from about two-thirds of total consumer spending at the beginning of the first century of Canada's nationhood to less than one half at the end of the century.

Some supplementary information [11] is available from Kuznets' study, presented below, which shows similar broad trends as are indicated in Summary Table 3.

SHARES IN TOTAL CONSUMER EXPENDITURES — PERCENT

	Food	Beverages and Tobacco	Clothing	Housing	Other [12]
1870 and 1890	32.2	5.7	16.9	26.7	18.5
1900 and 1910	30.0	6.5	17.0	24.8	21.7
1920 and 1930	29.8	5.7	15.0	26.0	23.5
1926-1930	26.4	5.2	13.8	28.2	26.4
1941-1950	27.1	8.2	14.2	24.5	26.0
1950-1959	23.7	8.3	10.2	21.2	36.6

---

[10] Canada is still considerably behind other industrialized countries in terms of resources devoted to research and development. The ratio in terms of Gross National Product is just a little over 1 per cent, about one-half the proportion applicable to the United Kingdom and one-third the proportion of the United States (see THE SCIENCE COUNCIL OF CANADA, *First Annual Report 1966-67*, Ottawa, Queen's Printer, 1967, p. 3).

[11] *Modern Economic Growth, op. cit.*, p. 267.

[12] Excludes expenditures on education, health and other services rendered directly by governments to consumers which should theoretically be included under household consumption (*ibid.*, p. 265).

To turn now to a discussion of the manner in which education contributes to economic development and is in turn affected by the growth process, or what may be described as the reciprocal relationship between education and economic growth.

SUMMARY TABLE 3. — CONSUMER EXPENDITURES ON GOODS AND SERVICES, ESSENTIAL AND OTHER, CANADA, 1870-1966.

YEAR	ESSENTIAL EXPENDITURES			SUB-TOTAL	OTHER EXPEND-ITURES	TOTAL EXPEND-ITURES	ESSEN-TIAL EXPEND-ITURES AS PERCENT OF TOTAL EXPEND-ITURES
	Food	Cloth-ing and Person-nal Fur-nishings	Shelter				
1870	141	66	55	262	142	404	64.9
1890	203	120	90	413	278	691	59.8
1910	487	291	234	1,012	665	1,677	60.3
1920	1,362	654	463	2,479	1,492	3,971	62.4
1945	1,920	1,040	832	3,792	3,177	6,969	54.4
1950	3,140	1,528	1,385	6,053	5,973	12,026	50.3
1965	7,114	2,972	4,907	14,993	17,070	32,063	46.8
1966	7,620	3,141	5,323	16,084	18,756	34,840	46.2

Source: For the Years 1945-1966, DOMINION BUREAU OF STATISTICS, *National Accounts, Income and Expenditure, 1966*, Ottawa, 1967, and earlier issues; for the years 1870-1920, O. J. FIRESTONE, *Canada's Economic Development, 1867-1953*, London, Bowes & Bowes, 1958.

EDUCATION AND STRUCTURAL CHANGES

Speaking generally, education is one of the factors contributing to structural changes, and in turn it is affected by them.

As education makes possible the advancement and the spread of knowledge, and as the latter is applied to developing new and improved goods and services and advanced technology, new industries come into existence or old industries are transformed in such a substantial manner as to be tantamount to new ones.

The application of advanced scientific knowledge in turn requires trained men and women who are the product of educational efforts and experience. Thus without adequate education and training facilities and people willing to learn, a country cannot make the rapid industrial progress which may be possible with advancing technology and greater managerial know-how.

Knowledge can be imported from abroad. But it requires skilled people in a country to put such knowledge to productive use. It is true, a nation can supplement its scientific and technical manpower through immigration and visiting experts, but there are limitations to this process. In the end, and over the longer term, there is no substitute for well-trained people brought up through an indigenous system of education, supplemented by whatever useful training can be obtained abroad, or through the importation of skills.

As new knowledge is introduced into the productive stream and contributes to change in economic structure, education is affected in two ways :

1. New and expanding industries require trained personnel and they are prepared, and in fact are able — usually because of productivity differentials and innovational advantages — to offer wages and salaries above the norm. High pay, in turn, will attract the number and the types of trained people needed, if not immediately, so over a period of time. Persistent demand for special skills and adequate remuneration become powerful factors in influencing people to acquire the education and training required to follow well rewarded occupations.

2. Gradually, society begins to recognize the benefits that accrue to the present and future generations from dynamic and continuing growth, accompanied by changes in the structure of the economy. As a result, the nation becomes increasingly willing to invest the large amounts of money involved in creating and maintaining the educational infra-structure, necessary to facilitate and encourage the training of men and women required in a technologically more complex age.

To formulate appropriate economic and social goals, to establish the necessary priorities and to develop effective policies and realistic programmes, governments in turn need the support of their citizens, both in terms of agreement in principle and willingness to take effective part in the implementation of measures proposed. Education contributes to public enlightenment. Thus it assists in creating a favourable climate for individual initiative and responsible social action.

Structural analysis could be greatly aided by the development of input-output matrices, which would make it possible to trace the effect of education on the formation of human capital, and as a corollary follow the flow of human capital to its final destination of employment in the various sectors that make up total economic activity.

One matrix would use educational activities as input and show the resulting effect on human capital formation. A broad concept of education could be used to include beside formal education also training and learning on the job.

The other matrix could treat human capital as input and show the end use of this resource factor by economic sectors. In other words, one matrix would be a Human Capital Budget showing what education affects whom and how. The other matrix would be a Human Sectoral Budget which would indicate the disposition of the various types of human capital by industries. [13]

Higgins has suggested :

A theoretically perfect approach would be to treat education as both an input and an output in the 'input-output matrix' of the economy as a whole. The value of education as an end in itself, quite apart from its contribution to increasing output of other goods and services, would be treated as a part of a national income. In addition, investment in education would be considered together with inputs of labor, raw materials, and capital equipment in the production of other goods and services. Both in choosing the product mix (the amounts of all goods and services to be produced) and in choosing the appropriate technology for producing each good and service in the product mix, education inputs would be considered along with inputs of other factors of production. [14]

---

[13] For suggestions of a new system of educational accounts proposed by Richard Stone, see Chapter 14.
[14] *Economic Development, Principles, Problems and Policies, op. cit.*, p. 412.

CHAPTER 14

Economic Implications of Education

EDUCATION AND CIVILIZATION

Education [1] facilitates an understanding of human and cultural values, of family and community traditions, and it contributes to the expansion of knowledge. Thus education assists in making man a better and a more knowledgeable one. In contributing to the enhancement and deepening of knowledge [2] education is only one of several factors serving this purpose, though it has increasingly become a particularly important one. Other factors include experience, experimentation and exposure to opportunities of learning.

Expansion of knowledge affects the improvement of civilization at four different levels.

1. Human qualities may be enhanced through personality development including the broadening of the learner's mind and attitudes, the acceptance of and the adherence to moral principles, the exercise of logic and discipline in making rational decisions, the stimulation of intellectual curiosity and the questioning of preconceived ideas, increasing spatial, occupational and social mobility, the growing individual flexibility and adaptability to changes in the technological, social, political and economic climate, etc.

2. Social advancement may be attained in the sense of improved relations among the members of a community and groups within a nation, the sharing of the hazards of living, e.g., social insurance and social security, the provision of social capital and social services to offer adequate opportunities for all to advance (of which state-supported compulsory public

---

[1] The term is used here to denote "formal" education, that is education offered in private and public institutions. Thus it excludes such learning as on-the-job training, through experience and self-development of knowledge.

[2] While it costs money and involves the use of scarce resources, man-time, to create knowledge, once it is created, it becomes a "free" good. Then when it is used to create goods and services, knowledge acquires an economic value which is incorporated in the market price of the final product.

schools and institutions for higher learning would be one example).

3. Political sophistication may be increased and this includes expanding political perception among citizens and raising the incidence of participation in political affairs, leading to greater democratization as well as more effective working of governments at different levels within a nation, and contributing to an increase in the understanding among governments and people in international affairs.

4. Economic progress may be achieved as greater knowledge improves man's chances and opportunities of controlling increasingly his destiny in his continuous struggle to wrest from nature and science the fruits of his labour which he then can translate either into a greater volume of goods and services to be consumed or invested (involving deferment of consumption), or into greater leisure to be enjoyed by reducing what David Ricardo has called the "irksomeness of labour". Thus increasing knowledge, if used effectively, not only makes it possible for man to increase the quantity and quality of material benefits he can create, but also to raise his capacity to pursue to a greater extent the non-material benefits which enable him to lead a fuller and more rewarding life.

EDUCATION AND ECONOMIC CHOICE

To the extent that education adds to the expansion of knowledge, and the latter in turn contributes to economic progress, a better way of life can be achieved by the individual and by society as a whole. But whether this "better" way of life consists of a greater volume and a higher quality of goods and services at the disposal of each person,[3] or whether it takes the form of greater leisure with consequent expansion of "joie-de-vivre", or a combination of both, is in most countries a matter of choice of the individual and of society as a whole.

---

[3] Availability of goods and services to an individual is usually measured in terms of consumer expenditures on goods and services per capita which reflect the supply availability, or in terms of personal disposable income per capita which reflect the income capacity to purchase a given quantity of goods and services. But such aggregate measurements do not fully reflect the range of differentials in living standards that exist in a society. Supplementary information on income distribution (after taxes) and the composition of consumer spending is required for an examination in depth, as well as other criteria.

This distinction is fundamental in any consideration of the reciprocal effect of education on economic growth. For if economic growth, development and progress are measured in terms of Gross National Product, total, per person working or per capita, or similar indicators of economic activity, then increasing education may contribute to one of two different results. If the choice is greater emphasis on leisure, the rate of expansion of economic growth as measured in real Gross National Product terms may indicate a slow-down if compared with an earlier period of expansion when a lesser input devoted to education may have produced a greater rate of increase in Gross National Product, simply because individuals and the nation as a whole chose more work in preference to more leisure.

On the other hand, if education stimulates consumer demand through greater willingness to accept innovations and acquire greater comforts of life, then the choice may be to take out the benefits arising from increased productivity in terms of higher real incomes to pay for expanded consumer purchases, rather than to increase leisure time. This, for example, was the case in Canada during the upswing phase in economic activity between 1961 and 1967. In that case, education contributes to raising the rate of growth of Gross National Product from the demand side, with supply factors responding to meet this demand.

What then are the effects of education on economic choice ? Increased education may contribute to expand the capacity of the economy to produce more goods and services. By deliberate choice, part of these enlarged capabilities may remain unused as society places greater values on leisure than on toil at one time, and opposing values at another time. The interaction between what are in essence economic and social phenomena, has been emphasized in a recent study :

> One consequence of increased education [. . .] might well be a reduction in the measured volume of economic activity, because people might with every justification choose to devote an increasing proportion of their time to non-economic activities in their pursuit of happiness. Such a development could still represent progress even in the economic sense since the productive potential of the community might be increasing at the same time. The fact that this capacity is not used would, if expressed in Gross National Product terms indicate

that the economy was declining. This would clearly be an inadequate representation of the true position. [4]

DISSEMINATION OF EDUCATION

There is another dimension to the link between education, knowledge and economic activity. For knowledge to achieve social and economic meaning, it has to be transmitted from one person to others. That process of communication, usually formalized in an institutional framework, is represented by education. But the extension of knowledge, in turn, is dependent on education, not only because education trains the teachers who are the future communicators of knowledge, but also because it trains the scientists and other professionals who become the originators of new knowledge.

This knowledge-producing process creates a sector of economic activity which can be described as the education industry. And this industry, through the wider and more effective diffusion of knowledge can bring economies of scale and external economies similar to those that occur in other industries.

Such production economies and the effect of the expansion of the education industry on economic growth has been explained in these terms :

> The economies of scale and external economies [...] arise from a wider diffusion of knowledge. Economies of scale occur, firstly, because as one piece of knowledge is transmitted to an increasing number of people the transmitter(s) will very likely become more specialized and more proficient and, secondly, as more people acquire any piece of knowledge there is a greated likelihood of a cross-fertilisation taking place between them which may result in stimulating new knowledge or in more effectively propagating existing knowledge. External economies also arise from the possession of knowledge because the possessors may be able to use it in a way that benefits other people as well as themselves.
>
> The knowledge-producing concept of education also throws light on the relationship between education and economic growth. Education can be both a cause and a consequence of economic growth — a consequence because as people become better off they may seek more education for its own sake, for the satisfaction it gives. Education may be a cause, in that education or specific aspects of it may be a

[4] *Investment in Education*, Report of the Survey Team appointed by the Minister of Education, Dublin, The Stationery Office, 1965, p. 386.

necessary condition for the production of some goods and services. To the extent that education is a cause of economic growth one must try to ascertain the amount and nature of the education needed to attain any given level of output. Viewed in this light, education as a knowledge-producing process may be thought of as contributing to economic growth in two ways. Firstly, there may be an increase in the total stock of knowledge in a community by the transmission of existing knowledge to a larger number of people; secondly, there may be an increase in the knowledge stock through the discovery or introduction of new knowledge. [5]

CONTINUING EDUCATION

For economic development to take place, a nation must be able to expand the capacity to produce and that means as far as labour input is concerned, to increase the productiveness of this particular factor of production. This can be done by exposing the young before they enter the labour force to increased opportunities for extended and higher quality education, by providing the active labour force with opportunities to avail themselves of added training and adult education, and by making it easier for inactive members of the labour force to return to the labour market following an updating of their educational attainments, the latter of particular significance for married women who in Canada, as in the United States, are returning to the labour market in increasing numbers. Hence, in a growth context, learning involves continuing education.

There are many other aspects to this relationship between increased education and greater national productivity. There is the question of matching supply and demand, bearing in mind the time factor. For it takes time to educate people and to give them the specialized knowledge and experience that modern technology requires.

The demand for experts in many fields is almost immediate when industry endeavours to introduce innovations in production and distribution fields or when governments embark on social programmes, such as a significantly stepped up demand for doctors and nurses, when a country introduces a national health programme encompassing prepaid public hospital and medical services.

---

[5] *Ibid.*, p. 376.

On this point, W. Arthur Lewis observes : "There cannot be too many technicians, engineers or scientists." [6] And he could have added doctors, nurses, teachers and many other occupations, including in particular managers, since the latter group represents perhaps the single most important occupation required to keep an economy innovating and growing.

MATCHING SUPPLY AND DEMAND

So far, social scientists have not come up with a fully satisfactory answer to the question whether there exists a specific correlation between supply of and demand for trained personnel at a given point of time and how this correlation changes under varying economic and social circumstances. [7] This subject is discussed further in this chapter in the section dealing with Cultural and Social Factors.

One of the reasons scientific manpower planning, i.e. relating education and training to projected labour force requirements (by age, sex, education, skills, training, experience, industry and location), has been such an elusive field of endeavour, has been due to the fact that in most developed countries the absorbtive capacity expanded more or less as rapidly as the supply of educated personnel increased. [8] Hence, there was, in the past at least, less pressure on developing manpower planning on a scientific basis.

The problems are more complex in countries that have not yet reached the stage of technological maturity. The difficulties an economist faces in advising the less developed countries where the number of people demanding education may exceed the foreseeable number of jobs has been described by Lewis in these terms:

> [An economist] can point out that a surplus of educated persons can only be a temporary phenomenon, since any econ-

---

[6] W. Arthur LEWIS, *Development Planning, The Essentials of Economic Policy*, New York, Harper and Row Publishers, Inc., 1966, p. 232.
[7] W. Arthur LEWIS, among others, has made some preliminary efforts to quantify the correlation between economic structure and education (*ibid.*, p. 106).
[8] This assumes that an economy is able to reach and maintain a "full" employment level resulting from the pursuit of effective economic growth policies by governments and other sectors of the economy.

omy can ultimately absorb any number of educated by reducing the premium for education and raising the educational qualifications for jobs. He can stress that a wide educational base is needed to find the best brains, which may make the crucial difference. He may welcome the fact that education raises aspirations, because low aspirations are one of the causes of low achievement. He can add that any kind of education must have some productivity, since it stretches the mind; but he cannot demonstrate that the marginal product of expenditure on education is bound to exceed that of other investments. Finally, he can remind the Government that education does not have to be productive in order to justify itself; it is valuable for its own sake. [9]

The implication is that there are also human and non-economic aspects to education that may justify the social costs involved in providing it on an expanding scale irrespective of economic rationale.

Imbalances in matching the supply of specific occupations with job opportunities adequately remunerated, will occur also in developed countries. [10] In Canada, as has been the experience in a number of industrialized nations, such imbalances have in the past been largely resolved through immigration or emigration. During most of the century as an independent nation, Canada has been a major beneficiary as well as contributor to the "brain-drain". [11]

Expanding the productive capacity of the labour force by itself will not lead to economic growth per se. There is also need to create sufficient effective demand to make efficient use of the expanding labour force equipped with greater knowledge and skills as a result of more and better education and training. This is a broad generalization, the practical implementation of which faces innumerable difficulties, particularly when it comes to formulating educational policies and programmes designed to dovetail with and facilitate economic

[9] *Ibid.*, p. 110.
[10] Education can be an important factor contributing to labour mobility, both in a locational and occupational sense, thus facilitating the matching of demand for and supply of labour. Hence, to the extent that education increases the mobility potential of the labour force, it contributes to maximizing output and productivity.
[11] For quantitative evidence, see Chapter 19.

growth. [12] Many countries have found it difficult to resolve such problems. The kind of questions that need answering before solutions can be found have been stated in these terms :

> We need to know *how* education enters into political or economic transformation, in what ways it interacts with other social processes, and in what sorts of time patterns. For which parts of the labor force is literacy essential? What, under various conditions, is the most fruitful allocation of resources between secondary and primary schooling, and with that distribution of responsibilities and costs? In what form and in which circumstances should technological training be given priority over academic? How do patterns of incentive and aspiration affect the outcome of this or that kind of schooling? How can incentives be modified to improve the contribution of education to diverse sorts of change? How different are the methods for transferring "know-how" from those that spread knowledge? When, where, and to what extent should resources be devoted to the formation of human capital rather than physical capital? Are there situations in which education may even obstruct economic advance? [13]

Notwithstanding difficulties of practical implementation, the objective of continuing economic growth and rapid economic development has been adopted by many countries the world over, encompassing industrialized and emerging nations alike as a cardinal principle of economic policy. One of the consequences has been to place increasing emphasis on education as a significant contributing factor to the growth process, notwithstanding the fact that social scientists have not so far developed the full array of techniques and analyses required to provide many of the answers that policy makers are seeking in this field. [14]

---

[12] Richard Stone has come forward with proposals for a new system of social accounts applicable to education which he describes as "a model of the educational system designed to work out the present implications of future levels of educational activity as determined by the evolution of the demand for places on the one hand and the economic demand for the products of education on the other." Such an educational growth model would in the first instance be separate from a general economic growth model, with the linking of the two models to take place at a later stage of development (see Richard STONE, "A Model of the Educational System", in *Minerva*, Volume II, No. 2, Winter 1965, pp. 172 ff.).

[13] Mary Jean BOWMAN and C. Arnold ANDERSON, "The Role of Education in Development", *Development of the Emerging Countries; an Agenda for Research*, The Brookings Institution, Washington, D.C., 1962, pp. 153 ff.

[14] Some progress is being made in developing concepts of education expenditures and educational capital consistent with economic theory (see for example, Dudley SEERS and Richard JOLLY, "The Treatment of Education in National Accounting", in *The Review of Income and Wealth*, No. 3, September 1966, pp. 195-209).

Thus both in theory and in practice a great deal of knowledge has still to be gained to understand more deeply the economic and social interrelationship between education and economic growth, development and progress. The increasing amount of research work now being done in this field is encouraging, though time is of the essence, since many developed and less developed nations are under great pressures to expand educational expenditures several times over during the next decade and to provide increasing economic opportunities for the educated.

EDUCATION — CONSUMPTION OR INVESTMENT

One aspect of the economic role of education that has received particular attention by academicians in recent years has been the examination of the theoretical and policy implications of considering education as either consumption or investment, or as a type of economic flow that under certain circumstances may serve one purpose, and under other circumstances may serve another purpose.

The literature on the subject is growing rapidly. [15] Without attempting to summarize the evolution of economic thinking on this subject, certain aspects of this type of analysis have a direct bearing on the question : Whether, to what extent and how does education contribute to economic growth, economic development and economic progress ? To explain briefly.

For education to take place, efforts have to be made. Most of these efforts go through the market place, the hiring of teachers and the payment of their salaries, the building of

---

[15] One of the leading economists who has been a pioneer in the field of the study of investment in human capital is Theodore W. Schultz. His publications include: "Investment in Man: An Economist's View", in *Social Service Review*, Vol. XXXIII, June 1959; "Capital Formation by Education, in *Journal of Political Economy*, Vol. LXVIII, No. 6, December 1960; "Investment in Human Capital", in *American Economic Review*, Vol. LI, March 1961; "Education and Economic Growth", in *Social Forces Influencing American Education*, The Sixtieth Yearbook of the National Society for the Study of Education, Part II, ed. Nelson B. HENRY, Chicago, The University of Chicago Press, 1961; *The Economic Value of Education*, Columbia University Press, New York, 1963; "Investing in Poor People: An Economist's View", in *American Economic Review*, Vol. LV, No. 2, May 1965, pp. 510-520; and "The Rate of Return in Allocating Investment Resources to Education", *op. cit.* For a particularly lucid exposition of the circumstances under which educational spending may be considered consumption or investment, see *Investment in Education, op. cit.*, pp. 378-385.

schools and other educational facilities, and the making of capital expenditures involved, the purchase of teaching aids and books involving current outlays for such purposes. Some educational efforts do not go through the market place, e.g. the contribution that parents may make to the education of their children or the educational self-improvement on the part of adults.

The part of educational efforts that goes through the market has a direct economic impact. For the making of expenditures for educational purposes, whether of a capital or operating nature provides jobs and incomes for teachers, for bricklayers working on a new school bulding, and for printers working in a publishing house of educational books.

Whether educational services are provided through the market place or outside, the resulting product represents knowledge acquired by the educated. He can put this acquired knowledge to two uses : economic and non-economic. The former enables him to pursue a gainful occupation and earn income, usually rising over most of a person's productive years. The latter enables him to pursue non-material objectives, to lead a better and fuller life, to make a greater contribution to society and to serve other worthwhile causes.

That part of the educational services that goes through the market entails the making of expenditures. From an economic point of view it matters whether such expenditures are consumption or investment.

Consumption involves outlays on goods and services which are currently used up and which provide direct benefits to the purchaser. Example: the purchase of food and clothing.

Investment involves the making of expenditures to purchase capital goods such as buildings and structures, machinery and equipment. Such expenditures are made in the expectation that the investment will yield a benefit in the future in the form of goods and services in the case of real investment, and in terms of monetary returns in the case of financial investment.

Three main aspects need to be considered :

1. Motivation (current enjoyment versus future expectations).

2. Financing (payment out of current or past income, i.e. savings versus borrowing, i.e. payment out of future earnings).

3. Economic impact (endogenous versus autonomous variables).

In the past, many economists used to consider education as consumption. But in the more recent period, economists have become increasingly aware of the important contribution which education makes to increase productivity both individual and national, and hence they have been inclined to the view that a good part of education, if not most of it, constitutes investment. [16] In fact, some economists, such as T. W. Schultz, have presented evidence which suggests that educational investment may bring in many instances higher returns than physical investment. [17]

PRODUCTIVE AND SOCIAL INVESTMENT

Some economists also make the distinction between "productive" and "social" investment. Productive investment is similar to the individual's concept of investment in the sense that the investor expects to recoup his total original investment plus a return on the investment which he considers adequate. Social investment covers expenditures made to obtain benefits for the community as a whole. The costs may be greater than the financial returns, for in making a social investment, the state may subsidize an undertaking or provide completely free services, e.g. free public schools and heavily subsidized university education.

---

[16] As Vaizey has pointed out, modern economists have distinguished predecessors, who at the turn of the century put forward somewhat similar hypotheses: "A. C. Pigou, *Wealth and Welfare*, London, 1912, argued that the marginal net product of resources wisely invested in persons is higher than that of resources wisely invested in material capital; a given sum wisely expended on the health and education of the people, and especially of the young, will increase production by a greater amount than the same sum wisely expended by private persons on the creation of new capital (pp. 355-6 and 163-4, quoted by Lord Dalton, London, *The Inequality of Incomes*, 1920, pp. 148-9). Cannan, as Lord Dalton points out, makes the same point. (*Wealth*, London, 1914)" (see *The Economics of Education, op. cit.,* p. 42).

[17] There is this further difference between physical and human capital investment. The former is completed when a structure is erected or a piece of equipment is installed ready for use. The latter rarely constitutes a finished product for education and training is a continuing process and young people, when leaving school, represent an unfinished product from an economic point of view.

Most individuals prefer current consumption to future consumption. Hence the individual tends to discount the future at a higher rate. On the other hand, the community as a whole takes a longer term point of view and it makes social investment in the expectation of serving future generations. Hence, if a nation's resources were allocated on the basis of preferences of individuals, the volume of investment might be smaller than if the latter is guided by society as a whole. Individual investment is financed out of current earnings and retained savings, while social investment is financed out of taxes and borrowing.

Applied to education, this distinction between productive and social investment means that less money would be spent on education if left to individual decision and more money would be spent if the decision is one of the community as a whole.

EDUCATION AND ECONOMIC DEVELOPMENT

To relate now the distinction between education as consumption and education as investment to the subject of economic development.

For economic development to take place on a continuing basis, an adequate volume of capital investment is required, partly because it contributes to the expansion and improvement of productive capacity, and partly because of its effects on employment and income levels. If education is considered a part of investment in human beings, then like capital formation in durable physical assets, structures, machinery and equipment,[18] an increasing volume of such expenditures is required to facilitate economic growth of an adequate rate on a sustainable basis. [19]

---

[18] Kuznets points out that in the United States, on the basis of the conventional concept of Gross Capital Formation, the latter comprised 30 per cent of Gross National Product (net of intermediate products) in 1956. If direct costs of normal education and some other investment in man are added, the proportion is raised to 42 per cent of Gross National Product. If earnings foregone by those receiving education are added to Gross National Product on the basis of the conventional concept which Kuznets calls the "pure" GNP total, the latter is raised by 10 per cent. And if the same earnings are added to total Capital Formation including human capital, the proportion the latter comprises of "pure" GNP is raised to 47 per cent (see *Modern Economic Growth: Rate, Structure, and Spread, op. cit.*, pp. 228-229).

[19] Kendrick presents a concept of *total* investment, including "all outlays designed primarily to increase output and income in future periods" (see John W. KENDRICK, "Restructuring the National Accounts for Investment and Growth Analysis", in *Särtryck ur Statistik tidskrift*, 1966:5, p. 354).

An expanding volume of investment in both physical durable assets and in human beings requires increasing amounts of savings. The latter can be increased by raising total income, or upping the savings-income ratio, or by using both approaches. When the savings ratio is raised, the ratio of consumer spending to income declines.

If education is considered a consumer service, then a case can be made to economize on it. If education is considered an investment, then a case can be made to expand it. This approach of necessity oversimplifies the complexity of the issues involved, but it serves the purpose of bringing into focus the possibility of a conflict arising on whether a nation should emphasize consumption or investment in travelling along a rapid growth path.

In part, the answer to resolving this conflict revolves around the question whether one endorses without reservation the concept of consumer sovereignty, or whether one accepts the premise that this concept must be blended with the concept of social responsibility.

EDUCATION AND CONSUMER SOVEREIGNTY

The concept of consumer sovereignty refers to the right of the consumer to decide what proportion of his earnings he wishes to save and what proportion he chooses to spend, what consumer goods and services he buys and where, what prices he pays for them and how he finances such purchases, from past savings, current earnings, or future income (through borrowing).

Some economists extend the concept of consumer sovereignty also to occupational choices. [20] Applying this concept to education, this means that the decision to obtain an education or not rests with the individual, or in the case of a minor, with his parents or guardian. In practice, the discretionary aspect of whether a person obtains an education or not is limited in many countries because of compulsory school attendance requirements, usually involving a school-leaving age at 14 or 16 years. There are however many countries without compulsory school attendance provisions, and even in countries where such regulations exist, large numbers of young people beyond school

---

[20] *Principles of Economic Policy, op. cit.*, pp. 142 and 144.

leaving age are in a position to exercise discretion in whether or not to acquire additional education and training.

In the more recent period, the exercise of consumer sovereignty in the field of education has become more circumscribed because of the growing interest of society in the use to which limited resources devoted to education are put. For increasingly, a larger portion of educational costs are borne by the state and governments have to decide on the priorities attached to such community investment, and the contribution which educational expenditures make to economic and social progress and human betterment.

There is the further point that at a certain stage in his life, a student represents a potential resource that is not yet fully developed. Society has invested some of its savings in the student. Social responsibility on the part of the learner means that society can expect a return from the educated person in terms of increased production. To maximize social returns on educational investment requires a student to obtain such education and training so as to enable him to perform effectively during his productive life and make the greatest possible contribution to economic progress that he is capable of.

POLICY IMPLICATIONS

Some of the major policy implications of considering education as an investment include :

1. The supply of educational capital and the scope of the educational establishment being adequate to provide the educational services required to meet the expanding and changing needs of society.

2. Educational curricula and training programmes must tie in with changing technological and skill requirements. To realize this objective requires a tie-in between educational planning and manpower planning on a continuing basis.

3. The process of matching supply of and demand for educated persons is growing increasingly complex. There is need to consider new and expanded incentives to encourage students to complete their education and training, improved methods of student counselling, and provision for the continuity of the educational process beyond the normal school-leaving age.

4. Increasing use of cost benefit analysis both in individual and social terms to examine the productivity of the educational system and that includes the economic benefits accruing to students and trainees, and the economic performance of the teaching staff, as well as the utilization of the investment in educational physical facilities. The days when professors could remain aloof and operate on cloud nine, untouched by reality, are gone. [21] There is need to combine academic achievements and the broadening of the intelligence horizons of individual students with an awareness that the knowledge acquired offers the student certain economic opportunities, but at the same time entails certain social responsibilities. For the community has a considerable investment in a social sense over his productive life. At the same time the academician has a responsibility not only to communicate knowledge, but also, to the extent he is capable, to contribute to new knowledge either directly through research, or indirectly through training the researchers of tomorrow.

ANALYTICAL IMPLICATIONS

To come back now to the point on why it may be useful in assessing the implications of education in macro-economic terms to make the distinction between economic growth, economic development and economic progress.

When education increases the productive capabilities of an individual, he represents a contribution to *potential* Gross National Product. But only when society makes use of this potential, will an increase in potential Gross National Product be translated into expansion of *actual* Gross National Product. And economic growth occurs, as defined earlier, when actual Gross National Product rises in real terms.

The rising productive capacity of an individual resulting from education may be used fully and effectively through com-

---

21 Schultz observes : "As economists we search for ways that will make producers most efficient. We tell everybody else how they can do their work better. But we fail to bring hard, analytical thinking to bear on our task as teachers. Surely the rate of obsolescence of what we teach and what students learn is higher than it need be" (see "The Rate of Return in Allocating Investment Resources to Education", *op. cit.*, p. 306). Harry G. Johnson also deals with this subject in his article "The Social Sciences in an Era of Opulence", in *Canadian Journal of Economics and Political Science*, Vol. 32, No. 4, November 1966, pp. 423-442.

bining human resources with other factors of production in a manner that maximizes output. Or it may be used only partially, e.g. using university graduates to do manual labour. If the human resource factor is used effectively, productivity will rise; if used ineffectively, it may level off or decline unless offset by other factors, e.g. availability and development of high quality natural resources.

For a nation to achieve continuing economic development, there is need for productivity to rise. Hence, if the benefits from education are to be maximized, it is necessary for society to make full and effective use of the educational product, a result hopefully achieved through fitting educational and employment goals into the broader framework of overall economic and social target-setting and policy formulation.

Education may also contribute to economic progress, as real Gross National Product expands at a more rapid rate than population, for in that case Gross National Product per capita increases. Or Gross National Product per capita may remain unchanged or even decline, but in that case the time available for leisure may expand because of a changing sense of values on the part of the population in dividing time between work and non-work.

Education will affect economic progress not only by contributing to rising Gross National Product and its more equitable distribution, to the choice between consumption now and consumption later, to the choice between work and leisure, but it may also have a bearing on a major variable of the growth process and that is the rate of population increase. Education may affect cultural, social and economic values, and the latter in turn may influence family size and family planning. [22]

Thus it can be said that education affects the state of civilization of nations, and their vitality and ability to survive in this restless and struggling world. And since knowledge knows no geographical boundaries and since education is an important aspect of economic development, the well-endowed nations have a responsibility on moral and humanitarian grounds, if not on

---

[22] For discussion of some of the social and cultural implications of education, see Chapter 15.

economic and political grounds, to assist the less well-endowed nations in speeding up advances in the process of education and training of their people. [23]

Education thus has moved through various stages of concern: from a family to a public responsibility, from a local to a regional concern, from a regional to a national task, and from a national to an international challenge.

---

[23] Canada participates in a number of programmes providing assistance in the field of education and training to other nations either bilaterally or multi-laterally. Such programmes include the Colombo Plan, the Special Commonwealth African Assistance Plan, Commonwealth Caribbean Assistance Programme, United Nations Educational, Scientific and Cultural Organisation, United Nations Development Programme, United Nations Training and Research Institute, and Commonwealth Scholarship and Fellowship Plan. Canada also assists in the recruitment of Canadian staff for educational projects for United Nations specialized agencies, such as U.N.E.S.C.O., I.L.O. and F.A.O. and undertakes to provide training in her country for trainees sponsored by a number of these organizations.

CHAPTER 15

Dual Effects of Education

DIFFERENT TYPES OF DUALITY

So far, the discussion has largely been concerned with the relationship between education and economic growth and development in aggregate and in structural terms. Education has been looked on primarily as a factor of input, that is the contribution it makes to increasing the capacity to produce, which, when fully used, will result in greater output. But education also contributes to increasing the demand for goods and services — quite apart from the desire for greater leisure. Thus education performs a dual function in the economic system.

One aspect of that duality is the contribution education makes to raising the capacity to consume and the capacity to produce. Another aspect of this duality is the contribution which education makes to expand production capabilities and human enjoyment, and to create the will and the effective demand to make use of the material and non-material benefits that flow from increased education.

There are still two other types of duality relating to the effect of education. One is the close interrelationship between economic and non-economic effects. The other revolves around the formulation of motivational factors. In addition to economic and humanistic factors, there are also cultural and social reasons for pursuing certain educational policies.

This chapter discusses the four types of duality of education under the following headings : Contribution to Capacity to Consume, Contribution to Capacity to Produce, Supply and Demand Effect, and Cultural and Social Factors.

CONTRIBUTION TO CAPACITY TO CONSUME

The capacity to consume and the desire to raise living standards may be affected by education for the following reasons :

    1. It widens the horizons of the consumer.

2. It aids the consumer to understand how to maximize the meeting of wants and thus obtain the greatest possible satisfaction from a given or obtainable quantity of resources.

3. It generates a desire to obtain access to a greater range of choice to meet existing or newly developed wants.

4. It fosters a willingness to experiment with new ways to obtain consumer satisfaction and thus encourages business firms to innovate by developing new or improved types of goods and services.

5. It creates increased opportunities to emulate living habits and standards of others, thus contributing to diversifying and expanding personal consumption of goods and services. [1]

6. It contributes to changes in consumer values, with the emphasis shifting from the bare necessities of life to greater demand for higher quality and greater variety of goods and services which yield increased consumer satisfaction.

7. It affects consumer attitudes towards material and non-material satisfaction obtainable from growing affluence.

8. It results in greater selectivity and critical assessment of the quality, serviceability and price of consumer goods and services coming on the market.

9. It makes it possible to translate the growing and more sophisticated capacity to consume into a higher, more variegated and more satisfying way of life that can be obtained from an effective blend of material achievement and spiritual choice.

10. It contributes to public enlightenment with consequent influence on government economic and social policies which in turn may significantly affect consumer spending and living standards.

The relationship between consumer needs and satisfaction and the contribution which education makes to the quality of life, has been stressed by Vaizey in these terms :

---

[1] James S. Duesenberry speaks of the "demonstration effect", that is the demonstration of the superiority of other products and of living habits of other people representing an inducement to consumers to do better for themselves (see James S. DUESENBERRY, *Income, Saving and the Theory of Consumer Behavior*, Cambridge, Massachusetts, Harvard University Press, 1949, p. 27).

Output satisfies "needs" and "needs" are not given; they change, and interact. It is here that education has a dual task. It can shift consumer satisfactions about; it can alter the enjoyment that people get out of goods and services, and what goods and services they want; it affects the quality of life. This is a point of enormous importance. [2]

Thus it can be said that education is a means of increasing the efficiency of consumption in the sense that education may assist the consumer in formulating rational choices, and as a result make it possible for him to obtain greater satisfaction from the exercise of his choice than he could have obtained from a less rational choice.

While education is one factor affecting consumer choice, there are many others. Consumer choices will also be influenced by business decisions, the manner in which entrepreneurs market and promote their products, and the product innovations they continuously offer to consumers thus widening their range of choice. And further, government fiscal and monetary policies may have a major effect on the capability of the consumer to meet his wants and to maximize his satisfaction.

Consumer spending is affected by many other factors as well, including levels and distribution of personal disposable income, current and future earnings, consumer assets and liabilities and the general mood and expectation of the consumer about his future well-being and the state of the economy. Thus it is important to bear in mind that educational attainments of the consuming public are only one variable, though perhaps an increasingly more important one in the process of determining consumer wants and consumer spending.

CONTRIBUTION TO CAPACITY TO PRODUCE

To turn now to the contribution which education makes to increase the capacity to produce, it is helpful to use a broad definition of education in this respect. The latter may be defined to include the formal acquisition of knowledge in schools and in institutions of higher learning, as well as technical training undertaken in vocational schools or on the job.

The capacity to produce may be raised through education for the following reasons :

---

[2] *The Economics of Education, op. cit.,* pp. 151 and 152.

1. It increases human skills and extends aptitudes which, if properly combined with the efficient use of other factors of production will increase individual and national productivity.

2. It raises managerial competence and entrepreneurial leadership, so essential to continuing economic progress.

3. It provides a basis in the everlasting search for scientific advancements, technological achievements and innovational accomplishments.

4. It pushes back the frontiers of risk-taking by both extending the opportunities to venture into new areas, and by minimizing the possibility of failure and by maximizing the potential for success through proper business and financial planning, and systematic and high-speed control measures.

5. It makes it possible to use the expanded capacity to produce so as to raise the nation's output and distribute it in a manner which contributes not only to maximizing consumer satisfaction but also makes possible the achievement of continued economic growth, higher levels of employment and real incomes, which in turn are prerequisites to raising standards of living and consumer welfare.

Supply and Demand Effects

Just as the Harrod-Domar model of economic growth allows for the dual impact of investment — its contribution to raising capacity and its effect on levels of employment and income [3] — so education can be said to have both a demand and a supply effect.

By turning out more knowledgeable and more sophisticated consumers, demand for goods and services is raised both in quantitative and qualitative terms. By training workmen to do a better job, and bringing to the fore business leaders who are productivity-conscious, innovation-oriented and risk-motivated,

---

[3] Roy F. Harrod, "An Essay in Dynamic Theory", in *Economic Journal* (Great Britain), Vol. XLIX, March 1939, pp. 14-33; id., *Towards a Dynamic Economics*, London, Macmillan, 1948 (especially Lecture 3); Evsey D. Domar, "Capital Expansion, Rate of Growth and Employment", in *Econometrica*, Vol. 14, No. 2, April 1946, p. 137 ff.; id., Expansion and Employment", in *American Economic Review*, Vol. XXXVII, No. 1, March 1947, p. 34-35; id., "Problems of Capital. Accumulation Formation", in *American Economic Review*, Vol. XXXVIII, No. 5, December 1948, pp. 777-794.

the capacity of the economy is expanded to produce more goods and services.

And as demand for more goods and services presses on the expanding capacity of the economy to produce more goods and services, the supply is increased. In the process, more employment and income is generated, not just because of the ensuing increases in demand for consumer goods and services, but also because the latter is accompanied by and at times preceded or followed by increases in demand for capital goods and government services. For a country to turn out an increased volume of goods and services, and to do so more efficiently, greater efforts are required to create the capital facilities and the governmental infra-structure. And beyond, there is need for increased international exchange of men, money and merchandise.

CULTURAL AND SOCIAL FACTORS

Many cultural and social factors affect both the quality and the extent of educational effort pursued and the results that flow from education to both the expansion of knowledge and the absorption of it by those who learn.

For the purpose of this study, only a few of the cultural and social factors are mentioned, and they include those that have a more direct bearing on the economic implications of education.

Cultural and social forces will affect the attitudes towards education (1) by those who are given opportunities to obtain education, that is the pupils, students and trainees, and those whose consent may be required, e.g. parents and guardians; (2) by those who do the educating, i.e. the teachers, professors and instructors of training courses; and (3) by society as a whole in deciding what proportion of the nation's resources is to be devoted to educational input and what use is to be made of educational output.

On the first point, people with different cultural and linguistic background may have varying views about the benefits of education. Some may be more interested in human improvement and some more in material rewards. Some may emphasize more the humanistic aspects of education and study to become lawyers, teachers, members of the clergy, musicians, artists, etc., while others may take a greater interest in the scientific aspects of education and become engineers, architects, mathematicians, physicists, chemists, etc.

In the former case, economic development of the country may be slowed down because of a shortage of the advanced skills required to develop and to introduce technological progress into the economic stream. In the latter case, a rapid rate of economic development may be facilitated, but this development may lack the balancing effect of human progress which involves advances on two fronts, the economic and the non-economic.

There may be differences on linguistic grounds, particularly important in a country like Canada with its two official languages, and even more significant in countries with more than two languages. When young people are educated and trained in one language without adequate knowledge of the other language or languages of the country, this type of education may limit the opportunities for economic advancement.

In terms of the individual, it may mean a lower return on his educational investment over his productive life. In terms of the nation, it may mean a lessening of the social return on human capital because language barriers affect labour mobility and thus reduce the optimum utilization of the human resource factor.

There may be varying attitudes towards education because of religious convictions and traditional beliefs, as well as political considerations. Such differences may become particularly noticeable between different political regional entities and between urban and rural areas. [4]

On the second point, in most countries — and Canada is no exception — the social status and the occupational image of educators have been lower than those of most other pro-

[4] "Farmers and farm workers in the province of Quebec have the lowest level of formal education in Canada. [...] While the upgrading of educational levels is quite apparent in other parts of Canada, it appears to have changed little among the farm workers of Quebec since 1941. Because of the differences in the educational systems of Quebec and other parts of Canada, it is difficult to draw absolute conclusions from these data, but they leave little doubt that rural Quebec lags behind the rest of Canada in the level of educational attainment among the male farm population" (see "Achievement and Opportunity in Rural Education", Marc-Adélard TREMBLAY and Walton J. ANDERSON, Eds., in *Rural Canada in Transition*, Ottawa. Agricultural Economics Research Council of Canada, 1966, p. 65.

fessions. Accompanying the lower priority attached to education as compared with other economic pursuits, is a level of teachers' earnings well below that of most other occupations involving similar training and experience. As a result, most teaching positions in the junior grades of the school system are filled with women, many of whom leave the teaching field when they get married and some of whom return when altered family circumstances make this possible in later years.

Where such teaching positions are filled by men, many of them are drawn into the teaching profession because of their dedication to a cause rather than because of material rewards, just as is the case with respect to many women teachers.

In most countries, salary differentials also apply to higher levels of education, e.g. universities, until a changing sense of social values leads a nation to devote a much higher proportion of its Gross National Product to educational expenditures, providing more adequate facilities for learning and higher pay to its educators, more or less comparable to other professional occupations with similar training and experience.

As the evidence presented in Chapter 16 indicates, this is what happened in Canada in the 1950's and 1960's when the proportion of Gross National Product devoted to education was materially raised, making it possible to recognize the valued services of educators, reflected in appropriate increases in the earnings of all teaching professions.

The discrimination against the teaching profession in terms of low earnings and social image in the earlier period of Canada's economic development as in many other countries moving through the various stages to that encompassing, technological maturity, had the effect of not attracting, in many instances, the potentially most promising young people, insofar as these people in choosing a profession were guided by considerations of financial reward and social prestige.

To the extent then, that some of the best brains of a country are syphoned off into areas of material advancement in non-educational occupations, and not enough men and women of comparable calibre are encouraged to enter the educational field, the contribution that education can make to the enhancement of knowledge and to its dissemination is not as great as it can be if the nation attached a high priority to educational efforts. As a result, economic development may not proceed at as rapid a pace as it is capable of reaching if the nation pursued a course of maximizing the expansion of knowledge and its application to economic pursuits.

On the third point, a country's economic development will be affected not only by society's decision of what proportion of its total resources is to be devoted to education, but also by the mix of the educational input and the economic use of the resulting output of trained people. [5]

Cultural and social factors may have a great bearing on the proportion of the Gross National Product a nation is prepared to devote to education. People living in rural areas frequently attach a lower value to education than people living in urban communities. People in lower income brackets may attach a lesser priority to education than people in medium or higher income brackets. People living in a society that is still struggling through the stages of take-off and drive to maturity may feel that they cannot afford, or they may not be prepared to make the sacrifices required to devote sufficient resources to education so as to maximize potential economic and social progress of future generations.

Within a society, people with different ethnic backgrounds may have varying views on the value of education to them, their children and to the community as a whole. Such different views may result in varying proportions of total resources devoted to education, and the type and quality of education obtained. As a consequence, wide differentials in earnings may occur, both actual as of a point of time, and potential over the productive life of individuals.

Such differentials will not only show up as between people with varying educational attainments, but also between people with comparable educational standards but coming from different ethnic backgrounds. The latter results indicate that edu-

---

[5] Schultz makes the point that "because education absorbs a large share of resources [. . .] misallocations *within* that sector and *between* education and alternative expenditures, could be wasteful" (see "The Rate of Return in Allocating Investment Resources to Education", *op. cit.*, p. 301).

cational attainments are only *one* variable in determining income levels — in addition to many others. [6]

As society becomes more perceptive as to its goals and aspirations and as each new generation formulates rising expectations, national views are likely to change materially with respect to the role that education may play in realizing a fuller and more rewarding life.

The human factor which reflects the philosophy and the character of a people becomes a significantly more important element in influencing the value which society attaches to education and its willingness to devote increasing resources to expanding both educational facilities and economic opportunities for the products of the learning process. [7]

The relationship between changing attitudes towards education and economic development has been explained in these terms : "Attitudes and preferences within a population strongly condition the interplay between education and other aspects of development; they are also variables subject to change and influenced by the nature of perceived opportunities." [8]

This discussion raises the broad question of educational planning and manpower planning, and there exists considerable literature on the subject. [9]

[6] The leading study on this subject in Canada has been three years in preparation: André RAYNAULT, Gérald MARION and Richard BÉLAND, *Distribution of Income by Ethnic Groups in Canada*, Study prepared for the Royal Commission on Bilingualism and Biculturalism, Queen's Printer, Ottawa, 1969. For a study dealing with the economic value of education and the welfare of low income minority groups in the United States, see Walter FOGEL, "Effects of Low Educational Attainment of Incomes: A Comparative Study of Selected Ethnic Groups", in *The Journal of Human Resources*, Vol. I, No. 2, Fall 1966, pp. 22-40.

[7] Hagen raises the question whether the argument that some countries train too many people for humanistic occupations and not enough for technical occupations, with the former group having difficulties to find adequate and remunerative employment, is really valid, and whether it does not "put the cart before the horse". He offers the suggestion that "the facile generalization that lack of demand for skills acquired is an important cause of social alienation needs empirical investigation" (see *The Economics of Development, op. cit.*, p. 215).

[8] "The Role of Education in Development", *op. cit.*, p. 155.

[9] See for example: Allan M. CARTTER, "A New Look at the Supply of College Teachers", in *Educational Record*, Summer 1965, pp. 267-277; ID., "The Supply of and Demand for College Teachers", in *The Journal of Human Resources*, Summer 1966, pp. 22-38; P. R. G. LAYARD and J. C. SAIGAL, "Educational and Occupational Characteristics of Manpower: An International Comparison", in *British Journal of Industrial Relations*, July 1966, pp. 224-266; Raymond F. LYONS, Ed., *Problems and*

The assumptions underlying "manpower-oriented planning have been criticized, as has been its neglect of differences in the costs of alternative ways of educating highly skilled manpower," [10] with manpower planning being described as "a flourishing practice with virtually no theory." [11] Other economists stress: "While manpower projections have appropriate uses in microanalyses, educational policy is not prudently to be based upon such projections in macro terms." [12]

As an alternative, economists have increasingly been making a case for using cost-benefit analysis as a guide for policy-makers to establish priorities for the allocation of educational expenditures, both in terms of totals and the main types of expenditures. [13]

QUANTITATIVE ASSESSMENT

Having presented an assessment of the economic implications of education and the different types of duality, the next task is to examine the quantitative aspects of the role of education in the Canadian economy over the last century.

Strategies of Educational Planning: Lessons from Latin America, Paris, International Institute of Educational Planning, 1966; Richard C. PORTER, "A Growth Model Forecast of Faculty Size and Salaries in United States Higher Education", in *Review of Economics and Statistics,* May 1965, pp. 191-197; B. C. ROBERTS and J. H. SMITH, Eds., *Manpower Policy and Employment Trends,* London, G. Bell & Sons, 1966; J. VAIZEY and R. KNIGHT, "Education", in W. BECKERMAN and others, Eds., *The British Economy in 1975,* Cambridge, England, Cambridge University Press, 1965; ORGANIZATION FOR ECONOMIC COOPERATION AND DEVELOPMENT, *Organizational Problems in Planning Educational Development,* Paris, O.E.C.D., 1966.

[10] Maureen WOODHALL, "The Economics of Education", in *Review of Educational Research,* October 1967, p. 392.

[11] E. R. RADO, "Manpower, Education and Economic Growth, in *Journal of Modern African Studies,* No. 1, 1966, pp. 83-93.

[12] C. Arnold ANDERSON, "The Adaptation of Education to a Mobile Society", in *The Journal of Human Resources,* Vol. II, No. 2, Spring 1967, p. 271.

[13] See *Economic Development, Principles, Problems, and Policies, op. cit.,* pp. 411-413; John W. KENDRICK, "Comments", in John VAIZEY, Ed., *The Residual Factor and Economic Growth,* Paris, O.E.C.D., pp. 216-217. Higgins makes the point: "Education inputs should be considered simultaneously with all other costs in determining returns to investment in various kinds of education, and in comparing returns on investment in education with returns on other forms of investment. The total size of the education budget will then be established by expanding investment in education until returns on further investment in education fall below the returns on other forms of investment. This is just another way of saying that the education budget would be determined by a 'cost-benefit' approach."

The approach in dealing with this subject is selective, with the data and analysis presented in Chapters 16 to 21, designed to throw light on eight specific questions.

1. To what extent have educational expenditures varied with rates of economic growth during the last one hundred years of Canada's development on the basis of a delineation of stages put forward by Rostow ?

2. To what extent has the school population and its learning capacity improved, and has education changed the training and quality of the labour force ?

3. To what extent has increased education contributed to higher earnings in the past ?

4. To what extent will different educational attainments affect lifetime earnings ?

5. To what extent do returns on educational investment differ ?

6. To what extent has Canada benefited from educational attainments abroad and to what extent has she contributed to other countries, and what is the net gain of educational capital from immigration and emigration ?

7. To what extent has the proximity of the United States, the country with the greatest educational and economic achievements in the world, affected Canada through emulation, sharing of knowledge and ready access to opportunities for higher learning and research.

8. To what extent has the rate of economic growth been affected by rising productivity associated with greater education and training ?

In dealing with these questions, a number of other questions, just as relevant, have been omitted. Subject matters that could usefully be explored but are not covered in this study include :

To what extent has the productivity of education been raised ? What were some of the technological changes affecting education ? How have modern means of mass communications affected education ? Has there been a change in the relative contribution which education and training (and that covers institutional and on the job training, as well as self-improvement) make to increasing knowledge and skills ? How has education affected the will to work, the desire for more leisure, and the attitude towards material and non-material rewards ? How has education affected spatial, occupational and social mobility ?

There are further some basic theoretical questions to be answered: Are expenditures on education considered investment or consumption ? And if the latter, should there be a distinction between productive investment and social investment ? [14] How imperfect is the market for education ? Why can the price system not be used to allocate resources as it does in most other sectors in western-type economies ? And what is the alternative to using the price system for allocating resources to education on a scientific basis ?

Still other questions may be raised in the field of applied economics : How adequate has education and training been to meet the skill requirements of rapidly changing technology and scientific advances ? And what about the obsolescence of education as new techniques, new forms and new objectives of education were evolved ? [15] How effective has been the balancing of training the teachers needed with the demands for fully educated persons in other occupations ? How dynamic has education been in sparking economic progress ?

Then there are questions in the social field : How strong have social factors and social pressures been in developing the educational system ? How has education affected the intellectual elite and leadership in the arts, professions and other major areas of economic pursuit ? Other questions could be added to these, both of a social and political nature. But perhaps enough has been said to indicate the enormity of the subject and the limitations of this study.

---

[14] "The 'productive category' is akin to the individual's concept of investment, in that the stream of benefits from a subject must have a money value sufficient to defray all of the costs incurred (including interest). 'Social investment' on the other hand, refers to projects whose benefits to the community are more valuable than the costs incurred, even though there may be a financial loss because the benefits are distributed free, or at a reduced price" (see *Investment in Education, op. cit.,* p. 373).

[15] Obsolescence of education raises the important question of "continuing" education to ensure that the educated keep up with the advances in knowledge.

One other caveat is desirable : In considering the economic effects of education, its implications on human resource development should not be overlooked. To quote two informed observers :

> The efforts to give greater emphasis to human resources in economic theory and the attempts to measure the contribution of education to economic growth are constructive. [...] It is incorrect to assume that the central purpose of human resource development is to maximize man's contribution to the creation of productive goods and services. Nor is it realistic to measure the return on education solely in terms of increases in individual incomes or the income of the economy as a whole. And increases in productivity certainly should not be taken as the exclusive test of the effectiveness of human resource development. [16]

The fact that education serves both economic *and* non-economic ends cannot be emphasized strongly enough.

---

[16] Frederick H. HARBISON and Charles A. MYERS, *Education, Manpower, and Economic Growth, Strategies of Human Resource Development*, New York, McGraw-Hill, Inc., 1964, p. 12.

CHAPTER 16

Education Industry

CHARACTERISTICS

What are the main characteristics of the Canadian education industry ?

1. It is an industry whose rate of growth exceeds the rate of expansion of most sectors of the Canadian economy.

2. It is an industry where the rate of technological progress, innovations and experimentation is being speeded up, resulting in an increase of the rate of obsolescence of both the output and the input. To illustrate the former, about one-half of knowledge acquired in institutions of higher learning by the medical profession, scientists and engineers working in industries with rapid product change is claimed to become obsolete in about ten years. To illustrate the latter, teachers need retraining, curricula have to be revised continuously, education aids are being replaced by new devices, mass communications require a revamping of the system of transmitting knowledge, buildings become cramped and inadequate, and equipment becomes obsolete.

3. It is an industry where supply is continuously lagging behind demand. This is due in part to the backlog of demand built up as a result of an inadequate rate of expansion in the past, in part to increasing affluency of individuals and society as a whole, and in part to changes in the public's attitude and valuation of the benefits of education, both in economic and non-material terms which have altered priority considerations.

4. It is an industry that operates in an imperfect market where the "buyers" of the product, that is the persons obtaining an education, are in many instances not the originators of the buying decisions (parents making decisions for their children), where demand is largely not a matter of choice (compulsory education to the age of sixteen), where the product is largely provided without *direct* charge to the buyer ("free" education at the public elementary and secondary level, though most

parents pay for education indirectly through taxes), where the buyers have inadequate knowledge of product alternatives (inadequate student counselling), and where the price system is ineffective in allocating resources (since a large part of the operations of the education industry is financed by governments, either directly or through grants, with social and political considerations frequently being the motivating factors rather than economic reasoning). [1]

5.   It is an industry with mixed ownership and direction, public and private, the former preponderant, with the two sectors guided by somewhat different motivation as to objectives and the best methods of realizing them. At the same time, it is a "sensitive" industry where such concepts as "teacher quality" and "academic freedom" loom large in affecting the operation, composition and output of the education sector.

6.   It is an industry where the scale of operations can be both a handicap and an advantage. Too small administrative units at the elementary and secondary school level, particularly in rural and semi-rural areas, have brought about many inefficiencies, inadequate quality of teaching, wasteful operations and misallocation of resources, necessitating the organization of larger and more efficient administrative units. At the same time, some of the institutions of higher learning have become so large that decentralization of organization and the creation of additional universities and junior colleges became necessary to achieve a combination of increased efficiency and high quality of teaching. Small classes make it possible for teachers to give more individual attention to pupils. Quality considerations of educational performance have produced a trend towards smaller classes, notwithstanding the great increase in numbers of those seeking education. The problem of reorganizing the educational system in Canada has been particularly complicated by factors of geography and demography. Most of Canada's population is concentrated in two dozen metropolitan centres and major cities, with the rest spread out thinly across the continent, some five thousand miles in length. Thus, providing adequate educational facilities has become in part a transportation problem.

---

[1]   These characteristics are common to most educational systems in operation in western countries.

7. It is an industry that operates in a federally constituted country, with ten provincial governments primarily responsible for education which they exercise in cooperation with many thousands of local administrative units (school boards, institutions of higher learning and vocational training, etc.). Standards of education lack uniformity and this is not without effect on the quality of education and the mobility of the labour force. The burden of financing Canadian education is heavy and it rests mainly on the shoulders of junior governments which are financially weaker than the central government. This has made it necessary for the federal authorities to offer assistance. A conflict ensued as to the form such assistance might take and it has led to continuing disputes between federal and provincial governments. While a modus vivendi exists, Canada is still far away from finding a solution to this puzzling problem acceptable to eleven different legislatures and governmental bodies, and the public at large.

8. It is an industry where pedagogic, social and economic research relating to both input and output are essential but where less work has been done than almost in any other major sector of economic activity in Canada.

It is against this background of the special characteristics of the Canadian education industry that the facts presented below about its size, growth and composition should be viewed.

TEACHERS, STUDENTS AND EXPENDITURES

Education in Canada represents an industry with a budget of over $4 billion, equivalent to about 7¼ per cent of the country's Gross National Product. It employs over a quarter of a million full-time teachers, about 3½ per cent of the labour force, together with tens of thousands of supplementary staff and part-time teachers. Educational capital expenditures involve over $1 billion annually, spent mainly on buildings and equipment, and representing about one-quarter of all outlays on social capital and equivalent to more than 10 per cent of business capital investment. About one-half of all local government spending, one-third of provincial government expenditures and about 5 per cent of federal government outlays are made to meet Canada's explosive growth of the education industry.

The great majority of teachers are employed in elementary and secondary schools, some 230,400 in about 20,600 institutions, with some 200,000 classrooms. Of these institutions, about 92 per cent are public and 8 per cent are private and they look after 5.3 million students.

About 20,700 full-time university teachers look after 233,000 full-time students, [2] registered in some 400 institutions of higher learning. The figures relate to the academic year 1966-1967 [3] which recorded a 13 per cent increase in university enrolment over the year previous. Remarked the traditionally cautious Dominion Bureau of Statistics : "If present trends continue, the 1965-66 full-time enrolment figure may be doubled in six years." [4]

The education industry caters to the needs of about 8.3 million Canadians, or 40 per cent of the total population. About 6 million people are obtaining education and training on a full-time basis, while 2.3 million are involved in adult education on a part-time basis. Thus education has become a way of life for many Canadians and the continuity of that process has become increasingly recognized (see Summary Table 4).

EDUCATIONAL EXPLOSION

With a nation where four out of ten people are learners, the education industry faces not only explosive growth but continuing pressures with the demand for well-trained staff, buildings, equipment, libraries and research facilities exceeding the supply in most institutions in this country. Bottle-necks and scarcities result and this is reflected particularly in shortages of scientific and professional personnel in certain occupational categories, from engineers to physicians, from social scientists to teachers, and from technicians to nurses.

---

[2] In addition, Canadian institutions of higher learning accommodated over 53,000 pre-matriculation students, that is, students enrolled in courses for which matriculation is not required, and some 99,000 part-time students. Among the full-time students, Canadian institutions provide training for more than 15,000 foreign students from some 150 countries. (Data of pre-matriculation students relate to 1965-66; all other date to 1966-67.)

[3] In that year, some 44,000 students received their bachelor and first professional degrees, with 6,250 being awarded graduate degrees.

[4] DOMINION BUREAU OF STATISTICS, *Preliminary Statistics of Education, 1965-66*, Ottawa, 1967, p. 24. (See also Edward F. SHEFFIELD, *Enrolment in Canadian Universities and Colleges to 1976-77, 1966 Projection*, Ottawa, Association of Universities and Colleges, 1966.)

The build-up of that pressure is indicated in Summary Table 4 which shows that during the stage of high mass-consumption, 1950-1967, Canada's population rose by about one-half while her school enrolment more than doubled, her total expenditures on formal education increased ninefold and her capital expenditures on schools and universities rose tenfold, while Gross National Product expanded threefold.

Remedies to deal with the educational explosion have been largely in the hands of provincial governments and local authorities with the British North America Act of 1867 (Act of Confederation) specifically placing education as a responsibility of the provinces. The situation is complicated by the fact that Canada has ten different provincially operated systems, with some unique features including the provision of education in English and French in a number of provinces.

The Federal Government has certain direct responsibilities in special areas including the two northern territories, the provision of education for Indians and Eskimos and for dependents of Canadian personnel employed abroad. In more recent years the Federal Government has provided increasing financial assistance to the education industry. [5]

KNOWLEDGE EXPLOSION

The growing pressures felt by the Canadian education industry have not been just the result of large increases in numbers. The concepts of what education entails and how the objective of learning can best be realized have undergone major changes. Emphasis has been directed towards keeping young people in school longer and in having them complete a vocational or academic course.

Quantitative changes have been accompanied by qualitative changes. Even with Canada's birthrate falling in the more recent period (and this trend is continuing), the pattern of age distribution and longer learning periods continue to add to the

---

[5] This has taken the form of grants to universities and payments for vocational and technical education, assistance under the Canada Student Loan Plan and research grants and scholarships through the National Research Council, the Medical Research Council, the Canada Council and a number of government departments and crown corporations.

SUMMARY TABLE 4. — POPULATION, SCHOOL ENROLMENT, TOTAL EXPENDITURES ON FORMAL EDUCATION AND CAPITAL EXPENDITURES ON SCHOOLS AND UNIVERSITIES, CANADA, 1950 AND 1967.

ITEM	1950 THOUS.	1967 THOUS.	PER CENT INCREASE 1950-1967
POPULATION [1]	13,712	20,405	48.8
ENROLMENT [2]			
Elementary and Secondary Schools			
Public	2,472	5,095	106.1
Private	107	190	77.6
Sub-Total	2,579	5,285	104.9
Vocational Education			
Public	—[3]	439[4]	—
Private [5]	35	39	11.4
Sub-Total	—[3]	478	—
Higher Education [6]	156[7]	233	} 76.9
Teacher Training	—	43	
Adult Education [8]	—	2,291	—
Sub-Total	—	2,567	—
Total	—	8,330	—
Public [9]	2,628	5,328	102.7
Private [10]	142	229	61.3
Total	2,770	5,557	100.6
TOTAL ENROLMENT AS PER CENT OF POPULATION	—.[3]	40.8	—
TOTAL EXPENDITURES ON FORMAL EDUCATION —$ Mill.	465	4,539	876.1 [11]
CAPITAL EXPENDITURES ON SCHOOLS AND UNIVERSITIES —$ Mill.	102	1,031	910.8 [12]
GROSS NATIONAL PRODUCT —$ Mill.	18,006	62,068	244.7 [13]

Source: *Preliminary Statistics of Education, 1966-1967, The Canada Year Book, 1952-53*, Ottawa, Queen's Printer, 1953; DOMINION BUREAU OF STATISTICS, *National Accounts, Income and Expenditure, 1966*, Ottawa, 1967, and earlier issues, ID., *National Accounts, Income and Expenditure, Fourth Quarter and Preliminary Annual 1967*, Ottawa, April 1968; DEPARTMENT OF TRADE AND COMMERCE, *Private and Public Investment in Canada, Outlook 1968*, Ottawa, 1968, and earlier issues.

[1] As of June.
[2] 1966-67; covers full-time except adult education.

heavy and growing demands of the education industry. At the same time an "explosion" in new knowledge has raised many problems at all levels. A variety of visual and auditory aids has been introduced into the classroom: television, the overhead projector, programmed instruction by machines, and language laboratories. Increasing use is being made of computers for marking papers, preparing reports, processing attendance and other reports, and for scheduling classes.

Under strong pressures, the Canadian education industry has expanded by leaps and bounds, particularly in the last decade and it has produced levels of education, scientific and technical training that, notwithstanding inadequacies and irritations, have served the economy well.

Still, discontent and dissent have been growing. Teachers were asking for greater self-determination and levels of remuneration comparable to those of other professions with similar qualifications. Students were demonstrating for "student power", basically asking for a reorientation of the purpose and method of learning, and full participation in academic matters and educational administration. The issues involved were complex because of differences of views among the dissenters and those in authority — the establishment which was increasingly buffeted from all directions and which could not with conviction defend the status quo though it was not quite prepared to venture into the unknown field of bold reforms asked for by the dissenters.

Dissent in educational matters was a problem that Canada shared with many countries of the world including the United States. The achievements of Canada's education industry had remained considerably behind those of the United States and this had a bearing on economic development, discussed later on.

---

3 Not available.
4 Figures relate to 1966.
5 Includes business colleges; data relate to 1950 and 1965.
6 Universities and colleges.
7 Includes teacher training.
8 Part-time; data relate to 1965.
9 Covers public elementary and secondary schools and institutions of higher learning.
10 Covers private elementary and secondary schools and private vocational schools.
11 This represents an increase in real terms of 501 per cent.
12 This represents an increase in real terms of 461 per cent.
13 This represents an increase in real terms of 112 per cent.

CHAPTER 17

Education and Stages of Economic Development

EDUCATION AND POVERTY

W. Arthur Lewis once remarked : "Poor countries cannot afford to pay as much for education as richer countries." [1] This observation can be reworded in historical perspective by saying : "Rich countries start out as poor countries, and during the period of poverty cannot afford to pay as much for education as later on when they are richer."

This has been Canada's experience. During their early history, Canadians could not afford to spend much on education. They had to devote their main efforts to developing a virgin country. Education was largely in the hands of the clergy. Separation between church and state in matters of education evolved slowly in Canada, and quite differently from the development in the United States. In that country the First Amendment to the Constitution with its "Free Exercise and Establishment Clauses" set out in specific terms the separation of functions. "With respect to education these provisions carried a twofold purpose: to ban the teaching of sectarian doctrines in public schools and to restrict the use of public funds exclusively for public education." [2]

With the main stem of Canada's population being largely French (Catholic) and English (Protestant), education during the first stage of Canada's economic development, the period before 1867, was greatly influenced by the varying role played by the church in maintaining control over learning in the elementary and secondary schools. The transformation to non-sectarian teaching came slowly and not without protracted controversy. [3]

---

[1] *Development Planning, op. cit.*, p. 104.
[2] V. T. THAYER, *Formative Ideas in American Education, From the Colonial Period to the Present*, New York, Dodd, Mead & Company, Inc., 1966, p. 41 (see also pp. 112 ff.).
[3] For example, action on a proposal made in Quebec in 1789 to introduce a system of elementary schools in villages, secondary schools in towns and a non-denominational collegiate institute for the teaching of the liberal arts and sciences, supported by local assessments, was

Very early in their attempts to change from non-secular to lay education, the settlers found that the provision of education required public support and that the lack of indigenous teachers had to be made up by importation from abroad. In the 1770's, English residents of Montreal raised one hundred pounds to bring in a school-master from New York. But the money did not last long and the residents petitioned the governor for financial assistance. By 1789, four such teachers were receiving grants of two hundred pounds each, [4] and the beginning to establish a publicly supported school system had been made.

PUBLIC SUPPORT OF EDUCATION

The development of the publicly supported school system, initially following the British pattern but increasingly influenced by modern ideas evolved in the United States, received great impetus in English-speaking provinces in the early nineteenth century, [5] while at about the same time Quebec, or Lower Canada as it was called then, established a new system for the operation of non-sectarian schools. [6]

Further major changes came in the 1840's with legislation enacted providing for separate denominational schools for a religious minority, supported by public funds, allotted "accord-

---

deferred for more than two decades because the plan was interpreted as an attempt by an unsympathetic government to get complete control over education (see Charles E. PHILLIPS, *Development of Education in Canada*, Toronto, W. J. Gage Ltd., 1957, p. 79).

[4] John E. CHEAL, *Investment in Canadian Youth, An Analysis of Input-Output Differences Among Canadian Provincial School Systems*, Toronto, The MacMillan Company of Canada Limited, 1963, p. 16.

[5] In Upper Canada (Ontario), the two main statutes were "An Act to Establish Public Schools in Each and Every District of this Province", 1807, and a more far-reaching Act following the American pattern, the "Common School Act of 1816". Common School Acts were passed in Nova Scotia in 1811 and in New Brunswick in 1816.

[6] "Act to Establish Free Schools and to Promote the Cause of Education", 1801. Pressures continued in Lower Canada for different types of sectarian education and denominational control. But the Legislative Assembly rejected such proposals giving as a reason in 1827 "the great jealousy existing between the religious creeds of the country which has retarded the progress of education". The case for free education was linked to the great poverty that affected most people in the Province. It was argued: "How could the common people be expected to support their children and at the same time give them an education when work was not to be got, or when scarcely any man could gain more than two shillings a day" (see statement by Dr. Joseph Blanchet, *The Star*, Montreal, February 28, 1829).

ing to their number, of the monies appropriated and raised by assessment for the support of Common Schools. [7]

While primary schooling developed early, [8] followed by secondary education, it took two centuries to develop institutions of higher learning. Some tentative beginnings were made in establishing the Séminaire de Québec, a Roman-Catholic College of Arts and Theology founded in 1663, which became a university in the modern sense in 1852 and was then renamed after the founder of the college, Bishop Laval. Before that date, English-language universities had been established in Halifax, Dalhousie University [9] in 1820, in Montreal, McGill University in 1821, the University of King's College in Upper Canada, 1827, later to become the University of Toronto, and in Fredericton, New Brunswick, King's College, to become later the secular university of New Brunswick in 1859.

Robert Gourlay, in assessing the educational system in Upper Canada (Ontario) lamented in 1822:

> There is no college in Upper Canada [...] no provision is made by law for free schools. The inhabitants of several townships are left to a voluntary support of schools, according to their own discretion. An act of the provincial legislature, in 1807, granted a hundred pounds a year to the teacher of one school, in each of the districts under the discretion of trustees. In some districts the school thus provided for is made a free school; but in other districts the salaries considered as a public encouragement of a teacher of literary eminence, in addition to the compensation received for the tuition of each scholar. [10]

---

[7] Act passed in 1841, 4 Vict. Cap. 18, Art. 11. This Act applied only to Upper Canada, with provisions made for Lower Canada in a separate statute in 1845, leading to the establishment in that province of two separate and distinct school corporations. Further amendments followed rounding out the system of separate schools before the advent of Confederation in 1867. Of these, the two most important statutes were the ones passed in Lower Canada in 1860 and in Upper Canada in 1863 (for further details see *Investment in Canadian Youth, op. cit.,* pp. 20 ff.).

[8] Though elementary schools controlled by the people did not become common until about 1820, with universal elementary education being achieved between 1850 and 1875.

[9] "In imitation of the University of Edinburgh." It followed the earlier establishment of a largely ecclesiastical institution, King's College, at Windsor, Nova Scotia.

[10] Robert GOURLAY, SIMPKIN & MARSHALL, *Statistical Account of Upper Canada, Compiled with a View to a Grant System of Emigration,* London, Stationers Court, 1822, pp. 244-245. Attending a university in Canada, as and when these became established, was a privilege largely

In the early stages, higher education placed major emphasis on the humanities and the arts, with interest in the sciences deferred to a later date when industrial development and growing awareness of educational achievements abroad (in the later period largely an emulation of American progress) began to exert a growing influence on the pattern of educational development in Canada.

FIRST STAGE

Looking at the role of education in Canada's first stage of economic development, the period before 1867, certain common characteristics can be noted:

The following passage relating to the Province of Ontario indicates that the Canadian school system developed by drawing on the experiences of many countries and adapting it to regional and local circumstances :

> Thus the Province is in a great degree indebted to New York for the machinery of our schools, to Massachusetts for the principle of local taxation upon which the schools are supported, to Ireland (originally) for the series of text-books, and to Germany for the system of Normal School training. All are, however, so modified and blended together to suit the wants and circumstances of the country, that they are no longer foreign, but are incorporated as part and parcel of our institutions. [11]

1. The pattern of educational development was shaped by religious, cultural, traditional and philosophical factors. During most of the period, economic considerations had either little or no influence.

2. The emphasis was on "basic" education at the primary and secondary levels, and on the humanities and the arts at the level of higher learning, with improvements at one level followed only after a considerable time lag by improvements

---

reserved for the sons, and later on the daughters of the well-to-do. But as early as 1824, William Lyon Mackenzie, who was to lead the Rebellion of 1837, pleaded for the establishment of a university in Upper Canada which would provide free higher education (see his article in the first issue of the *Colonial Advocate*, May 18, 1824).

[11] "Education in Ontario", Abbreviated from a report prepared under the direction of the Provincial Minister of Education, in *Canadian Economics,* Proceedings of the Conference of British Association for the Advancement of Science, held in Montreal in 1884, Montreal, Dawson Brothers, 1885, p. 315.

in the next higher level. Development of technical training at the post-primary level and scientific orientation at the university level had to await the greater advances in technology and expanded industrialization which only developed as Canada moved through the stages of the pre-conditions of take-off and the take-off.

3. The strong denominational character of education and the development of the separate school system, differing from province to province, had far-reaching consequences on the quality of education and the development of skills, necessary to advance the country's economy from one stage to another. In essence, the type of educational system evolving in Canada in the Pre-Confederation period was a contributing factor to delaying the take-off stage in the northern half of the continent as compared with the rate of growth and type of industrial progress experienced in the United States. [12]   W. W. Rostow places the take-off stage for the United States between 1843 and 1860, as compared with 1896-1914 for Canada. [13]

Inadequate information is available to assess the retarding effects on the rate of economic growth in the colonial period resulting from the slow progress made in expanding and improving the educational system and in particular the retarding effects of the denominational school system. But some studies relating to the more recent past exist which are suggestive of what some of the economic implications might have been.

Based on an examination of the relationship between input and output of different educational systems in operation in Canada during the 1950's, evidence obtainable appeared to support the following conclusions :

---

[12] While the Canadian provinces were struggling to resolve the issues between denominational and non-denominational schooling and the separation between church and state in matters of education, and school attendance and participation were still on an irregular basis towards the middle of the nineteenth century while university training was largely available to the privileged few, by 1840 something like one-half of the children in the New England states were given free public education and about one-sixth of those in the western states. "By 1850 some 2,000 academies were serving over 250,000 students and the 9 colleges of the colonial period had increased in number to some 200 colleges and universities. By 1850, also, secondary education was no longer a monopoly of privately supported academies. Public high schools as well as public elementary schools were rapidly becoming an inherent part of state school systems" (*Formative Ideas in American Education, op. cit.*, p. 85).

[13] *The Stages of Economic Growth, op. cit.*, p. 38.

A significant negative correlation was found between educational output and the degree of denominationalism in provincial school systems. This negative relationship was supported also in a comparison of the outputs of the dual school systems of Quebec and the public and separate school systems of Alberta. Factors found to be associated with denominationalism were lower per-pupil expenditure, lower teacher salaries and qualifications, lower personal incomes, and greater educational need in terms of both the number of children to be educated and the number of years of schooling in the adult population. It was also found that several provinces higher in denominationalism were making more effort relative to ability than provinces with less denominationalism, but were nevertheless achieving a lower output. The denominational factor in Canada's provincial school systems would seem to have a significant association with the regional differences that have been found in educational inputs and outputs. This factor would seem to be related to cultural variables that find expression in attitudes towards education, which may play a significant role in determining the retention power of the schools and, subsequently, the productive power of the population. [14]

4. Colonial administrators placed a low priority on education in the early period. And later when the settlements were given a reasonable degree of self-determination in domestic affairs, low levels of incomes and the comparatively high costs of education — for some teachers had to be attracted from abroad and paid higher than the going wage-scales — limited the capacity of the provinces to raise education to the levels required that would bring forth an adequate flow of young people trained to cope with the requirements of a society which was slowly moving from a rural and agricultural pioneering community to a more urbanized, more commercially active, and ultimately more industrially oriented nation.

The social scientist wishing to establish what proportion of Canada's Gross National Product was devoted to expenditures on education at the time of Confederation and through the remainder of the nineteenth century faces major data problems. However, a general impression can be gained from partial data covering a major sector of government expenditures on education. Statistics are available of receipts of publicly controlled

---

[14]   *Investment in Canadian Youth, op. cit.*, p. 119.

elementary and secondary schools going back to 1870 and continuing to the present. [15]

For the period 1926 to date, comprehensive estimates of total expenditures on formal education, prepared by the Dominion Bureau of Statistics, are available. During this period, expenditures by publicly controlled schools have comprised between 60 per cent and 70 per cent of total education expenditures for most years (see Appendix B).

Allowing for non-coverage and as a first approximation, it appears that Canadians spent about $1 per capita (plus or minus) on education in 1867 and they devoted less than 1 per cent of their Gross National Product for that purpose (see Summary Table 5).

SECOND TO FOURTH STAGE

Piecing together the incomplete data available for the first six decades with the more complete estimates obtainable from official sources in the last four decades, [16] the following tentative conclusions can be offered about the relationship between education and economic growth in Canada between 1867 and 1967. [17]

1. During the preconditions for take-off stage, 1867-1896, Canada's population grew at an annual average rate of 1.4 per cent and Gross National Product in real terms by 3.3 per cent. During this period per capita expenditures on formal education rose from $1 to $2.50. [18] The ratio of educational expenditures to Gross National Product rose from less than 1 per cent in 1867 to about 1¼ per cent in 1896. [19]

---

[15] These cover provincial grants and receipts from local assessments. Total revenues are close to total government expenditures made for publicly supported elementary and secondary schools covering both operating and capital outlays. The data are reported on a provincial basis with figures missing for some provinces for certain years. Adjustments have been made to facilitate comparison over the period and estimates were prepared for 1867 on the basis of trend analysis.

[16] See Table 3 in Appendix A.

[17] These conclusions are subject to revision in the light of additional evidence becoming available.

[18] The figures represent first approximations and they should be considered as $1, plus or minus, $2.50, plus or minus, and $7, plus or minus (for 1914).

[19] Again the percentages are approximate, 1¼ per cent, plus or minus, for 1896, and 2 per cent, plus or minus, for 1914.

In the take-off stage, 1896-1914, population grew more rapidly and so did the Gross National Product in constant dollars, 2.4 per cent and 3.7 per cent respectively. Still, the proportion of the nation's output devoted to education rose only slowly, reaching about 2 per cent in 1914, with per capita educational spending of about $7.

Prices had changed comparatively little between 1867 and 1896, but they rose significantly over the next stage, by about one-half, between 1896 and 1914 (see Table 1 in Appendix A). Thus in terms of 1914 purchasing power, the $2.50 spent in 1896 were equivalent to about $3.75, indicating that the improvement in educational spending in real terms was considerably less than is indicated in current dollar terms.

In the next stage, the drive to maturity, 1914-1950, Canada's population rose at an annual average rate of 1.5 per cent and Gross National Product in constant dollars by 3 per cent. During this period, education responded to technological changes and scientific requirements of a new age and expenditures increased fairly rapidly. Still in terms of the ratio of expenditures on formal education to Gross National Product, there was remarkably little change over the long term though there were significant differences in the ratios at various points in the intervening period, largely affected by cyclical factors and the exigencies of World War II.

From about 2 per cent of Gross National Product devoted to education in 1914, the ratio rose to 2.7 per cent in 1926. By 1950, 24 years later, when Canada had reached the stage of industrial maturity, the ratio was almost unchanged, 2.6 per cent.

In the intervening period, the ratio varied little in the 1920's, but it moved to 4.2 per cent in 1933, the bottom of the Great Depression, as expenditures in education could not be cut back in line with the sharp decline of Gross National Product. As the economy expanded again in the latter part of the 1930's, the ratio returned to 2.7 per cent at the time World War II broke out. During the peak year of the war effort, the ratio reached its lowest point in the stage of drive to maturity, 1.5 per cent in 1944. After the war the ratio moved up gradually, to 2.6 per cent by 1950, still a shade below the 1926 ratio (see Summary Table 5).

SUMMARY TABLE 5. — EXPENDITURES ON FORMAL EDUCATION, TOTALS AND PER CAPITA, AND RATES OF ECONOMIC GROWTH, CANADA, 1867-1967.

YEAR OR PERIOD	ANNUAL RATE OF GROWTH PER CENT [1]		EXPENDITURES ON FORMAL EDUCATION		
	Population	Gross National Product [2]	Amount [3]		Per Cent of Gross National Product [4]
			Total $ Mill.	Per Capita $	
1867-1896	1.4	2.3	—	$(1\pm)^5$	$(1\pm)^5$
1896-1915	2.4	3.7	—	$(2\pm)^5$	$(1\frac{1}{4}\pm)^5$
1914-1950	1.5	3.0	—	$(7\pm)^5$	$(2\pm)^5$
1926	—	—	142	15	2.7
1929	—	—	160	16	2.6
1933	—	—	147	14	4.2
1939	—	—	154	14	2.7
1944	—	—	173	14	1.5
1945	—	—	195	16	1.6
1950-1967	2.4	4.5	465 [5]	34 [5]	2.6 [5]
1956	—	—	909	57	3.0
1961	—	—	1,873	103	5.0
1966	—	—	3,946	197	6.8
1967	—	—	4,539	222	7.3

Source: Based on Tables 1 and 3 in Appendix A. The figures shown in brackets are first approximations based on partial data available of expenditures on elementary and secondary schools (see Appendix B).

---

[1] Compound rate.

[2] Based on constant (1957) dollars.

[3] In current dollars.

[4] In view of the unavailability of price index of education costs, the implied price index in Gross National Expenditure was used to deflate expenditures on formal education as per Table 6. This is the same technique as used by the Dominion Bureau of Statistics (see *Survey of Education Finance, 1963*, Ottawa, 1967, pp. 10 and 11). On this basis the proportion of expenditures on formal education to Gross National Product would be the same whether expressed in current or in constant dollars. To the extent that rates of growth of an education cost index would vary from the implied price index in Gross National Expenditure, the above ratios would vary correspondingly.

[5] Beginning of period.

Per capita expenditures on education had increased from $7 in 1914 to $15 in 1926. Prices rose by about 55 per cent during this period. Thus in terms of 1926 purchasing power (based on the implied price index in Gross National Expenditure) per capita expenditures on education were the equivalent of close to $11, again suggesting a more moderate improvement in real terms than is indicated in current dollars estimates.

Over the next two decades, educational expenditures per capita moved in the $14 to $16 range. Since prices rose by about 12 per cent between 1926 and 1945, this meant that in real terms, Canadians were actually spending less on education when World War II ended than they had spent on a per capita basis during the middle of the 1920's.

FIFTH STAGE

The most rapid growth of the Canadian economy and the educational explosion commenced with the period of techno- logical maturity in the middle of the twentieth century. Between 1950 and 1967, population grew at an annual rate of 2.4 per cent and Gross National Product in real terms by 4.5 per cent (see Summary Table 5). The ratio of expenditures on formal education rose from 2.6 per cent in 1950, to 5 per cent by 1961, to 6.8 per cent in 1966, and to 7.3 per cent in 1967.

Per capita expenditures rose from $34 in 1950 to $222 in 1967. Even allowing for the substantial increases in the general price level that took place during that period, about 63 per cent, the rate of growth in educational expenditures per capita is substantial indeed, involving an expansion of four times the former level in constant dollar terms.

The great difference of what a nation can afford on educa- tion, higher learning, research and training once it reaches the stage of industrial maturity, compared with the preceding stage, is illustrated below.

ANNUAL AVERAGE RATE OF INCREASE [20] — PER CENT.

	Gross National Product [21]	Total Educational Expenditures [22]
1926-1950	3.5	3.2
1950-1967	4.5	11.1

[20] Compound rates in constant (1957) dollars.
[21] Based on Table 1 in Appendix A.
[22] Based on Table 6 in Appendix A.

The annual rate of economic growth, reflected in total Gross National Product in real terms moves up only 1 percentage point, from 3½ per cent during 1926-1950 to 4½ per cent during 1950-1967. But total expenditures on formal education in constant dollars rise from an annual average rate of increase of 3.2 per cent to 11.1 per cent, a more than threefold improvement in terms of the rate of growth between the two periods.

One of the main reasons for the significant rate of growth in total educational expenditures was the need to expand rapidly the capital facilities which proved to be increasingly inadequate to cope with the growing volume of educational services required. Rates of growth were even more pronounced in building up university facilities than expanding primary and secondary schools, as indicated below.

TOTAL CAPITAL EXPENDITURES, [23] ANNUAL
AVERAGE RATE OF INCREASE [24] — PER CENT.

	Schools	Universities	Schools and Universities
1926-1950	3.8	2.8	3.6
1950-1967	9.0	16.5	10.7

Educational capital expenditures as a proportion of total social capital formation declined from 7.7 per cent in 1926 to 6.8 per cent in 1950, but then rose rapidly in the ensuing period to 17.7 per cent in 1967. In terms of the ratio to business gross capital formation, [25] educational capital expenditures over the same period rose from 2.6 per cent to 8.3 per cent (see Summary Table 6).

The suggestion is sometimes made that the rapid expansion of educational efforts is frequently the result of the growth of the middle class and in fact contributes significantly to increasing the relative size of this class in society as a whole.

There are some preliminary indications that Canada's middle class expanded significantly after the end of World War I, partly because of the result of success in many and varied business and financial ventures initiated during the period of the preceding global conflict, and partly because of the increas-

---

23 Based on Tables 4 and 6 in Appendix A.
24 Compound rates in constant (1957) dollars.
25 As per National Accounts.

ing number of persons entering professional occupations. It would require a special study to trace the historical growth of the middle class in Canada over the last century. But if there is one period during which Canada's middle class appears to have expanded at a particularly rapid rate, it is in the 1920's.

Traditionally, the middle class has been more security-conscious than families in lower income brackets for whom adequate provision for their old age was in an earlier period of Canada's economic and social history an unattainable objective. As for families in high income brackets, the "wealthy" class, properties, investments and business ownership offered in most instances a full assurance against the hazards of life and old age.

Hence, amounts of life insurance in force could be one general indicator of the growth of the middle class in Canada if such data are adjusted to take account of price changes. Such data are available on a per capita basis expressed in constant dollars. [26] They show the following increases :

LIFE INSURANCE IN FORCE PER CAPITA
IN CONSTANT (1935-1939) DOLLARS

	Amount $	Per Cent Increase over Preceding Period
1900	139	—
1910	163	17
1920	213	30
1929	510	139
1939	585	14
1945	642	9
1950	662	31

The 139 per cent increase of life insurance in force in constant dollars per capita during the 1920's is more than eight times the increase recorded in the first decade of the twentieth century and more than four times in the second decade, and substantially greater than anything achieved in Canada in a subsequent decade. Hence the data illustrate the growing awareness on the part of Canadians for the need to provide for increased security against the hazards of life, a desirable objective shared by most people in this country but given particular impetus apparently by the growth of the middle class in Canada.

---

[26] O. J. FIRESTONE, *Canada's Economic Development 1867-1953*, London, England, Bowes & Bowes, 1958, p. 91.

But what is rather curious is, that notwithstanding the rapid growth of the middle class in Canada in the period between the two world wars, this growth was not accompanied by corresponding increases in the proportion of educational expenditures to Gross National Product. Canada had to wait for the stepped-up pace of technological and economic advances of the post-World War II years for educational efforts to be expanded materially, at a considerably more rapid rate than the expansion of total output of goods and services.

Not only did resources devoted to education expand rapidly in both absolute and relative terms in the more recent stage of Canadian economic development, but the objectives of education were also altered. The pendulum which had swung from teaching the humanities to teaching the sciences after World War I and particularly after World War II, was swinging back again. Emphasis was growing on education serving the main aim of creating a more rounded person. This was explained :

> Education in Canada is directed towards the natural aptitudes and spirations of the total population and towards the rapidly proliferating demands of business, industry, the professions and other public agencies. Of one thing we are certain: that we have to supply the country's manpower needs as quickly and as economically as possible without sacrificing that sense of individual fulfilment for our people that is so crucial to national stability; thus, while the pattern of Canadian education becomes more closely oriented to the technological age, it also must become more inclusive as far as basic education subjects are concerned, with English and the humanities, mathematics, science and the social sciences carefully integrated into all programs of study at every level, if the two aims of education are to be served. [27]

Another major change in the more recent period consisted of a re-orientation of the contents of education, particularly at the primary and secondary levels. In the English-speaking provinces great emphasis was placed on British culture and history, and in the Province of Quebec on the contributions of French explorers, missionaries, colonizers, artists and literary figures. Observed a critic of the Canadian educational system :

---

[27] *Basic Vocational Education,* Paper prepared by the Department of Education of the Province of Ontario, submitted by the Government of Canada to the Fourth Commonwealth Education Conference, London, England, November 1967, CEC(67)C/2, p. 2.

> It is only within the last few years that Canadians have been seriously challenging the character of their public school systems: the curricula are being revised with an emphasis upon national culture; biographical dictionaries of "great ancestors" are being compiled and Canadians generally are experiencing a quickening of national consciousness. [28]

Another major contribution in the quickening pace of Canadianization of the education system was the work done by two Commissions of Enquiry, leading to the tabling of the Parent Report in the Legislature of the Province of Quebec and the Hall-Dennis Report in the Legislature of the Province of Ontario. [29]

The Royal Commission on Bilingualism and Biculturalism stressed the vital importance of much greater acceptance of English and French as the two official languages in Canada, [30] with a number of the recommendations of this Royal Commission being endorsed by the Federal Government and some of the provincial governments.

DIFFERENTIALS IN RATES OF GROWTH

The analysis presented above of relating educational expenditures to Gross National Product can be supplemented by an examination of rate of growth of both flows over four sub-periods and for Canada's first century as a whole. Data are available of revenues received by publicly supported elementary and secondary schools, and these can be compared with increases in Gross National Product, with both sets of data shown in constant dollar terms. In so doing, the limitations of the data should be borne in mind yielding only a first approximation of the order of changes. [31]

---

[28] Howard ADAMS, *The Education of Canadians, 1800-1867, The Roots of Separatism*, Montreal, Harvest House, 1968, p. 117.

[29] *Report of the Royal Commission of Inquiry on Education in the Province of Quebec*, Quebec, Queen's Printer, 1963-1966; *Report of the Provincial Committee on Aims and Objectives of Education in the Schools of Ontario*, Toronto, Queen's Printer, 1968.

[30] Royal Commission on Bilingualism and Biculturalism, *Report*, Ottawa, Queen's Printer, 1967, Volume I.

[31] See Appendix B.

SUMMARY TABLE 6. — CAPITAL EXPENDITURES ON SCHOOLS AND UNIVERSITIES COMPARED WITH CAPITAL FORMATION, SOCIAL, BUSINESS AND TOTAL, AND GROSS NATIONAL PRODUCT, CANADA, 1926, 1950 AND 1967.

ITEM	1926	1950	1967
Capital Expenditures — $ Mill.			
Schools	20	88	694
Universities	4	14	337
Sub-Total	24	102	1,031
Other Social Capital Formation	312	1,396	4,804
Total Social Capital Formation	336	1,498	5,835
Total Business Capital Formation	581	2,317	9,339
Total Business Gross Capital Formation [1]	702	3,348	12,365
Total Private and Public Capital Formation	917	3,815	15,174
Capital Expenditures on Schools and Universities as Per Cent of			
Total Social Capital Formation	7.7	6.8	17.7
Total Business Capital Formation	4.1	4.4	11.0
Total Business Gross Capital Formation [1]	2.6	4.4	8.3
Total Private and Public Capital Formation	3.4	3.1	6.8
Gross National Product	0.5	0.6	1.7

Source: Based on Tables 1 and 4 in Appendix A.

[1] As per National Accounts.

ANNUAL AVERAGE RATE OF INCREASE [32] — PER CENT.

	Gross National Product [33]	School Revenues [34]
1867-1896	2.3	4.8
1896-1914	3.7	6.3
1914-1950	3.0	3.7
1950-1967	4.5	9.5
1867-1967	3.5	3.1

The data suggest that during the stage of preconditions for take-off education expenditures rose more rapidly than total economic activity, 4.8 per cent compared with 2.3 per cent. In the following stage, the take-off, educational expenditures

[32] Compound rates in constant (1957) dollars.
[33] Based on Table 1 in Appendix A.
[34] Covers publicly supported elementary and secondary schools, based on Table 3 in Appendix A.

continued to be ahead at a considerably more rapid rate than the economy as a whole, 6.3 per cent, as compared with 3.7 per cent.

In the period of the drive to maturity, the economy expanded fairly rapidly at an annual growth rate of 3 per cent with education moderately ahead, 3.7 per cent. In the following stage of technological maturity and high mass-consumption the situation changed dramatically. While the economy commenced expansion along a rapid growth rate, educational expenditures rose considerably more quickly, 4.5 per cent, compared with 9.5 per cent. [35]

Over the century as a whole encompassing four of Rostow's stages, the economy and education grew at about the same annual rate, with education only fractionally behind, 3.5 per cent compared with 3.0 per cent. But if truly comparable data on *total* expenditures on formal education were available, they would probably show a considerably greater increase of educational efforts in Canada than is indicated in terms of growth of total economic activity. The main reason appears to be structural changes in educational efforts, with much greater importance being attached to higher learning and technical and other post-secondary education in the post-World War II period as compared with earlier stages in Canadian economic history.

Such structural changes are not reflected in data dealing with the expansion of elementary and secondary schools, with expenditures in this sector rising at a considerably slower rate than expenditures in the sector covering "other" educational pursuits. The tentative data presented on the rising proportion of

---

[35] The unevenness of progress in education in Canada and its economic implications have been stressed by the Economic Council of Canada: in the latter part of the nineteenth century and into the early part of the twentieth century "spectacular advances were made in education [. . .] literacy and elementary education for all citizens were strongly promoted [. . .]. But educational advances appear to have tapered off by 1920; the earlier momentum at the primary school was not maintained and there were only limited advances at the secondary school level. Renewed dynamism has clearly characterized major segments of Canadian education in the post-war years." The Council concluded that over the century the Canadian economy benefited greatly "from the improved quality of its labour force as reflected in enhanced educational attainments. But this improvement has been uneven, and has fallen well short of what could have been achieved" (see ECONOMIC COUNCIL OF CANADA, *Towards Sustained and Balanced Economic Growth,* Second Annual Review, Ottawa, Queen's Printer, 1965, p. 75).

total educational expenditures to Gross National Product support this assertion.

The following general conclusions may be advanced on the basis of evidence available in Canada relating education to economic development over the last century.

During the first half of the century covering the period of the pre-conditions of take-off and the take-off stage, Canada devoted between 1 and 2 per cent of her Gross National Product to education. In the next approximately 3½ decades, the drive to maturity stage, the proportion of the nation's resources devoted to education continued to rise slowly, to a little over 2½ per cent by 1950. Only when Canada reached technological maturity and a period of high mass consumption was she able to respond in a substantial way to the need of devoting increasing resources to education (including higher learning, technical training and research), with the ratio rising to about 7¼ per cent by 1967.

REASONS FOR DIFFERENTIALS

Does this mean that Canada could not afford to devote during the first eight decades of her economic development as a nation more than between 1 per cent and about 2½ per cent of her Gross National Product to education ?

Or does it mean that education in the political and social environment of that period was accorded a lower priority than some other requirements which were considered relatively more urgent, as for example the building up of a social and production infra-structure including transportation and communication services across the continent in the latter part of the nineteenth century, and large urban and public service facilities, together with industrial, commercial and financial institutions, in the first half of the twentieth century ?

Or was it a question of not recognizing earlier in Canada's history the importance of the economic consequences of education which may bring results in many instances only after a considerable time interval ? [36]

---

[36] Such studies, undertaken in the United States, became known in Canada. An example would be the study undertaken by H. Thomas James which reported that "a high correlation was found to exist between

Or was it a question of waiting until the pressures of demand for better trained men and women to meet the needs of technological and scientific progress became so urgent that the nation had no alternative but to embark on a very large and broadly based educational expansion programme ?

Or was it that emulation of American progress made in education and the results it was bringing in terms of greater productivity increases and leading to a "brain-drain" of professionally and technically trained personnel added new urgency to Canada making up for lost time in improving educational opportunities at home as well as economic rewards for the educated ? [37]

Or was it a widening in international orientation of the Canadian economy, accompanied by the growing recognition that expanding trade and other economic relations with the rest of the world involved increasing competition among the nations and that in order to keep in the forefront of advancing countries, Canada had to have an adequate supply of well-trained managers, scientists, teachers, technicians and other skilled personnel ?

Probably all these factors had something to do with the slow secular growth rates of educational expenditures as compared with rates of expansion of Gross National Product in real terms for the first eighty years of Canada's economic history as a nation, even though the differentials in rates of growth were quite substantial for particular subperiods. Similarly, these factors are likely to have contributed to the significant speed-up in expanding educational facilities and the stock of educational capital by devoting a considerably greater proportion of the nation's resources to education in the more recent period.

INDUSTRIALIZATION AND EDUCATION

Tentatively then, the suggestion can be put forward on the basis of Canadian experience, that until a nation has become fully industrialized, it may not be able to accord or it may not

expenditures for education by states in one period and personal income payments a quarter of a century later" (see *School Revenue Systems in Five States*, Stanford, Stanford University, School of Education, 1961). J. E. Cheal referred to the James study in assessing Canadian developments (see *Investment in Canadian Youth, op. cit.*, pp. 47-49).
    [37]   See chapter 20.

wish to accord the high priority required to devote a large enough proportion of its limited resources to human improvements which may bring results in economic terms several decades hence. The pay-off for human investment involves a much longer period than the pay-off for physical investment whether business or social capital, and this may be a factor in guiding priority allotments of the nation's resources.

The latter inference may be drawn from the Canadian experience over the first eight decades of her economic development as a nation. But public thinking and business and government orientation have been changing in the last two decades. The emphasis has shifted to longer term considerations and planning, and this change in orientation appears to have favoured growing emphasis on investment in human capital.

TAKE-OFF IN EDUCATION

This is not to suggest that the Canadian experience is necessarily a guide to developments in other countries, for there are many cultural, traditional, political and other non-economic factors [38] that have greatly influenced rates of growth of educational efforts and of national output in Canada.

Each country's environmental and institutional factors and sources of growth will vary. Hence, without claiming that the Canadian experience will be applicable to other developing nations, all that can be said is : that rates of general economic growth and increases in productivity appear to set certain limitations on the ability of a country to speed up the process of improving human resources through education. While progress can be telescoped as a result of a high priority attached to education [39] and with help from abroad, the fact remains that

---

[38] That would include demographic factors which have also certain economic implications.

[39] Many economists make the point that "the provision of educational opportunities [...] should have a top priority in a newly developing country" (see, for example, W. J. WAINES, "The Role of Education in the Development of Underdeveloped Countries", in *The Canadian Journal of Economics and Political Science,* Vol. XXIX, No. 4, November 1963, p. 439). But the problem is not so much whether to attach a top priority to creating additional educational facilities but one of deciding, once such a priority has been established, where the resources would come from to the extent and of the type required to expand the education industry at what is considered an "adequate" rate and how to absorb into the economic system the increasing flow of educated and better trained people.

the pay-off period of newly acquired learning and training is lengthy and it takes time to transform an economy from a traditional society to a highly industrialized nation that can absorb the products of education and reward them at satisfactory rates of pay.

The Canadian experience suggests that educational progress and economic growth go hand-in-hand during the first four stages of economic development, and that the educational take-off comes in the stage of technological maturity and high mass-consumption, something like 50 years after the industrial take-off.

The challenge which less developed countries face during the second half of the twentieth century is to decide whether and how they can reduce a fifty-year gap between what they want to do and what they can do in the field of education and economic progress. In their labours to reconcile aspirations and reality, the less developed countries deserve the full understanding and support of the well-to-do nations.

CHAPTER 18

Effect on Labour Force and Earnings

EDUCATIONAL ATTAINMENTS

What have been the results of devoting an increasing proportion of the economic resources of the nation to education over the last one hundred years ?

This question is dealt with selectively, as far as the impact of expanding the stock of educational capital on the labour force is concerned, in the following terms :

1. Greater number of young and not-so-young people going to school. [1]

2. Greater attendance as a result of increasing school enrolment of the school-age population.

3. Greater attendance in terms of increases in the number of years of formal education.

4. Greater attendance in terms of number of days per school year.

5. Greater shift to higher learning and technical training.

6. Greater quality of teaching including changes in student-teacher ratios.

GREATER SCHOOL ENROLMENT IN AGGREGATE

Over the last century the number of pupils enrolled in publicly controlled elementary and secondary schools rose from 726,000 to 5.1 million, and the number of pupils enrolled per thousand population from 210 to 250 (see Summary Table 7). The annual average rate of increase [2] of the total number of pupils enrolled for the period 1867-1967 was 2 per cent.

The rates of growth were comparatively low in stage 2, 1867-1896, pre-conditions for take-off, 1.3 per cent, and stage 4,

---

[1] The latter group includes part-time and adult education, "mature" students, learning by immigrants, etc.

[2] Compound rates.

1914-1950, drive to maturity, 1.2 per cent. They were somewhat higher in the period of mass-immigration, following the turn of the century which coincides with stage 3, 1896-1914, take-off, 2.2 per cent, and they reached the highest level in stage 5, the age of high mass-consumption, 1950-1967 (and continuing), 4.6 per cent (see Summary Table 8).

SUMMARY TABLE 7. — ENROLMENT, ATTENDANCE, AND TEACH-ERS, PUBLICLY CONTROLLED ELEMENTARY AND SECONDARY SCHOOLS, CANADA, SELECTED YEARS, 1867-1967.

ITEM	1867	1896	1914	1950[1]	1967
Pupils Enrolled					
Total — Thous.	726.0	1,056.8	1,555.6	2,377.5	5,095.3
Per 1,000 Population	209.6	208.3	197.4	173.4	249.7
Per Teacher	60.0	40.3	33.6	27.0	23.7
Average Daily Attendance					
Total — Thous.	387.3	633.4	1,052.0	2,065.6	4,743.0
Per Pupil	0.53	0.60	0.68	0.87	0.93
Teachers					
Total — Thous.	12.1	26.2	88.2	88.2	215.4
Per 1,000 Persons Employed	1.14	1.54	1.75	1.75	2.88

Source: Based on Table 2 in Appendix A.

[1] Commencing 1950 includes Newfoundland.

The data suggest a quickening of the pace of school attendance as the nation moved from the period of precondition for take-off to the stage of the actual take-off, as the need for more personnel achieved much greater urgency, and in fact became a prerequisite for technological advances and a broadening of the economic base of the country.

In the following stage the efforts of bringing more young people to school and providing them with greater educational opportunities slackened off. This was in part associated with the slower rate of population growth and changes in the age distribution pattern, and in part because of lesser priority attached to devoting resources to the build-up of educational capital.

SUMMARY TABLE 8. — ENROLMENT, ATTENDANCE AND TEACHERS, PUBLICLY CONTROLLED ELEMENTARY AND SECONDARY SCHOOLS, TOTALS FOR FIVE PERIODS AND ANNUAL RATES,[1] CANADA, 1867-1967.

ITEM	1867-1896		1896-1914		1914-1950		1950-1967		1867-1967	
	TOTAL	ANNUAL RATE	TOTAL	ANNUAL RATE	TOTAL	ANNUAL RATE	TOTAL	ANNUAL RATE	TOTAL	ANNUAL RATE
Pupils Enrolled										
Total	45.6	1.3	47.6	2.2	52.8	1.2	114.3	4.6	601.8	2.0
Per 1,000 Population	—0.6	—0.3	—5.2	—0.3	—12.2	—0.4	44.5	2.2	19.0	0.2
Per Teacher	—32.8	—1.4	—16.6	—1.0	—19.6	—0.6	—15.1	—0.8	—60.5	—0.5
Average Daily Attendance										
Total	63.5	1.7	66.1	2.8	96.3	1.9	129.6	5.0	1,124.6	2.4
Per Pupil	13.2	0.4	13.3	0.7	27.9	0.7	6.9	0.4	75.5	0.6
Teachers										
Total	116.5	2.7	76.7	3.2	90.5	1.8	152.8	5.6	1,680.1	2.9
Per 1,000 Employed	35.1	1.0	3.9	0.2	9.4	0.2	70.4	3.2	152.6	0.9

Source: Based on Table 2 in Appendix A.

[1] Compound rates.

During this period, the drive to maturity, the emphasis was on industrial development and the expansion of international trade, with the provision of social capital being considered of secondary importance. This, among other things, affected the development of educational capital and the provision of educational services. As a result the pace of educational progress slackened even though, as the estimates presented earlier suggest, the proportion of Gross National Product devoted to education rose moderately, from about 2 per cent in 1914 to approximatively 2½ per cent in 1950.

GREATER SCHOOL ENROLMENT AND SCHOOL AGE POPULATION

The greater number of young people attending schools in Canada was not just due to demographic factors, in the sense of changing age distribution. To a more important extent it was the result of increasing school attendance within each age group of the potential school population.

The rate of increase in school attendance per age group varied considerably, from 88.9 per cent of school population age 10-14 in 1921 to 97.2 per cent in 1961, as compared with increases over the same period from 3.1 per cent to 11.6 per cent age 20-24 (see Summary Table 9).

Between 1921 and 1961, school enrolment in the age groups 5-9 and 10-14 rose at an annual rate of about 2 per cent, as compared with rates of increases for the 15-19 age group of 4 per cent and the 20-24 age group of 4.6 per cent. The trend for more education for every age group is apparent, with the main impetus coming from the older age groups that were desirous to obtain greater and more intensive education.

School enrolment in Canada compares favourably with that of most countries in the world, largely the result of increased school attendance of young people in the age groups in which school attendance is not obligatory, and this covers the later years of secondary schools and beyond. A recent research study throws light on the subject :

"Due to past demographic developments, Canada has one of the youngest populations of any major industrialized country, with about half the population under 25 years of age. Given the high, and still rising, high school and university enrolment ratios, this means that Canada now also has one of the highest proportions of the young population attending school. The five and a half million Canadians who attended various educational institutions last year (1966) represented almost three-quarters of the population in the 5-24 age group. This proportion is about 10 to 20 percentage points higher than comparable proportions in all other major Western countries except the United States. The favourable position which Canada holds in such a comparison is mainly due to relatively high and rising enrolment rates at the secondary and post-secondary levels-rates which appear to be rising more rapidly in this country than elsewhere, and which, over the next 10 years, are estimated to approach those reached in the United States in the mid-1960's." [3]

GREATER NUMBER OF SCHOOL YEARS

The data shown below of the mean years of schooling of the male labour force age 25-64 [4] indicate that Canadians have increased educational capital invested in their work force by about two fifths over the last half century in terms of years of education.

MEAN YEARS OF SCHOOLING

1911	6.60
1921	7.06
1931	7.43
1941	8.02
1951	8.62
1961	9.15

---

[3] Wolfgang M. ILLING and Zoltan E. ZSIGMOND, *Enrollment in Schools and Universities, 1951-52 to 1975-76*, Staff Study No. 20, prepared for the Economic Council of Canada, Ottawa, Queen's Printer, 1967, pp. 3 and 4. See also *L'Enseignement dans les pays du Marché Commun, Étude comparative sur l'organisation et l'état de développement de l'enseignement dans les pays du Marché Commun, aux Etats-Unis, en Grande-Bretagne et en U.R.S.S.*, Paris, Institut pédagogique national, 1965.
[4] Gordon W. BERTRAM, *The Contribution of Education to Economic Growth*, study prepared for the Economic Council of Canada, Ottawa, Queen's Printer, 1966, p. 14.

SUMMARY TABLE 9. — POPULATION AND SCHOOL ENROLMENT, MALES, AGED 5-24, CANADA,[1] 1921-1961.

ITEM	1921	1931	1941	1951	1961	PER CENT INCREASE 1921-1961	
	Thous.	Thous.	Thous.	Thous.	Thous.	Total	Annual Average [2]
Population — Ages							
5-9	529	572	528	689	1,029	94.5	1.6
10-14	461	542	556	556	916	98.7	1.7
15-19	404	525	565	516	706	74.8	1.4
20-24	352	464	517	522	570	61.9	1.2
Total	1,746	2,103	2,166	2,283	3,221	84.5	1.5
Enrolment — Ages							
5-9	345	391	352	449	774	124.3	2.1
10-14	409	507	524	518	890	117.6	2.0
15-19	92	170	191	211	434	371.7	4.0
20-24	11	17	23	34	66	500.0	4.6
Total	857	1,085	1,090	1,212	2,164	152.5	2.3
Enrolment as Percent of Population							
5-9	65.2	68.4	66.7	65.2	75.2	—	—
10-15	88.7	93.5	94.2	93.2	97.2	—	—
15-19	22.8	32.4	33.8	40.9	61.5	—	—
20-24	3.1	3.7	4.4	6.5	11.6	—	—
Total	49.1	51.6	50.3	53.1	67.2	—	—

Source: DOMINION BUREAU OF STATISTICS, *Census of Canada, 1961*, Ottawa.

[1] Excludes Newfoundland which joined Canada in 1949.
[2] Compound rates.

The trend of extending schooling is continuing. This is illustrated by the data shown below of the greater number of mean years of school attendance of younger age groups in the more recent period. [5]

MEAN YEARS OF SCHOOLING

25-34	9.68
35-44	9.22
45-54	8.57
55-64	7.57
25-64	9.15

The educational attainments of the younger age groups are notably ahead of the older age groups, about 2.1 years between the 25-34 year-olds and the 55-64 year-olds. "This difference can be viewed as approximating the change in the average level of education over an average of 30 years, and demonstrates that the average level per man rose over this period by about 28 per cent." [6]

Another way of illustrating the trends towards more education in Canada is to consider the proportion of those in the male labour force who have completed university education, by age groups. [7]

PER CENT OF TOTAL

25-34	6.0
35-44	6.3
45-54	5.0
55-64	4.2
25-64	5.6

The data indicate a difference of 1.8 percentage points between the 25-34 age group and the 55-64 group. This differential implies that there exists demand about 43 per cent greater to obtain a full university education today, as compared with the situation thirty years ago. [8]

[5] Ibid., p. 17.
[6] Ibid.
[7] Ibid., p. 20.
[8] 1.8 per cent as a proportion of 4.2 per cent.

GREATER NUMBER OF SCHOOL DAYS

Average daily school attendance amounted to 53 per cent in 1867. It rose to 93 per cent by 1967 (see Summary Table 7).

Over the century, progress varied, with rates of increases rising only slowly in stages 2 and 4, 1.7 per cent and 1.9 per cent respectively, increasing more rapidly in stage 3, 2.8 per cent and very rapidly in stage 5, about 5 per cent. The average annual rate of improvement over the century was 2.4 per cent (see Summary Table 7). Thus the data on school attendance support the observation made earlier that educational progress in Canada during the last one hundred years was uneven, with a period of slow progress followed by one of more rapid progress, with the situation again changing, with a reduction and then a speed-up in the rate in the subsequent two stages of economic development.

Available evidence suggests that the average school year in Canada during most of the twentieth century consisted of 200 school days. [9] On that basis, average daily school attendance consisted of 136 days in 1914, 174 days in 1950, and 186 days in 1967. [10]

At the time of Confederation average school attendance per pupil was less than 100 days. [11] The data imply that the average young person in Canada spent in 1967 about twice as many days in school than did his great-grandfather when he was a child a hundred years ago. Presumably, increasing school attendance has been a factor in improving the output of the school system, thus adding to educational capital.

Gordon W. Bertram estimates that between 1911 and 1961, the average number of days of school attendance per year of school completed by the male labour force increased by about 50 per cent. He observes :

> Particularly important in explaining this considerable rise in the actual time spent in school was the continuing shift in the population from rural to urban areas. This

---

[9] *Ibid.*, pp. 38 and 111-114.
[10] Gordon W. Bertram using somewhat different source material arrives at estimates of a similar order: 130 days in 1911 and 184 days in 1961 (*ibid.*, p. 3).
[11] Gordon W. Bertram's estimate of 90 days for 1867 may be a little on the low side (*ibid.*, p. 39).

movement, clearly discernible in Canada from the 1870's onward, represented the process of urbanization as commercial and industrial localization and specialization developed in the economy. In a predominantly rural society, the real cost of sending children continuously to school for the entire term consisted of the work which they could otherwise do on the farm. The shift to urban communities, however, did not end the competing opportunity of employment, for in the cities, industrial employment was still a possible alternative to attending high school in the early part of this century. Provincial legislation restricting the employment of children and establishing compulsory school attendance laws was a significant source of increases in the average days of school attended. [12]

GREATER EMPHASIS ON HIGHER LEARNING

Reference has already been made to the fact that as the number of school years increased, the emphasis shifted from primary and secondary to post-secondary school education. This more advanced type of education took various forms, including attendance at university and colleges, teacher and nursing training, attendance at technical and vocational schools, and the taking of courses at business colleges.

The data in Summary Table 10 show that between 1911 and 1961, the total number of the male labour force age 25-64 increased at an annual average rate of 1.8 per cent. The rate of increase of those that had completed 8 years of elementary schooling or less, was less, 0.8 per cent, while the rate of increase of those with secondary schooling, 1-4 years, was greater, 3 per cent. Those with some university training [13] show the greatest rate of increase, 5.7 per cent, followed by those who completed their university education, 3.5 per cent.

Demographic factors have so far delayed the full impact to be felt by Canadian institutions of higher learning of the large numbers seeking university entrance. As Summary Table 4 shows, school enrolment in public and secondary schools more than doubled between 1950 and 1967, as compared with an increase of approximately one-half for university enrolment. But with the much larger number of young persons reaching

---

[12] *Ibid.*
[13] These include young persons completing Grade 13 in high schools in some provinces.

SUMMARY TABLE 10. — MALE LABOUR FORCE, 25-64 YEARS, [1] BY
YEARS OF SCHOOLING, CANADA, 1911-1961.

YEAR	ELEMEN-SCHOOL 8 YEARS OR LESS	HIGH SCHOOL 1-4 YEARS	SOME UNIVER-SITY [2]	COM-PLETE UNIVER-SITY	TOTAL	PER CENT OF TOTAL	
						Some Univer-sity [2]	Com-plete Univer-sity
	Thous.	Thous.	Thous.	Thous.	Thous.		
1911	1,130	322	23	36	1,511	1.5	2.4
1921	1,319	451	39	61	1,869	2.1	3.3
1931	1,401	542	66	77	2,085	3.2	3.7
1941	1,522	758	132	108	2,520	5.2	4.3
1951	1,594	1,051	228	157	3,029	7.5	5.2
1961	1,708	1,425	376	208	3,717	10.1	5.6
Percent Increase 1911-1961 Total	51.2	342.5	1,534	477.8	146.0	—	—
Annual Aver-age [3]	0.8	3.0	5.7	3.5	1.8	—	—

Source: Gordon W. Bertram, *The Contribution of Education to Economic
Growth*, Economic Council of Canada, Ottawa, Queen's Printer, 1966,
pp. 73-75.

[1] Estimations by cohort method.
[2] Includes Grade 13.
[3] Compound rates.

university age and with the much greater facilities becoming
available including many new universities, junior colleges, and
technical and vocational institutions established in Canada
during the last decade, the shift towards greater emphasis on
increasing further the stock of educational capital in Canada's
labour force is well underway.

The point deserves emphasis that this is a more recent
trend, in part encouraged by the incentives for greater economic
rewards offered to those obtaining higher education and training,
and in part facilitated by the expanding capacity of society to
provide young people with growing opportunities to obtain a

more extensive education, including the ability of the economy to carry these young people for a longer period before they reach the productive stage of full entry into the labour force.

GREATER QUALITY OF TEACHING

The quality of teaching, as far as its economic impact is concerned, is not easily measured. Usually it is associated with better-trained teachers who are presumably better paid, greater teaching facilities and aids, and improved curricula and student participation.

One limited way of looking at possible improvements in the quality of teaching over the longer term is to consider the ratio of pupils to teachers on the assumption that the smaller classes make it possible for teachers to do a better job by giving pupils more individual attention. This may not be the case in a number of instances because of the many other variables affecting teaching quality. But to the extent that smaller classes per teacher do affect quality, the following trends representing one hundred years of Canadian experience may be noted.

The number of teachers in publicly supported primary and secondary schools in Canada rose from about 12,000 in 1867, to 215,400 in 1967. The average class dropped in size from 60 in 1867 to 40 in 1896, to 34 in 1914, to 27 in 1950, and to about 24 in 1967 (see Summary Table 7).

The improvements were more notable in stages 2 and 3 with an annual average rate of decrease in the number of pupils per teacher of 1.4 per cent and 1 per cent respectively. The improvement slowed down in stages 4 and 5 to about 0.5 per cent and 0.8 per cent respectively on an annual average basis.

This pattern of change differs from that suggested by data of total number of pupils enrolled and increases in the rate of average daily attendance which indicated somewhat greater progress being made in stages 3 and 5 as compared with stage 2.

One possible explanation would be the process of urbanization in the eastern parts of Canada contrasted with the thinly spread out settlements in western Canada in the latter part of the nineteenth century and in the early part of the twentieth century requiring an increasing number of teachers to serve a large number of small communities in what became known as the one-room log school.

By relating data of the number of teachers to the total number of persons employed, a measure becomes available of the resources devoted by the nation to education. As Summary Table 7 shows, teachers comprised 1.14 per cent of the total number of persons working, rising to 1.54 per cent in 1896, to 1.60 per cent in 1914, to 1.75 per cent in 1950 and to 2.88 per cent in 1967. The dramatic improvement in the ratio in the stage of high mass-consumption, 1950-1967 is quite apparent.

The improvement of 1.13 percentage points in the latter period comprising 17 years exceeds by a considerable margin the rate of improvement in the preceding stage consisting of 0.15 percentage points over 34 years. During these two periods the number of pupils per teacher in publicly controlled primary and secondary schools, with an annual average rate of 0.6 per cent and 0.8 per cent respectively was lower than in the preceding two stages (see Summary Tables 7 and 8).

It appears that it was not just the pressure to reduce size of classes that contributed to increasing the number of teachers — though such demands were a factor — but rather it was the necessity of increasing the supply of teachers in line with the growing numbers of young people seeking greater educational opportunities, requiring specialized attention and appropriately qualified teachers, and also in line with changing location factors, particularly the result of the rapid rate of urbanization.

The data presented above are indicative of the notable progress made in upgrading the educational stock of the Canadian people, and particularly its labour force. But this progress has been uneven, at times taking place only after intervals of a slow-down, and accompanied by considerable lags between the time new educational developments took place and the time their economic impact became felt. The Economic Council of Canada explained the reasons for the uneven rates of progress of building up educational capital in Canada in these terms :

Such factors include the

...changing age distribution patterns in the total population resulting in temporary bulges or dips in the numbers of new entrants to the labour force; stepped-up or lagging efforts to promote higher educational attainments; changes in legal school-leaving ages, legislation limiting the employment of children and other such institutional factors; marked changes in the availability of new job opportunities; the movement of population from rural to urban areas (children of urban families generally spend more years in school than children of farm families); and a host of additional influences. [14]

Concluded the Council :

> The dominating fact about changes in the education stock is that an extremely powerful combination of factors is probably required to bring about any substantial short-term or medium term change in this stock. At the same time, basic factors may have prolonged and cumulative effects stretching over many decades. For example, ... the higher school retention rates and the increased enrolment ratios in the 1950's did not have much effect in that decade, but will tend to have longer term effects on the rising stock of education in the 1960's and 1970's and beyond. [15]

Having established that significant progress has been made in raising the stock of educational capital in Canada in quantitative and qualitative terms and in instilling a new orientation that stems from increasing knowledge into the labour force, the question arises : What are some of the economic consequences of this growing investment in Canada's human resources. Three particular aspects are examined in the sections that follow : the effect on individual income, the return on educational investment, and the social impact in terms of economic growth and rising levels of national income.

EFFECTS ON PAST EARNINGS

Education is one of the main factors affecting the level of annual earnings. [16] There are many other factors as well and they may be grouped into five categories :

1. Economic factors — short run. These include the state of the economy, levels of employment, full-time and part-time, and unemployment, wage and salary rates, illness and other reasons for non-working besides unemployment, number of

---

[14] *Towards Sustained and Balanced Economic Growth, op. cit.,* pp. 77 and 78.
[15] *Ibid.,* p. 78.
[16] Some economists hold that other factors are just as important in affecting income levels as education: "Learning, both on and off the job, and other activities appear to have exactly the same effects on observed earnings as do education, training and other traditional investments in human capital" (Gary S. BECKER, in "Investment in Human Capital: A Theoretical Analysis", in *The Journal of Political Economy,* Vol. LXX, No. 5, Part 2, Supplement, October 1962, p. 49).

hours worked per week, the degree of overtime pay or under-employment, seasonal factors, etc.

2. Economic factors — long run. These include sex of persons employed, their age, occupation, education, training, experience and place of residence (higher wages being paid in cities and lower wages in rural areas), changes in structure of industry, differentials in productivity, etc.

3. Human factors. These include native ability, intelli-gence, health, the will to work, emulation, ability to grasp opportunities, etc.

4. Institutional and social factors. These include the effectiveness of unions in management-labour negotiations, minimum wage laws, employment practices based on different attitudes towards sex and age, community, cultural and family influences, etc.

5. Statistical factors. These include the difficulties of measuring net income for self-employed personnel, separating income earned from work from other sources of income, particu-larly distinguishing returns for labour from returns for capital, say in the case of a working proprietor, etc.

How important are differentials in educational attainment in influencing earnings ? The data in Summary Table 11 indicate :

First, the higher the educational attainment, the higher the income. The average incomes of males with university degrees in Canada in 1961 was $8,866 or 165 per cent higher than the average income of a person having completed ele-mentary school (eight years) and 84 per cent higher than that of a person having completed an additional four to five years of secondary schooling.

Second, irrespective of educational levels reached, expe-rience and training add to income over time until the age level of 45-54 years is reached. After that, during the last decade of active life [17] the average level of income declines, in part as a result of a drop in labour productivity in some occupations and

---

[17] The age 65 is a customary retirement age in Canada, though a certain proportion of persons in the over-65 years age category continue to work.

greater difficulties of older workers finding and retaining employment, and in part as a result of the hazards of living, e.g., the incidence of ill-health, etc. The relative decline is greatest for the least educated and smallest for the highest educated.

Third, annual earnings of females are about one-half those of males, with the greater incidence of part-time employment a major factor, besides the practice of unequal pay for equal work in many occupations. The differentials in earnings depending on education are quite similar for both females and males, 165 per cent between those completing elementary school and those with a university degree, and 68 per cent between those completing secondary school and those with a university degree. But in one respect female income earners do not follow the pattern of males. In two of the three categories shown in Summary Table 11, incomes of females rise in the age category 55-64, rather than fall as is the case for males, and this applies to females who have completed secondary schooling or obtained a university degree.

The question arises, what proportion of the higher incomes Canadians enjoy has been due to greater educational attainments ? A study prepared by Gordon W. Bertram throws some light on this question, using techniques similar to those developed by Edward F. Denison. [18]

Bertram's estimates provide an indication of what the real income of male income earners would have been in 1961 if the quality of those working had not changed since 1911, as far as their educational attainments are concerned. The meaningfulness of the estimates depends to an important extent on the validity of the assumptions underlying them. The Economic Council of Canada which used these estimates in its Second Annual Review, suggested that they should be regarded as "minimum" estimates and it reasoned :

> It [the estimate] takes no account, for example, of increased education and training outside the elementary and secondary schools and universities, or of the increased quality of education over time. Nor does it, of course, reflect the indirect impact of higher education on such factors as the development of improved research and technology, better

---

[18] Edward F. DENISON, *The Sources of Economic Growth in the United States and the Alternatives Before Us*, Supplementary Paper No. 13, New York, Committee for Economic Development, January 1962.

SUMMARY TABLE 11. — AVERAGE EARNINGS OF NON-FARM
LABOUR FORCE, BY LEVEL OF SCHOOL, AGE AND SEX,
CANADA, 1961.

SCHOOLING AND AGE	MALE $	FEMALE $	FEMALE AS PER CENT OF MALE
Elementary School			
Under 25	1,928	1,227	0.64
25-34	3,311	1,521	0.46
35-44	3,653	1,627	0.45
45-64	3,648	1,664	0.46
55-64	3,480	1,617	0.46
Total	3,345	1,537	0.46
Secondary School, 4-5 years			
Under 25	2,497	2,000	0.80
25-34	4,760	2,437	0.51
35-44	5,779	2,577	0.45
45-64	6,130	2,548	0.42
55-64	5,944	2,920	0.49
Total	4,813	2,438	0.51
University Degree			
Under 25	3,406	2,699	0.79
25-34	6,909	3,873	0.56
35-44	9,966	4,256	0.43
45-64	10,821	4,866	0.45
55-64	10,609	5,055	0.48
Total	8,866	4,067	0.46
Percent Difference Elementary School and University Degree — Total	165.1	146.6	—

Source: J. R. PODOLUK, *Data from Census of Canada, 1961; Monograph Incomes of Individuals,* summarized in *Earnings and Education,* Ottawa, Dominion Bureau of Statistics, 1965.

organization for production, and the general advance of knowledge. [19]

Bearing these qualifications in mind, the Bertram estimates are as follows: [20]

---

[19] *Towards Sustained and Balanced Economic Growth, op. cit.,* p. 92.
[20] *The Contribution of Education to Economic Growth, op. cit.,* p. 51.

RISE IN MEAN INCOME PER MAN DUE TO
INCREASES IN YEARS OF SCHOOLING, 1911-61

1911	100.0
1921	102.2
1931	103.8
1941	106.5
1951	109.5
1961	112.0

According to these estimates, the average income per man in the male labour force, 25-64 years of age, rose by about 12 per cent "due to improved education over the last fifty years". [21] The index of improvement in real earnings due to education for the period 1911-1951 (which approximates Rostow's stage of the drive to maturity, 1914-1950) shows an increase of 9.5 percentage points while the rise in the decade 1951-1961 which forms part of Rostow's stage of high mass consumption indicates a growth of 2.5 percentage points. In other words, the improvement in real earnings due to education during the last decade has not been very different from the average for the previous four decades.

How can this finding be reconciled with the observation made earlier that during the period of industrial maturity, Canada stepped up considerably the ratio of resources devoted to education, from 2.6 per cent of the Gross National Product in 1950, to 5 per cent in 1961 (and to an even greater extent in the period following 1961) ?

One possible explanation has been mentioned earlier : It may take a considerable period of time until the results of investment in human resources are reflected in higher productivity and hence in higher national income. The implication is that the large amounts that Canadians have been spending on education in the last decade or two may not show up in tangible form to any significant extent for another decade or two.

EFFECTS ON ANTICIPATED EARNINGS

So far, the discussion has been concerned with the effects of education on past earnings. What about the effects of education on future earnings ?

---

[21] *Ibid.*, p. 50.

A study prepared by Miss J. R. Podoluk of the Dominion Bureau of Statistics throws some light on this question by presenting estimates of future life-time earnings of male members of the non-farm labour force by degree of schooling. The results for the age groups 25-64 by occupations, adjusted for mortality but not for labour force participation rates, are shown in Summary Table 12 and for the age group 15-64, by major groupings of education attainments, total for career as a whole and discounted to the present at a rate of 5 per cent are shown in Summary Table 13. [22]

The estimates of life-time earnings are based on the 1961 Census with certain modifications. The distinction between the two sets of estimates should be noted for one covers the age group 25-64 and the other the age group 15-64. On the latter basis, the differential between the earning of the low and high schooling categories is reduced if compared with the former set of estimates.

Average life-time earnings rise with each occupational category as educational attainments increase. [23] Labourers with elementary schooling of eight years or less have the lowest earning prospects, $114,000 over their life of gainful employment while the managerial occupations with university degrees have the highest average expectation, $423,000. The expectations of the latter group are greater than those of the professional occupations with university degrees whose average life-time earnings are placed at $354,000.

There are great differences between each occupational category, even with similar educational attainments. For example, the professional category lists physicians and surgeons as the potentially highest income earners in that group, $584,000 [24] and members of the clergy with the lowest income, $133,000. Professional engineers and university professors occupy a middle position with estimated career earnings of $337,000 and $358,000 respectively.

---

[22]   J. R. PODOLUK, *Earnings and Education*, Dominion Bureau of Statistics, Ottawa, 1965, pp. 54-60.
[23]   There are two exceptions, with life-time earnings of approximately the same order for craftsmen and clerical workers with high-school education, 4-5 years, and some university education.
[24]   The medical profession has the highest life-time earnings of any occupation in Canada.   The next highest category is managers in manufacturing, $491,000, while executives in the public service have expectations slightly below those of professional engineers, $328,000.

SUMMARY TABLE 12. — AVERAGE LIFETIME EARNINGS BY OC-
CUPATIONAL GROUP AND LEVEL OF EDUCATION, MALE NON-
FARM LABOUR FORCE, AGED 25-64, CANADA, 1961.

($ Thous.)

OCCUPATION	ELEMEN-TARY SCHOOL 8 YEARS OR LESS	HIGH SCHOOL 1-3 YEARS	HIGH SCHOOL 4-5 YEARS	SOME UNIVER-SITY	UNIVER-SITY DEGREE	PER CENT DIFFER-ENCE ELEMEN-TARY SCHOOL AND UNIVER-SITY DEGREE
Labourers	114	112	118	—	—	—
Craftsmen	135	157	171	170	194	43.7
Miners and quarrymen	150	172	185	—	—	—
Transportation and communication occupations	136	161	183	196	—	—
Service and recreation	112	142	164	191	245	118.8
Sales	142	175	210	217	256	80.3
Clerical	135	150	161	160	173	28.1
Professional occupations	171	196	224	225	354	107.1
Managerial occupations	201	233	284	316	423	110.4
All occupations	131	168	209	234	354	170.2

Source: J. R. Podoluk, *Earnings and Education,* Ottawa, Dominion Bureau
of Statistics, 1965.

The difference in life-time earnings between the average
for all occupations with eight years of elementary schooling
or less, $131,000, and the average with a university degree,
$354,000, is 170 per cent (see Summary Table 12). The dif-
ference for the same grouping on a slightly adjusted basis as
shown in Summary Table 13 is 158 per cent. [25]

If the comparison is made on the basis of the 19-64 age
grouping, the difference is reduced to 142 per cent and on the

---

[25] See footnote 1 in Summary Table 13.

SUMMARY TABLE 13. — AVERAGE LIFE-TIME EARNINGS, TOTAL
AND DISCOUNTED BY LEVELS OF EDUCATION, MALE, NON-
FARM LABOUR FORCE, CANADA, 1961.

($ Thous.)

AGE GROUP	ELEMEN-TARY SCHOOL 5-8 YEARS	SECOND-ARY SCHOOL 4-5 YEARS	UNIVER-SITY DEGREE	PER CENT DIFFER-ENCE ELEMEN-TARY SCHOOL AND UNIVER-SITY DEGREE
Total Life Time Earnings				
25-64	137[1]	209	354	158.4
19-64	148	223	358	141.9
15-64	152	222	356	134.2
Discounted Life Time Earnings [2]				
15-64	48	64	92	91.7

Source: J. R. PODOLUK, *Earnings and Education,* Ottawa, Dominion Bureau of Statistics, 1965.

[1] The reason for the slight difference between this figure and the corresponding figure in Summary Table 12 is that the latter includes income earners with less than 5 years of schooling.
[2] At a rate of 5 per cent.

basis of the 15-64 age grouping to 134 per cent. The reason is that young people who leave school early usually have some earnings between the ages of 15 and 24 and this reduces the difference with the earnings of those who have obtained a university degree and who during their period of study have either only limited or no earnings from partial employment.

The differential is further reduced if the basis of comparison is life-time earnings discounted to the present. At the rate of 5 per cent discount, life-time earnings of persons having completed between 5 and 8 years of elementary schooling in the 15-64 age group are estimated at $48,000 and this compares with $92,000 for those with university degrees, a difference of about 92 per cent.

Whatever method of comparison is used, persons with greater education can expect considerably higher career earnings than persons with less education. The difference varies, depending on the method of measurement, with university educated males probably earning between double and two and a half times as much as their less successful compatriots who have completed only elementary schooling.

The author of the estimates offers these qualifications :

> The criticism of this method of relating earnings and education is that it ignores the costs involved in obtaining the education and that it does not take into account the fact that age-earnings profiles differ for different groups. As a result, such unadjusted lifetime earnings show much greater differences between the earnings accruing to persons with higher levels of education and to those with lower levels of education than alternative methods of estimations. [26]

The Economic Council of Canada in using these estimates has made the further comment that there appear to be some offsetting factors relating to the differences in incomes of those with lower levels of education compared to those of higher levels :

> At least under post-war conditions of general scarcity of many of the more highly educated occupational groups, the average incomes for individuals in these groups have been rising more rapidly than the average of all incomes, and much more rapidly than the average incomes of the groups of individuals with generally lower educational attainments. [27]

RETURN ON EDUCATIONAL INVESTMENT

Does it "pay" to get a higher education ? The data presented in the preceding two sections indicate that the answer is : "Yes". The higher real earnings of individuals [28] are reflected in higher national income. And rising aggregate income contributes to increases in the rate of economic growth.

But the assessment so far is incomplete because no account has been taken of the costs incurred in acquiring the added education. For, if the costs involved were to exceed the ultimate

---

[26] *Ibid.*, p. 56.
[27] *Towards Sustained and Balanced Economic Growth, op. cit.*, p. 87.
[28] In addition to higher individual earnings "there may be large indirect economic returns to education, through external or diffusion effects, that are not reflected in individual income increments" (see M. J. BOWMAN, "Educational Shortage and Excess", in *The Canadian Journal of Economics and Political Science*, Vol. XXIV, No. 4, November 1963, p. 456).

benefits, no net gain would have resulted if the measurement were limited to economic consideration only. Or if the return from such additional investment in education were to be less than a return obtainable from alternative investment possibilities, say investment in physical capital, then a case could be made purely on the ground of maximizing returns on resources used, to devote limited factors of production to more profitable investment rather than to less profitable investment. [29]

This is a purely hypothetical question. In real life, quite apart from the greater profitability of investment in human resource development than investment of other types, indicated below, large and increasing expenditures on education would likely continue to be made whatever the results of statistical or economic analysis because of overriding social and human considerations and because of strong public pressures, a real factor in the democratic decision-making process.

Miss Podoluk has extended her estimates of life-time earnings to include also rates of return on investment in education. These are defined as the benefits derived from additional income flows which accrue from obtaining more education. The technique used was to estimate average earnings

> ... for each age and education group [...] on the assumption of a cohort of persons starting a career at some specific age. The anticipated average earnings estimated are the average earnings per initial entrant. [...] For some particular level of schooling, for example, completion of a university degree, the returns to extra education would be the difference between the average earnings per person with a university degree minus the average earnings per person with a high school diploma in each age group. [30]

---

[29] Seymour E. Harris brings out the interesting point that the law of diminishing returns applicable to investment in physical capital does not necessarily apply to investment in human capital: "In general, as more resources are invested in a particular factor of production the returns tend to decline; this conclusion generally applies to further investments in capital. But it is not clear that similar trends should consistently be applied to investments in human capital, that is in education. It is conceivable, and often probable, that present investment in human beings may yield increased rather than declining returns. This conclusion applies especially when, by better selection, the students to be educated tend to improve in quality as compared to earlier groups" (see "Returns on Investment in Education", in *Economic Aspects of Higher Education*, Study Group in the Economics of Education, Paris, Organisation for Economic Co-operation and Development, 1964, p. 47).

[30] *Earnings and Education, op. cit.*, p. 60.

The resulting estimates represent rates of return for private investment and they are shown in two different forms.

One method "is to treat the costs of schooling as negative income during the years of school attendance." [31] These estimates are summarized in columns 2 and 3 of Summary Table 14. They show "the estimated earnings differentials for cohorts of males who have completed high school and for cohorts of males who have completed university. For high school graduates the earnings differentials are those between high school graduates and males with only five to eight years of elementary schooling, while for university graduates the differentials are those between university graduates and males with four to five years of high school." [32]

The other method follows the techniques developed by W. Lee Hansen of treating costs as investment instead of negative income. [33] The return on investment is then

> ... calculated to be that rate of interest which made the present value of the investment equal to the present value of the income stream. This method yields the same results as the previous approach but eliminates the use of negative figures. [...] The statistics show the cost to an elementary school graduate of securing both a high school graduation diploma and university degree and the net earnings differentials between a university degree and an elementary school education by age groups. [34]

The estimates in columns 2 and 3 in Summary Table 14 show that returns based on earnings before taxes are higher on investment in university education than for investment in high school education, 20 per cent as compared with 16 per cent.

Relating the additional earnings per year at each age resulting from further schooling, assuming a working life between 23 and 64 years, to private costs [35] of elementary school gra-

   31   *Ibid.* This technique is similar to that advanced in NATIONAL BUREAU OF ECONOMIC RESEARCH, *Human Capital: A Theoretical and Empirical Analysis, with Special Reference to Education*, Princeton, Princeton University Press, 1964.
   32   *Earnings and Education, op. cit.*, p. 60.
   33   W. Lee HANSEN, "Total and Private Rates of Returns to Investment in Schooling", in *Journal of Political Economy*, Vol. LXXI, No. 2, April 1963.
   34   *Earnings and Education, op. cit.*, p. 61.
   35   Private costs include both expenses incurred in obtaining an education and foregone earnings while studying.

duates from completing elementary school to completing university, as per columns 4 and 5 of Summary Table 14 indicates a return on investment of 17 per cent.

SUMMARY TABLE 14. — RETURN ON PRIVATE INVESTMENT IN EDUCATION, BY LEVELS OF EDUCATION, MALE NONFARM, LABOUR FORCE, CANADA, 1961.

(Dollars)

AGE	ADDITIONAL INCOME RECEIVED WHEN COMPLETING		PRIVATE INVESTMENT IN EDUCATION [2]	ADDITIONAL INCOME [3]
	Secondary School 4-5 years [1]	University Degree [3]		
15	—725[4]	—	725	—
16	—924[4]	—	924	—
17	—1,122[4]	—	1,122	—
18	—1,346[4]	—	1,346	—
19	50	—1,493[4]	1,493	—
20	198	—1,526[4]	1,526	—
21	497	—2,022[4]	2,022	—
22	595	—2,366[4]	2,366	—
23	668	447	—	1,113
24	839	694	—	1,531
25-34	1,310	2,117	—	3,418
35-44	1,887	4,040	—	5,910
45-54	2,092	4,323	—	6,396
55-64	1,816	3,798	—	5,597
Rate of Return — Per Cent	16.3	19.7	17.1	—

Source: J. R. PODOLUK, *Earnings and Education*, Ottawa, Dominion Bureau of Statistics, 1965.

[1] For the ages 25 to 64 the earnings figures are the additional earnings per year at each age resulting from additional schooling. For high school graduates these are the additional earnings received by graduates as compared with persons having only five to eight years of elementary schooling. For university graduates it is the increment in earnings over the earnings of persons with four to five years of high school.

[2] Covers private costs to elementary school graduates from completing elementary school to completing university.

[3] Covers the additional earnings per year at each age resulting from additional schooling.

[4] The private costs of schooling are treated as negative income.

These estimates are based on the assumption that all education costs are investment. If a part of these costs were considered consumption, the rates of return would be higher. The Economic Council of Canada, in using these estimates, made the point that they support the claim that investment in human capital may bring significantly higher returns than most investments in physical capital. To quote :

> These rates of return [. . .] are rates of return to individuals. The calculations have not taken public costs of education into account — either capital or operating costs. These costs, however, are probably small in relation to the private costs to individuals, including foregone income. This would imply that even the over-all rates of return to the economy for total investment in education would be relatively high — perhaps in the range of 10 to 15 per cent. Indeed, such rates would appear to compare favourably with the rates of return (even on a pre-tax basis) which typically accrue to total capital investment in physical and financial assets. [36]

The estimates are subject to certain limitations. For one, they relate to the situation in 1961. Since then substantial increases have occurred in earning potential associated with rising educational attainments. Further the estimates are based on gross earnings and thus they do not take account of differentials in higher marginal tax rates. From a social point of view, they do not reflect the impact of education on advancing knowledge, technology, management techniques, and a better understanding of the working of the economic system which in turn may affect rates of economic growth.

The validity of the estimates are sometimes questioned on the ground that "the inaccuracies and imperfections inherent in a price system render such calculations of little value for the whole economy though they may, of course, be of interest for any one individual".[37]

Other comments relate to the fact that the rates of return are private rather than social rates. In the case of education, the latter rates may be higher than the former rates. [38] Thus any

---

[36] *Towards Sustained and Balanced Economic Growth, op. cit.*, p. 91.
[37] *Investment in Education, op. cit.*, p. 384.
[38] This assumes that social gross income (or benefits) is greater than the social costs of education. Studies in the United States indicate that this situation may not necessarily apply. Gary S. Becker, for example, estimates that private returns on educational investment, that is the extra benefits accruing to an individual from additional schooling,

decisions that are made on the basis of individual rates could result in an under-investment on the basis of social returns. [39]

The preceding economic analysis has been based on quantifying returns on educational investment on an aggregate basis, that is by treating educational expenditures as a homogenous entity which, of course, they are not. Just as there are different returns on investment in different types of physical capital, so presumably returns differ on investment in different types of educational capital. Commented one professional observer:

> Though we know something about the relative rates of return to high school education as compared with university education [...] there is little information to my knowledge of the relative rates of return to increased expenditures on technical secondary schooling as compared with university history courses. [...] We need to investigate the existence of differential rates of return within education, with the aim of providing our educational policy makers with information about return which will enable them to be more selective in their application of funds. [40]

amounted to more than 12 per cent in the case of university education (after taxes) and that they exceeded social returns (see *Human Capital, op. cit.*, p. 114).

[39] This subject is examined in C. H. WILLIAMS, "Relationships of Education to Economic and Social Goals", in *Working Papers, Interprovincial Conference on Education and the Development of Human Resources*, Montreal, September 8-10, 1966, issued by the Ontario Department of Education, Toronto, 1966, pp. 16 ff.

[40] *Ibid.*, pp. 18 and 19.

CHAPTER 19

Effect of Net Migration

EXTENT OF NET MIGRATION

So far the discussion has been in economic terms of what education may do for individuals and for society as a whole without regard to where the education takes place. There is now need to take account of the fact that knowledge knows no boundaries and that man can learn not only from his compatriots but can also obtain, at times even greater knowledge from abroad. This sharing of the progress of knowledge on an international plane takes many forms, from students studying abroad, to importing educators, from obtaining the results of foreign research to immigration of professionals and skilled technicians.

Two aspects are considered in this study. The first is the flow of educational attainments from abroad and the economic benefits obtained by Canada from the costs of educational investment incurred by foreign countries, as well as Canada's contribution to other nations in what has become known as the "brain-drain". The second is the effect of U.S. educational attainments on Canadian development.

Over the last one hundred years, 8.6 million immigrants came to Canada's shores and 6.9 million emigrants left this country. Thus Canada obtained a net inflow of 1.7 million immigrants during this period (see Summary Table 15).

During the nineteenth century, while Canada struggled to build up a viable nation, this country lost close to 700,000 people (net). But, in the twentieth century, Canada more than made up for this outward flow, with net immigration totalling 2.4 million, with the inward movement largely concentrated in the first and in the last decade.

EFFECT ON STOCK OF EDUCATION

How have these flows of immigrants and emigrants affected the stock of education in Canada ? This was one of the subjects of enquiry by the Economic Council of Canada which found that while immigration added significantly to increasing the stock of knowledge it did not produce "any major or decisive shifts in the stock of education in Canada over the past half century". [1]

SUMMARY TABLE 15. — POPULATION, IMMIGRATION AND EMI-
GRATION, CANADA, BY DECADES, 1861-1961.
(Thous.)

PERIOD	POPU-LATION [1]	IMMI-GRATION	EMI-GRATION [2]	NET IMMIGRATION	
				Number	Per cent [3]
1861-1871	3,689	187	379	—192	—5.9
1871-1881	4,325	353	440	—87	—2.3
1881-1891	4,833	903	1,109	—206	—4.8
1891-1901	5,371	326	506	—180	—3.7
1901-1911	7,207	1,759	1,043	+716	+13.3
1911-1921	8,788	1,612	1,381	+231	+3.2
1921-1931	10,377	1,203	974	+229	+2.6
1931-1941	11,507	150	242	—92	—0.9
1941-1951	13,648[4]	548	379	+169	+1.5
1951-1961	18,238[5]	1,543	462	+1,081	+7.7
Total	—	8,548	6,915	1,669	—

Source: Data on population from *Census of Canada 1961*; data on immigration and emigration from *The Basic 1961 Census Data of Immigration and Citizenship*, Department of Citizenship and Immigration,
Ottawa, 1963, and supplementary estimates by the Dominion Bureau of Statistics.

1   As of end of decade.
2   Estimated on a residual basis.
3   Per cent of population at beginning of period.
4   Excludes Newfoundland with a population of 361,416 which
became a province of Canada in 1949.
5   Includes Newfoundland.

One of the main reasons has been that the educational level of the immigrating labour force has not been substantially different from the average level of the Canadian labour force. This can be illustrated by data available for the decade 1951-1961 when net immigration to Canada was particularly heavy. During this period, "the median years of schooling of both male immigrants coming into the labour force and male emigrants

---

1   *Towards Sustained and Balanced Economic Growth, op. cit.*, p. 78.

leaving the labour force [. . .] was about 9.6 years. This compares with the median years of schooling of the total Canadian labour force of 8.8 years in 1951 and 9.4 years in 1961." [2]

In terms of immigrants with university degrees, Canada turned out to be a net gainer. In 1961, about 5.6 per cent of the Canadian male labour force had university degrees. Of male immigrants entering the Canadian labour force during 1951-1961, some 6.3 per cent had a university degree, while male emigrants with university degrees comprised a lesser proportion, 5.8 per cent. In terms of total numbers, the former were four times as numerous as the latter. Concluded the Economic Council of Canada : "The over-all effect of this migration was to bring about some increase in the average educational level of the male labour force in Canada." [3]

Accepting the premise that there exists a correlation between improvement in education and improvement in productivity, the data, even in this brief exposition, are suggestive of four general conclusions :

1. That in the period of industrial maturity, Canada's absorbtive capacity to offer challenging and rewarding opportunities, expanded greatly, notably for people with higher educational attainments and skills, leading to the greatest net inflow of immigrants in the country's history.

2. That as Canada prospered and offered greater opportunities for economic advancement at home, the outflow of skilled persons, the "brain-drain" lost some of its momentum and thus Canada's growing stock of educational capital was less adversely affected.

3. That the loss in educational capital that did occur, particularly through the emigration of professional and technical personnel to the United States, was more than made up by a gain of educational capital through an inflow of well-trained professional and technical personnel, fourfold the size of the outflow, with educational attainments, which on an average were slightly higher than that of the outflow.

4. That the net gain in educational capital accruing to Canada took not only the form of an increase in quantity, bu'

---

[2] *Ibid.*, p. 79.
[3] *Ibid.*

also in terms of increases in quality. The latter is reflected in increasing somewhat the educational attainments of the Canadian labour force as a whole as a result of higher standards of education and greater training abroad by immigrants joining the labour force. More highly skilled workmen were able to command higher wages. Demonstration of opportunities to earn greater incomes in turn represented incentives to native Canadians to acquire more education and training. Further, the higher wage levels of skilled trades represented a "pull" force contributing to moving up wages of workers with lesser training.

VALUATION OF EDUCATIONAL CAPITAL

How can these net additions to Canada's stock of educational capital be measured ? Bruce W. Wilkinson has prepared estimates for the decade 1951-1961 of the years of educational attainment and the costs involved covering both immigrants and emigrants separately for members of the labour force and the non-labour force. The data are shown in Summary Table 16. [4]

The estimates are subject to a number of limitations. One of these is the lack of adequate statistics of emigration. The author has presented estimates of emigration of Canadian-born persons to the United States only, and these represent the bulk of Canadian emigrants. [5] Two emigration estimates are presented. The high estimate is based on the gross number of Canadian-born immigrants into the United States as reported by the U.S. Immigration and Naturalization Service for the period July 1, 1951 to June 30, 1961, less the number of Canadians recorded as having returned to Canada during this period. The low emigration estimate is based on the decline of Canadian-born residents in the United States between 1950 and 1960, as recorded in the population censuses, adjusted for deaths of Canadian-born residents based on mortality tables. [6]

During 1951-1961, Canada added to the stock of educational capital of her labour force the results of 6.3 million years

<hr/>

[4] Bruce W. WILKINSON, *Studies in the Economics of Education,* Occasional Paper, Economic and Research Branch, No. 4, Department of Labour, Queen's Printer, Ottawa, 1965, pp. 56 ff.   The author has also presented estimates of other cost items including settlers' effects, migrants' funds and cost of child rearing (*Ibid.*, pp. 73-77).
[5] See Footnote 1 in Summary Table 16.
[6] *Ibid.*, pp. 62 and 64.

SUMMARY TABLE 16. — TOTAL YEARS OF EDUCATION AND COSTS OF EDUCATION, IMMIGRANTS AND EMIGRANTS, CANADA, 1951-1961.

ITEM	IMMIGRANTS		EMIGRANTS [1]			
			HIGH ESTIMATES		LOW ESTIMATES	
	Years of Education	Costs of Education [2]	Years of Education	Costs of Education [2]	Years of Education	Costs of Education [2]
	Thous.	$ Mill.	Thous.	$ Mill.	Thous.	$ Mill.
Labour Force						
Professional	1,081	1,403	458	594	259	336
Other	5,254	2,924	846	555	578	313
Subtotal	6,335	4,327	1,304	1,149	737	649
Non-Labour Force						
Housewives	2,210	1,033	538	364	304	206
Children	1,144	290	327[3]	153[3]	185[3]	86[3]
Other	408	250	78	63	44	38
Subtotal	3,762	1,572	943	580	533	330
Total	10,097	5,890	2,246	1,729	1,270	979

Source: Bruce W. WILKINSON, *Studies in the Economics of Education,* Department of Labour, Economics and Research Branch, Occasional Paper No. 4, Ottawa, Queen's Printer, July 1965, pp. 67 ff.

[1] Covers Canadian-born emigrants to the United States, estimated to represent 94 per cent of total Canadian-born living abroad (see *United Nations Demographic Yearbook,* New York, 1966).

[2] Covers institutional outlays for current expenses, implicit interest and depreciation, opportunity costs and incidental expenses of attending school.

[3] Includes students.

of learning. This country contributed to the United States between ¾ million and 1.3 million years of education. Thus Canada's net gain exceeded 5 million years of education.

If other members of households are added, including wives and children, Canada's total gross gain was 10.1 million years of education, her loss was between 1.3 million and 2.2 million, and her net gain was approximately 8 million years of education (or better, even after allowing for non-coverage of emigrants going to countries other than the United States).

It costs the countries which educated the people leaving subsequently for Canada some $5.9 billion during 1951-1961. Over the same period, Canadians spent on the education of emigrants and their families going to the United States between $1 billion and $1.7 billion. Hence, Canada's net gain exceeded $4 billion during the decade.

Taking one-tenth of the $5.9 billion of costs of education of immigrants for the decade as representing the average for 1960, the resulting $590 million is equivalent to 1.6 per cent of the Gross National Product and 36 per cent of total expenditures on formal education spent in that year.

Taking the average in the net value of education for the decade, that is allowing for a half-way estimate of the educational cost of emigrants, between the low and high estimates, yields a total of $4,544 million. This amount is "nearly 52 per cent of the monetary capital inflow to Canada during this ten-year period. One-tenth of this average net value ($454 millions), is 102 per cent of new issues of Canadian securities during 1960, and 70 per cent of total foreign, direct investment in Canada for the same year." [7]

Seen in perspective, Canada has gained greatly by drawing on educational capital generated abroad and this gain has been particularly marked in the period after Canada reached industrial maturity. This suggests that there is no time limit as to the stages of economic development during which a nation may benefit from drawing on education from abroad, and that the benefits from international sharing of knowledge are continuing and universal.

---

[7] *Ibid.*, p. 73.

CHAPTER 20

United States Influence

EDUCATION AND PRODUCTIVITY DIFFERENTIALS

The United States reached the stage of technological maturity and high mass consumption at the turn of this century. [1] And this led to a much earlier take-off in educational progress in that country, preceding Canada by about half a century.

Considering that the United States has a population about ten times and a Gross National Product about fourteen times that of Canada, and that the two countries enjoy close trade and other economic relations, it is quite understandable that the much earlier and more rapid advances affect Canadian economic and educational development. This in fact is what has happened. While evolving in many respects an indigenous educational system, the shape of progress in Canada was greatly influenced by forces of emulation, a free flow of students and professors, access to and participation in research and many other related factors.

During most of the twentieth century, Gross National Product per capita in Canada has been running about one-quarter below that of the United States. [2] In terms of output per person, the differential is somewhat less, below one-fifth in the more recent period. Among the reasons are differences in the labour force participation rate between the two countries, differences in age distribution of the population and a lesser ratio of women working.

Of the many factors that can be cited to explain differentials in productivity rates between the two countries, the factor of particular concern in this study is : the difference in the quality of the labour force to the extent that this is a result of variations in educational input. Research work initiated by the Economic Council of Canada led it to the following conclusion :

> The relatively much higher level of educational attainment in the United States than in the Canadian labour

---

[1] *The Stages of Economic Growth, op. cit.,* p. 59.
[2] *The Contribution of Education to Economic Growth, op. cit.,* p. 57.

force ... has been calculated in very rough terms to account
for well over a third of the productivity difference between the
two countries. Two elements are involved in the income
difference associated with differences in education — the relatively much larger share of the labour force in the United
States which has completed high school or acquired a university degree, and the significantly higher average incomes accruing to those with higher education. [3]

EDUCATION AND INCOME DIFFERENTIALS

The two key variables of education and income for Canada
and the United States can be quantified as follows : [4]

1. During the period 1910 to 1960, years of education per
person in the male labour force in the United States rose at
an average rate of between 9 and 10 per cent per decade, as
compared with a range of between 5 and 8 per cent for the
Canadian male labour force.

2. By 1961-1962, median years of schooling of the male
labour force in the United States were between one-fifth and
one-quarter higher than in Canada, covering the age group 25-54,
with the proportion somewhat smaller for the age group 55-64.

3. In 1960-1961, about 11 per cent of the U.S. male labour
force had university degrees, as compared with about 5½ per
cent for Canada.

4. In 1960-1961, the gap between the two countries was
widening further, with 45 per cent of the age group 25-34
having a secondary school education or better in the United
States, as compared with 24 per cent for Canada.

5. Over the last half century, the total stock of education
in the male labour force in the United States rose by better
than one-third that of the Canadian labour force, taking
account of changes in years of schooling and average daily
attendance. [5]

------

[3] *Towards Sustained and Balanced Economic Growth, op. cit.*, p. 58.
[4] *Ibid.*, pp. 80-90, based largely on the study undertaken for the
Economic Council of Canada by Gordon W. BERTRAM, *op. cit.*
[5] Between 1910 and 1960 average years of schooling rose: Canada
39 per cent, United States 59 per cent; average days attended per year
rose: Canada 50 per cent, United States 56 per cent; average total days
attended rose: Canada 107 per cent, United States 147 per cent. (The
Canadian data relate to 1911-1961.)

6. Accompanying the more rapid build-up of stock of educational capital in the United States, increases in incomes attributable to education were more marked in that country than in Canada.

> Over the period 1911-1961, income per man, considering only years of schooling, increased almost twice as much in the United States (21.2 per cent) as in Canada (12 per cent). The percentage change in average years of schooling in the same period was 58.5 per cent in the United States and 38.6 per cent in Canada — the Canadian achievement being two-thirds of the U.S. achievement.[6]

The cumulative effect of differentials is particularly marked in the decade 1951-1961. Over this period, labour income per man, considering only years of education, rose by 4.7 per cent in the United States as compared with 2.3 per cent in Canada, or more than twice.

7. Average incomes of the more highly educated rose in the United States, as it did in Canada. But with relatively more people receiving more education per person, the dynamic effect on raising income levels due to education was more marked in the United States than in Canada. The pattern of differentiation in income levels by educational attainments is not uniform. Special factors affect average incomes of university graduates in Canada and in the United States.

MEDIAN INCOMES OF MALE LABOUR FORCE[7]

	Canada $	United States $	United States as Percent of Canada
Elementary School, 8 years or less	3,074	3,262	106
High School, 1-3 years	4,233	4,936	117
High School, 4-5 years	4,941	5,520	112
Some University	5,368	6,045	113
University Degree	7,956	7,693	97

Generally speaking, the above figures indicate that incomes for comparable levels of education are on an average between 6 and 13 per cent higher in the United States than in Canada.

---

6 *The Contribution of Education to Economic Growth, op. cit.,* p. 52.
7 Covers persons age 25 years and over of the non-farm male labour force. The data for Canada relate to 1960 and for the United States for 1959 and they are expressed in Canadian and U.S. dollars respectively. The data are from the *Census of Canada 1961* and the *United States Census of Population 1960.*

In the case of university graduates, Canadian incomes were about 3 per cent higher in 1960 than corresponding incomes in the United States.

Looking at the broad sweep of the twentieth century, it can be said that during most periods the United States made more rapid progress in educational advancement than Canada, not only in absolute terms as could be expected from a country ten times the size of Canada in terms of population and fourteen times in terms of Gross National Product, but also in terms of rates of increases reflecting the greater priority attached to education in the United States as compared with Canada.

As a result, the gap in educational attainments between the two countries has been growing. But in the more recent period, the trend appears to have been reversed, with Canadians making relatively greater efforts than their neighbours to the south, to make up for lost time and missed opportunities to advance the cause of education in their country.

Estimates prepared by the Economic Council of Canada presented below, [8] indicate that the number of students enrolled in Canadian universities as a proportion of the 18-24 year olds rose from 5 per cent in 1955-1966 to 11 per cent in 1965-1966, or by 120 per cent. The comparable increases for the United States were from a ratio of 14 per cent to one of 21 per cent, or by 50 per cent.

Over the decade to 1975-1976, the Economic Council of Canada foresees a rise in the ratio in Canada to 20 per cent, representing an increase of 82 per cent, as against a ratio in the United States of 25 per cent, involving an increase of approximately 20 per cent.

In fact, if the United States data of university enrolment are compared with the proportion shown for post-secondary enrolment in Canada, the two ratios are fairly close, 25 per cent and 24 per cent respectively. This suggests the possibility that Canada may be approaching United States educational standards by 1975-1976 in terms of the relative number of young people engaged in the pursuit of higher learning.

---

[8] ECONOMIC COUNCIL OF CANADA, *The Canadian Economy from the 1960's to the 1970's*, Fourth Annual Review, Ottawa, Queen's Printer, 1967, p. 69.

POST-SECONDARY ENROLMENT AS A PERCENTAGE OF THE
18-24 YEAR OLD POPULATION

| | Canada | | United States |
	Post-Secondary [9]	University	University
1955-1956	6	5	14
1960-1961	9	7	17
1965-1966	13	11	21
1970-1971	20	16	23
1975-1976	24	20	25

REASONS FOR DIFFERENTIALS

Even though the situation appears to be changing in favour of Canada, some more specific explanation is needed for the differentials in incomes and educational attainments for Canada and the United States shown above. Three reasons have been advanced. [10]

First, there are more university graduates in the United States labour force than there are in Canada. The relatively greater scarcity of highly educated personnel has led to premium payments in Canada.

Second, there is a greater concentration in Canada of university graduates in occupations with higher incomes, e.g., professional and technical occupations and relatively fewer graduates in such occupations as sales.

Third, there is a heavy concentration of young university graduates in the male labour force in the United States, more so than is the case in Canada. The incomes of these young graduates would initially be lower than those of the older graduates, with the situation changing significantly as the younger graduates grow older and their incomes rise with greater experience and expanded opportunities.

In broad perspective, the United States has made more rapid progress in educational attainments than Canada and this has brought greater benefits to their people in terms of higher incomes, to the extent that such increased earnings flow from higher education. Hence, educational differentials have widened

---

[9] Includes enrolment in universities, teachers' colleges and technical institutes, and enrolment in technical courses at community colleges.
[10] *Towards Sustained and Balanced Economic Growth, op. cit.*, p. 90.

rather than narrowed "differences in income and productivity between the two countries". [11]

OFFSET TO LAGGING EDUCATION

Fortunately for Canada, other factors contributed to offset slow economic progress resulting from lagging educational efforts. Among these are the availability of abundant natural resources that Canada could develop economically and the products of which could be sold in world markets at generally rising prices over the longer term. Another important factor is the greater relative role of international specialization in Canadian economic growth as compared with American economic growth, with foreign trade being about four times as important for Canada in relation to Gross National Product as compared with the United States. Another factor which is less clear and in fact subject to different interpretation, is the claim made that there exists some evidence which suggests the possibility that the ratio of capital per worker in the non-farm sector is higher in Canada, than in the United States. The Economic Council of Canada, for example, suggests that in 1961, "capital per employed person in Canada was about one-eighth higher in manufacturing and over two-fifths higher in other non-farm sectors than in the United States". [12]

As a result of such offsetting factors, the gap in income differentials between Canada and the United States did not change materially during the twentieth century and Canada was able to keep pace with American progress in raising levels of real income and standards of living. The data support the conclusion that given the existence of other favourable factors including the endowments of nature, greater reliance on international trade, and the degree of capital intensity of her industries, Canada could have exceeded the rate of economic progress of the United States if her educational efforts had not lagged behind those of the United States in relative terms. But there were, as suggested earlier, good reasons for the lag.

This presentation of differentials in educational attainments and economic rewards associated with them, between Canadian

---

[11] *Ibid.*, p. 93.
[12] *Ibid.*, p. 59.

and American income earners is quite limited [13] and study in greater depth would be required than has been attempted here to probe the basic causes of the differentials observed.

What the data illustrate is that a country with a smaller economic base and younger in age of industrial maturity, like Canada, cannot expect to make as great progress in educational attainments with corresponding economic rewards as the wealthy United States, though it can with appropriate efforts and priority allocation of resources narrow the gap that exists.

The point was made earlier that cultural factors, in addition to economic and other forces may affect materially the extent and the kind of educational opportunities offered to the young. Considering the wide variations in educational attainments of Canadians, as compared with those of Americans, the question arises whether cultural factors are among the main reasons for the differences noted.

Views differ whether cultural similarities of the two nations are substantial or not. But the very fact that in recent years successive Canadian governments, both conservative and liberal, have endeavoured to encourage the evolvement of a distinct Canadian culture as a means of growing self-identification and reassertion of nationalism, is illustrative of the concern that cultural similarities between Canadians and Americans may be inimical to political sovereignty of Canada over the longer term, in the sense that cultural absorption together with overwhelming economic control may lead to political absorption. [14]

Differences in cultural attitudes do not appear to constitute significant elements in accounting for the variations in educational standards between Canada and the United States, and

[13] On the basis of the limited evidence available and after adjustments of the estimates to insure comparability, Gordon W. Bertram observes that "Canadian rates of return to education compare favourably, not only with those on alternative returns typically accruing from total capital investment in physical and financial assets, but also with the similar U.S. rates of return to education. Further research is needed to clarify such comparisons of Canadian and U.S. rates of return — both for private and social rates of return to education" (see *The Contribution of Education to Economic Growth, op. cit.*, pp. 63 and 64).

[14] For an assessment of some of the measures taken and their implications, see Edwin R. BLACK, "Canadian Public Policy and the Mass Media", in *The Canadian Journal of Economics*, Vol. I, No. 2, May 1968, pp. 368-379.

the consequent differentials in economic performance. For the outlook of Canadians and their way of life is as North American as is the living pattern of Americans.

It is not cultural similarities or differences that have been largely responsible for Canadians to maintain their political independence and to pay the price of substantial differences in national economic achievements and individual educational attainments. Rather, it has been in part the conscious and in part the instinctive desire of Canadians to evolve a pattern of life which in social and economic terms is similar to that of Americans, but in political and historical terms is quite different to that of their neighbours to the south. Or, as one scholar put it : "In the absence of significant cultural differences, tolerance of that gap depends on the amount of legitimacy accorded to the Canadian political system by its citizenry." [15]

Negative and Positive Effects

It could be reasoned that there is no need for a smaller country like Canada to keep pace with the educational advances of the United States and that it would be more appropriate for Canada to grow at her own pace and in her own way. While such an argument can be made rather persuasively, it does not take full account of certain implications of the effects of U.S. educational attainments on Canadian development. These are of two kinds: negative and positive effects.

The negative implications are, the "brain-drain", the falling behind in research efforts and scientific progress, and a lessening in the rate of potential productivity improvement.

As long as educational facilities remain inadequate in Canada in comparison with those in the United States, Canadian students will continue to go to that country in increasing numbers to take up graduate studies. Many of them find jobs and then stay there if permitted to do so by U.S. authorities. Greater research opportunities and higher incomes attract many scientists and other professional and technical personnel to the United States reducing Canada's stock of educational capital in one of the most vital areas affecting economic development.

---

[15] The above reference is to the economic gap, that is the fact that Canadian average levels of income have been running at three quarters of those of American (*ibid.*, p. 379).

To the extent that education contributes to increasing productivity, a lesser relative educational effort on the part of Canada reduces the economy's potential of competing with the United States on the basis of approximate equality of productivity improvements over the longer term. Canada depends on expanding world trade for economic development and growth to a much greater extent than the United States. In a situation like this what matters is that Canada must remain competitive in world markets if she is to prosper. And this in turn means keeping up with productivity increases of other major trading nations with which Canada competes in foreign markets.

The situation is further complicated by the increasing insistence of Canadian unions for wage parity with American workers. This is particularly the case in such industries as motor cars, steel, etc., even though there exist notable differentials in productivity between the United States and Canada.

Hence, Canada faces even greater cost-push pressures than the United States, that is, costs of production including wages rising more rapidly than productivity. Thus the urgency to achieve an increase in the rate of productivity improvement is even greater in Canada than in the United States, and for many reasons more difficult to achieve. Such reasons include differences in scale of operations, size of markets, advances in technology, extent of research work undertaken, availability of investment capital, etc.

One way of overcoming such handicaps is specialization, not only in terms of production, but also in terms of developing specialized skills that can match the best to be found anywhere in the world. In other words, there are certain realities that Canadians must recognize. Their country cannot match the United States in terms of wealth. But it should be possible for Canada to give her people the type and quality of educational training which will make it possible to compete effectively with people of equivalent training in other countries, and particularly in the United States, whose geographic proximity and remarkable economic progress have been important factors in providing both a stimulus and an incentive for Canadians to do better.

There are some positive implications to the U.S. influence on Canadian educational progress. They relate to the "demonstration" effect of educational attainments, the sharing of knowledge resulting from research, both basic and applied, and the opportunities provided for many Canadians to benefit directly from U.S. educational progress.

The "demonstration" effect refers to the desire on the part of Canadians to emulate U.S. educational advances, realizing the many benefits that education brings in economic as well as in non-economic terms, the latter including human, social and political values. American scientists share their growing knowledge freely with the rest of the world and Canadians as neighbours have particularly close relationships among the professions of the two countries.

Further, many Canadian firms, being subsidiaries of American corporations, have ready access to new discoveries and innovations taking place in the United States and so have many other Canadian firms which manufacture and distribute products under license from American companies. [16] Thousands of students at the undergraduate and graduate levels attend American institutions of higher learning and a large number of scholars participate in U.S. research projects or obtain financial grants from American sources.

The net impact of these influences, moving in opposite directions, varies from time to time, with Canada's gain greater at one stage and less at another stage. But such forces exist and their impact cannot be overlooked in an assessment of education on economic development. For the Canadian experience suggests that the international spread of knowledge, enhanced by greater educational attainments abroad, has a distinct bearing, and in recent decades an increasing impact on national economic development.

---

[16] Canadian experience supports the following conclusion offered by Denison: "Adoption of another nation's production practices, and their adaptation to local conditions, is quicker, cheaper, and easier than development of new knowledge. But it nonetheless requires a large effort and use of resources (as well as, often, competititve pressure). Among other things, it probably requires much the same kind of technical and managerial talent as does new research. For this reason, it is quite likely that, by facilitating the adoption of known techniques, expansion of the number of engineers, scientists, and well educated management personnel can contribute more to growth in Europe than it can in the United States." (And he could have added: Canada; see Edward F. DENISON, "Measuring the Contribution of Education (and the Residual) to Economic Growth", in *The Residual Factor and Economic Growth*, Paris, Organisation for Economic Co-operation and Development, 1964, p. 55.)

CHAPTER 21

Education and Economic Growth

CAUSE AND CONSEQUENCE

In turning now to the effects of education on economic growth, development and progress as evidenced by Canadian experience over the last century, let it be said at the outset that such an assessment deals with only one side of the coin. For education affects not only economic development, but economic development affects also education since the latter can be both a cause and a consequence of economic advancement.

The several aspects of the duality of the interrelationship between education and economic growth has been mentioned previously but the point cannot be emphasized strongly enough. For what can be observed is the end result of this duality and attempts to isolate quantitatively the two flows of effects moving in opposite directions are still in their infancy. The point was made earlier that high priority considerations for business and social capital, other than education, were one contributing factor to generally limiting the proportion of the nation's resources going to the education industry during the first eight decades, with the situation changing markedly in the last two decades.

Further, changes in industrial structure, scientific and technological advances and growing international competition in the stage of industrial maturity, the stage in which Canada experienced her most rapid rate of economic growth, put much greater pressures on expanding the facilities of and the services provided by the education industry.

Social scientists have been endeavouring to quantify the contribution education makes to economic growth and to expand the understanding of the interrelationship between education and economic development. A breakthrough in the search for answers was Denison's estimate of the "residual", which included the contribution of education and technical knowledge to economic growth. [1]

---

[1] Denison made the point that about 23 per cent of the recent growth of the national income of the United States was the result of increased education of the labour force (see *The Residual Factor of Economic Growth, op. cit.,* pp. 13-55).

Other economists who either preceded Denison or followed him and who made important contributions in this field include : Blaug, [2] Becker, [3] Bowman, [4] Fabricant, [5] Kendrick, [6] Myint, [7] Schultz, [8] Solow, [9] and Vaizey. [10]

Still, with all the research work done and analytical comments offered, a recent investigation suggested that social scientists have barely scratched the surface and that the conclusions so far offered on the basis of incomplete evidence and unsubstantiated assumptions were in many respects "so simplified as to be misleading". [11] The following suggestion was made :

> By examining such questions as, for example, whether or not the available knowledge stock is being fully utilised, whether or not the education industry is producing adequate

[2] Mark BLAUG, "The Rate of Return on Investment in Education in Great Britain", in *Manchester School of Economic and Social Studies*, September 1965, pp. 205-262; ID., "An Economic Interpretation of the Private Demand for Education", in *Economica*, May 1966, pp. 166-182; ID., "Literacy and Economic Development", in *School Review*, Fall 1966, pp. 393-418.

[3] Gary S. BECKER, "Investment in Human Capital: A Theoretical Analysis", *op. cit.*; ID., *Human Capital: A Theoretical and Empirical Analysis with Special Reference to Education, op. cit.*; Gary S. BECKER and Barry R. CHISWICK, "Education and the Distribution of Earnings", in *American Economic Review*, May 1966, pp. 358-369.

[4] Mary Jean BOWMAN, "Schultz, Denison and the Contribution of 'Eds' to National Income Growth", in *Journal of Political Economy*, October 1964, pp. 450-464; ID., "The Requirements of the Labour-Market and the Education Explosion", in George Z. F. BEREDAY and Joseph A. LAWERYS, Eds., *Education Explosion, World Yearbook of Education 1965*, New York, Harcourt, Brace and World, 1965, pp. 64-80; ID., "The Human Investment Revolution in Economic Thought", in *Sociology of Education*, Spring 1966, pp. 111-137; ID., "The New Economics of Education", in *International Journal of the Educational Sciences*, No. 1, 1966, pp. 29-46; ID., "Educational Shortage and Excess", *op. cit.*; ID., "The Role of Education in Development", *op. cit.*

[5] Solomon FABRICANT, *Basic Facts on Productivity Change*, Occasional Paper 63, National Bureau of Economic Research, New York, 1959.

[6] John W. KENDRICK, *Productivity Trends in the United States*, National Bureau of Economic Research, Princeton, Princeton University Press, 1961.

[7] H. MYINT, "Education and Economic Development", in *Social and Economic Studies*, March 1965, pp. 8-21.

[8] See footnote 15, p. 145.

[9] Robert M. SOLOW, "Technical Change and Aggregate Production Function", in *Review of Economics and Statistics*, Vol. XXXIX, No. 3, August 1957, pp. 312-320.

[10] John VAIZEY, *The Costs of Education*, London, Allen and Unwin, Ltd., 1958; *The Place of Education in the Strategy of Economic Development*, Study Group in the Economics of Education, No. 3, Organization for Economic Cooperation and Development, Paris, 1961; *The Economics of Education, op. cit.*

[11] *Investment in Education, op. cit.*, p. 377.

supplies of people with the appropriate knowledge needed for present and future production, whether or not there is scope or need for introducing some knowledge which is available abroad into the country, economists may do much useful work on the relationship between education and economic growth. [12]

QUANTIFYING EDUCATION'S CONTRIBUTION TO ECONOMIC GROWTH

For the period 1911 to 1961, the Bertram estimates for Canada indicate the following relationship between education and economic development.

1. Output per employed person or total productivity per man grew by 1.67 per cent. [13]

2. Labour share in net national output amounted to some 76 per cent. [14]

3. Labour productivity [15] rose by 0.52 per cent per annum as a result of improved education.

4. Total production per man rose by 0.40 per cent per annum as a result of improved education. [16]

5. Educational improvements accounted for almost one-quarter of the rise of productivity per employed person. [17]

Denison prepared estimates for the United States covering the contribution of education to economic growth for two periods, 1909-1929 and 1929-1957. Having completed the estimates for Canada for the period 1911-1961, Bertram then proceeded to provide roughly comparable rates for Canada for the period 1929-1957 (see below) :

---

[12] *Ibid.*, p. 376.

[13] On the basis of the data shown in Table 1 in Appendix A and preparing a special estimate of persons employed in 1911, Gross National Product per person working in constant (1957) dollars rose from $2,647 to $5,680 over the period 1911-1961, or at an annual average rate of 1.53 per cent, slightly below the rate of 1.67 per cent indicated by Bertram (*The Contribution of Education to Economic Growth, op. cit.*, p. 55).

[14] Based on average of 1929-1957 (*ibid.*, p. 124).

[15] Measured in terms of labour income per man based on total days of education (*ibid.*, pp. 52 and 55).

[16] 76 per cent of 52 per cent (*ibid.*, p. 55).

[17] 0.40 per cent of 1.67 per cent. Bertram explains some possible bias inherent in this type of calculation (*ibid.*, pp. 55 and 115-121).

1929-1957 — Per cent

Contribution of Improvements in Education to	Canada [18]	United States [19]
Productivity per employed person	20.0	42.0
Real national income	11.4	23.0

The estimates suggest that the lesser resources devoted by Canada to the development of education, referred to earlier, has resulted in education making a smaller contribution to economic growth in this country than in the United States, about one-half of the American figure over approximately three decades. Comparing the situation between Canada and the United States, the Economic Council of Canada observed that the "greater contribution of education to growth in the United States indicates that education has apparently been a factor tending to widen rather than narrow differences in income and productivity between the two countries". [20]

The Council concluded :

> Very considerable scope would appear to exist in Canada to promote the growth of average per capita income by improving the educational stock of the labour force. The accumulating evidence and analysis suggest that the benefits from such improvements can be substantial for both the individuals and the economy as a whole. [21]

In fact, the Economic Council of Canada has presented evidence supporting the claim that education was becoming a more important factor in increasing the rate of economic growth in Canada.

The contribution of education as a factor input to the annual rate of increase of real net national income averaged 0.3 per cent out of a total increase of 3.6 per cent for the period 1955-1962. This contribution to the growth of national income, according to estimates prepared by the Economic Council, was likely to rise to 0.5 per cent out of a total increase of 4.6 per cent over the period 1970-1975. [22] This would mean that education

---

[18]   *Ibid.*, pp. 55 and 56.
[19]   *The Sources of Economic Growth in the United States and the Alternative Before Us, op. cit.,* p. 73.
[20]   *Towards Sustained and Balanced Economic Growth, op. cit.,* p. 93.
[21]   *Ibid.*
[22]   *The Canadian Economy From the 1960's to the 1970's, op. cit.,* p. 91.

which contributed about 8 per cent to the annual average increase in real national income during the period 1955-1962 would contribute approximately 11 per cent during the period 1970-1975. [23] Concluded the Economic Council :

> The result will be that the contribution of education to growth in Canada will move up into the range of the contribution which it has been making to growth in the United States in recent years. Moreover [. . .] the Canada — U.S. differences in the educational attainments of younger people coming into the labour force will be narrowing in the future. [24]

The contribution which education can make in increasing productivity may under favourable circumstances be even more pronounced than its contribution to raising the annual rate of increase of real national income. This can be illustrated by reference to changes in Gross National Product in constant dollars per person employed. Bearing in mind that such data represent an oversimplification of measurement, [25] the Economic Council has presented estimates which illustrate the growing contribution that can be expected as education and training begins to pay off in economic terms.

Education is estimated to have contributed 0.3 per cent to the annual increase in real Gross National Product per person employed, totalling 1.5 per cent, as the average for the period 1955-1962. [26] During the period 1970-1975, according to estima-

---

[23]   That is 0.3 as per cent of 3.6 and 0.5 as per cent of 4.6.

[24]   *Ibid.*, p. 93.

[25]   Changes in real Gross National Product per man-hour would be a preferable measurement to take account of variations in the numbers of hours worked per week.   Nevertheless, the Gross National Product data per person working, that is per man-year, appear to be a reasonable indicator of productivity changes since the Economic Council assumed the same annual average percentage change of —0.2 due to reduction in hours worked, for both the 1955-1962 and 1970-1975 periods (*ibid.*, p. 95).

[26]   The major factor contributing to the increase in real Gross National Product per person employed was the "residual", involving 1.0 per cent for the period 1955-1962 and 1.1 per cent for the period 1970-1975.   Many elements affect this residual, including "all those factors which have a bearing on the efficient use of labour and capital inputs — shifts of resources from lower to higher productivity uses; advancing industrial technology and knowledge; increased scale and specialization in production; changes in the mobility and adaptability of labour and other productive resources under changing economic conditions; changes in attitudes, efforts and enterprise of both managements and labour; and a whole host of other factors, including environmental and institutional factors, affecting many different facets of economic activity" (*ibid.*).

tes presented by the Economic Council, the ratio is expected to rise to 0.6 per cent contributing to a total increase of 2 per cent per annum. [27] This suggests an increase in the relative contribution of education to productivity improvements from 20 per cent in the 1955-1962 period to 30 per cent in the 1970-1975 period. [28]

INDUSTRIAL AND HUMAN DEVELOPMENT

The evidence presented in this study supports the claim that Canada has reached the stage of development where economic advancement in the future depends to a greater extent than ever before on increasing the stock of educational capital. This country has now the resources to devote a much greater proportion of its productive capacity to education if it recognizes the necessity and has the will to do so. Failure to expand the stock of educational capital at an *adequate* rate is likely to stunt Canada's economic growth rate, as well as affect the quality of the growth process.

The point is that a country can only achieve full development in industrial terms if it also achieves full development in human terms. Hence, educational underdevelopment is a major retarding factor in the economic growth process, and growth and development policies without appropriate educational and training programmes and priorities are bound to bring less than the desired results.

Denison's estimates have been subject to a number of critical assessments [29] and they have brought forth a spirited rejoinder from the author. [30] Denison himself admitted that he had no illusions that "specific estimates are other than crude" [31] while Bertram emphasized the "preliminary" character of his estimates. [32]

---

[27] *Ibid.*
[28] That is 0.3 as per cent of 1.5 and 0.6 as per cent of 2.0.
[29] See for example Comments by Friedrich Edding, Edmond Malinvaud, Erik Lundberg, and J. Sandee, in *The Residual Factor and Economic Growth, op. cit.*, pp. 56-76.
[30] *Ibid.*, pp. 77-85.
[31] *Ibid.*, p. 85.
[32] *The Contribution of Education to Economic Growth, op. cit.*, p. 4.

Nevertheless the Denison estimates for the United States and eight West European countries, [33] and the Bertram estimates for Canada, the latter covering a more limited area, present a significant step forward in the search of finding ways and means to quantify the effects of education and other factors on economic growth and development. The hope is that future progress in this field can be telescoped so that social scientists can come forward with an answer on a systematic and theoretically consistent basis to the pressing question : What contribution can education make to change the age of scarcity to the age of abundance — for the individual, for the nation and for the world community ?

That this is a very difficult task is indicated by the following statement of one scholar who stresses that measurement of economic phenomena alone is not enough and that there is need to do more theoretical work to establish *why* education furthers economic growth and development.

> Though several have made the effort, as yet no one has been able to isolate quantitatively the role of education in economic growth, for no one has been able to establish a context which removes all normative aspects from measurement of the internal rate of return and the effect of education upon growth. Furthermore, excessive preoccupation by most economists with the problems of statistical measurement has caused them to neglect questions of reform and, by indicating that the return from education is substantial, may have obscured the need for increasing the efficiency of the existing system of education. Whatever the cause, economists working on problems of measurement have failed to state comprehensively just why they think education promotes economic growth. [34]

CONCLUSION

To draw together six general conclusions as they relate to education and economic growth, developed in this study:

1. Education is an engine of economic growth. Increasingly, theoretical analysis and empirical evidence suggest the possibility that investment in human capital of which education

---

[33] Edward F. DENISON, assisted by Jean-Pierre POULLIER, *Why Growth Rates Differ, Postwar Experience in Nine Western Countries*, Washington, D.C., The Brookings Institution, 1967.
[34] William L. MILLER, "Education as a Source of Economic Growth", in *Journal of Economic Issues*, Vol. I, No. 4, December 1967, p. 296.

is a major means, may bring society greater returns than investment in physical capital.

2. Education and economic growth are interrelated. Education contributes to the expansion of knowledge, which, if
applied effectively, facilitates economic growth, economic development and economic progress, and it creates the educated
manpower, essential to translate potential economic growth into
actual economic growth of an adequate rate on a continuing
and sustainable basis. As the nation's economic resources
expand, more of these both in absolute and in relative terms
can be devoted to education. Thus a perpetual process is set
into motion. More economic growth may permit more education.
More education may speed up the rate of economic growth.

3. Education is a major factor of assisting the breaking
down of the barriers of economic development and economic
progress. Such barriers may be particularly numerous when a
country is in an early stage of economic development and they
may include the lack of an adequate private and public infra-
structure, traditional beliefs and limiting social and cultural
attitudes leading to resistance to change and innovations, inadequate training and experience of the working and managerial
classes, etc. In such a situation, education, if wisely evolved
and appropriately applied, can substitute forward-looking enlightenment for restrictive ignorance.

4. Education, by contributing to increasing knowledge and
enhancing the stock of human capital may increase the mobility
of human capital and its substitution for physical capital, and
vice versa. Mechanization replaces certain routine manual
functions. Certain skills are developed higher up the ladder of
technical knowledge to operate the machines. Automation follows, with advanced types of equipment and processes replacing
certain routine thinking and supervision. Again man climbs up
the ladder of knowledge to construct new types of equipment,
to create new human wants and to push back the frontiers of
material and non-material achievements.

5. Education contributes to structural changes, all the way
from altering the industrial mix (change in industrial structure)
to dividing the nation's output as between different uses (that is
altering the composition of Gross National Expenditure) and
among different users (that is altering the composition of Gross

National Product including a redistribution of income). In turn, changes in economic structure may affect education. In part, this is due to the fact that changes in industrial structure will frequently lead to productivity improvements which make it possible for society to change its sense of values and to establish priorities to devote increasing resources to tasks that may in an earlier age have been somewhat neglected, and this is particularly true in the case of educational efforts. In part this is due to advancing educational technology which makes mass education both possible and more effective.

6. Education opens new horizons for human progress. It also makes man more aware of the limitations of his potential at a given point of time. For there is a rate of economic growth beyond which even the greatest advances in knowledge do not yield tangible results for the present — though they may do so at some stage in the future. There is the further point that as society becomes more affluent, education offers man increasing opportunities for creativeness and fulfilment of human aspirations. But at the same time man becomes more conscious of the inadequacies of a system that permits widespread poverty in the midst of plenty, uncared illness in the midst of revolutionary progress in the health sciences, ignorance and illiteracy in the midst of great advances in educational facilities and teaching techniques, lack of adequate economic opportunities and discrimination in the midst of full employment and rising standards of living, political strife and military conflict among nations in the midst of increasing goodwill among men and the growing understanding that world peace and universal prosperity are indivisible.

There is a positive aspect of man's growing recognition of his limitations, and that is to conquer the three F's of human frailty : Failure, Fear and Frustration. It represents a challenge to his ingenuity and creativeness. And the better man becomes educated, the better he is equipped to understand his destiny and to realize his potential.

CHAPITRE 22

Sommaire

1. *Effet double de l'éducation.* — La IIe partie de cet
ouvrage établit les relations entre l'éducation et la croissance,
l'essor et le progrès économiques en termes d'ensemble, de
structures et de micro-économique, durant le premier centenaire
de l'expérience canadienne. L'éducation est considérée comme
un facteur d'intrant; c'est-à-dire, la connaissance résultant d'une
éducation plus poussée augmente la capacité de production qui,
lorsqu'elle est pleinement utilisée, va donner un plus grand
rendement. Elle est également considérée comme un facteur
contribuant à augmenter la demande de marchandises et de
services, ainsi que le désir de loisirs plus longs. On y souligne
la double fonction de l'éducation, son effet sur l'offre et la
demande, ainsi que sa contribution au progrès culturel et social.

2. *Causes et effets.* — On y examine l'éducation comme
cause et effet de la croissance, de l'essor et du progrès économiques, ainsi que son rapport à l'amélioration de la qualité de
la main-d'œuvre, en augmentant le rendement et en activant
le rythme de la croissance économique et des améliorations
dans la physionomie de l'essor économique. Lentement et
graduellement, la société passe de l'âge de la pénurie à celui
d'une pénurie moindre, puis se dirige vers un stade proche de
l'abondance, pour atteindre enfin l'âge de l'abondance, quant
à l'ensemble — bien qu'à ce stade, la pauvreté puisse continuer
en certaines régions et que certaines ressources puissent être
encore sous-utilisées, comme cela se passe aujourd'hui au milieu
de l'opulente société des États-Unis. A mesure que l'économie
devient plus prospère, une plus grande abondance de ressources
peuvent être et sont habituellement consacrées à l'éducation.
Les résultats de tels efforts accrus — une population plus
instruite et mieux qualifiée — contribuent à leur tour à accélerer
le processus de la croissance qui est déjà amorcé. Cet ouvrage
scrute les relations sans cesse changeantes entre l'éducation,
la science et la croissance économique.

3. *Stades de la croissance économique.* — Comme cadres
de cette enquête, nous utilisons les cinq stades de Rostow,

l'évolution des structures industrielles de Colin Clark et le processus de croissance de Simon Kuznets, tel qu'expliqué dans ses études comparatives d'ensemble sur la croissance économique à l'échelle internationale. Appliqués au Canada, les cinq stades peuvent se définir ainsi : la société traditionnelle, 1605-1867; la préparation au démarrage, 1867-1896; le démarrage, 1896-1914; la poussée vers la maturité, 1914-1950; l'âge de la consommation de masse et de la maturité technologique, 1950-1968 (actuellement en cours). Le premier stade s'étend sur toute la période coloniale, durant laquelle l'éducation a exercé peu d'influence sur le mode de développement de ce qui fut, durant presque toute la période, une société de pionniers. Le dernier siècle contient toute l'histoire de la croissance du Canada en tant que nation. Durant cette période, l'éducation a contribué largement à l'essor économique; cet apport a varié grandement en intensité et en qualité au cours des quatre stades de l'histoire économique.

4. *L'éducation et l'essor économique.* — 1° Durant le stade de préparation au départ, 1867-1896, le taux annuel moyen de croissance de la population fut de 1,4% et celui du produit national brut de 3,3%, en termes de valeur réelle, alors que le coût par tête de l'éducation s'est élevé de $1 à $2,50. La proportion du coût de l'éducation, comparée à la production nationale brute, s'est élevée de moins de 1% qu'elle était en 1867, à 1¼% en 1896. Durant cette période, le niveau des prix a peu changé. 2° Durant le stade de démarrage, 1896-1914, le taux de l'accroissement annuel de la population fut de 2,4% et celui du produit national brut, de 3,7%, en termes de la valeur réelle. La proportion du revenu national consacrée à l'éducation s'est accrue lentement, atteignant 2% en 1914, le coût de l'éducation par tête s'élevant environ à $7. Durant cette période, les prix ont monté considérablement, soit environ 50%, de sorte que les $2,50 dépensés en 1896 étaient équivalents à un pouvoir d'achat de $3,75 en 1914. 3° Durant le stade de la poussée vers la maturité, 1914-1950, le taux moyen d'accroissement annuel de la population fut de 1,5%; celui du produit national brut, de 3%, en termes de la valeur réelle. La proportion du coût de l'éducation par rapport au produit national brut, s'est élevée de 2 à 2,6%. Cette proportion a fluctué notablement au

cours de la période : 2,7% en 1926, 4,2% en 1933, au plus
fort de la grande dépression économique, 2,7% en 1939, au
début de la Deuxième Grande Guerre; 1,5% en 1944, l'année
de pointe de l'effort de guerre. Le coût par tête de l'éducation
a passé de $7 en 1914 à $15 en 1926. Si l'on tient compte
de la majoration des prix — 55% — durant cette période,
les $7 dépensés par tête en 1914 équivalaient à $11 en 1926.
Durant les deux décennies suivantes, le coût per capita de
l'éducation a passé de $14 à $16. Étant donné que les prix
ont monté d'environ 12% entre 1926 et 1945, il ressort que
les Canadiens dépensaient proportionnellement moins par tête
pour l'éducation à la fin de la Deuxième Grande Guerre, qu'ils
ne le faisaient au milieu des années 1920. 4° Durant le
stade de la consommation de masse et de la maturité technologique, 1950-1968 (actuellement en cours), l'économie du
Canada s'est développée à un rythme beaucoup plus accéléré
que dans les périodes précédentes de son histoire économique
et l'éducation a connu une transformation extraordinaire.
Durant cette période, le taux annuel d'accroissement de la
population fut de 2,3% ; celui du produit national brut,
4,5% en termes de valeur réelle. La proportion du coût
de l'éducation, de 2,6% qu'elle était en 1950, s'est élevée
à 5% en 1961, à 6,5% en 1966 et à 6,7% en 1967. Durant
cette période, prise dans son ensemble, le coût par tête de
l'éducation a passé de $34 à un peu plus de $200. Si l'on
tient compte de l'augmentation de 61% du niveau général
des prix, le coût par tête de l'éducation a été quatre fois plus
élevé, en termes de valeur réelle, en 1967 qu'en 1950.

5. *Taux de l'accroissement durant le premier siècle.* —
Si l'on compare le produit national brut, en termes de la valeur
réelle, avec les statistiques sur les revenus des écoles publiques, primaires et secondaires, représentant entre 60 et 70%
du coût total de l'éducation, pour la plupart des années — ces
revenus étant réduits à l'échelle des prix en conformité avec les
dépenses nationales brutes — on obtient le pourcentage suivant
de fluctuation de l'accroissement annuel (composé) pour les
quatre stades de Rostow, ainsi que pour l'ensemble du siècle :

	Produit national brut	*Revenu des écoles*
1867-1896	3,3	3,5
1896-1914	3,7	3,7
1914-1950	3,0	1,9
1950-1967	4,5	9,5
1867-1967	3,5	3,1

6. *Variations aux différents stades.* — Durant la première moitié du siècle, le Canada a consacré à l'éducation entre 1 et 2% de son produit national brut. Cette proportion s'éleva lentement durant les trente-cinq années suivantes pour atteindre un peu plus de 2½% en 1950. C'est seulement lorsque le Canada eut atteint le stade de la maturité technologique et de la très grande consommation (selon le sens de l'expression employé par de Rostow), que le pays réussit à élever notablement cette proportion, soit 7% en 1967.

7. *Causes de ces variations.* — 1° La concurrence serrée dans l'utilisation de ressources limitées nécessaires à la création d'une production adéquate et à l'élaboration d'une infrastructure sociale (autre que l'éducation); 2° le peu d'importance que le public et les gouvernements attachaient à l'éducation durant les huit premières décennies; 3° on ne reconnaissait pas suffisamment les avantages économiques de l'éducation, durant cette période initiale; 4° au début, le besoin de personnel instruit et qualifié était satisfait au moyen de l'immigration, puis le besoin se fit sentir de plus en plus de personnel entraîné au pays, car l'industrialisation et le progrès technique menaçaient de retarder la croissance économique, à moins d'obtenir plus d'ouvriers qualifiés que l'immigration n'en pouvait fournir; 5° le « drainage » vers les États-Unis des savants et des techniciens; 6° la concurrence internationale croissante dans le commerce et les autres domaines économiques, à laquelle on ne pouvait faire face qu'en accélérant constamment le taux du rendement national, ce dernier étant affecté à son tour par le niveau d'éducation atteint par la main-d'œuvre canadienne; 7° une pléiade de facteurs étrangers au domaine économique : facteurs culturels, linguistiques (le Canada est un pays bilingue, français et anglais), sociaux, institutionnels, constitutionnels, légaux et politiques (comprenant le processus lent de la séparation de l'Église et de l'État en matière d'éducation, le retard causé par le système des écoles confessionnelles et l'accent donné aux humanités dans les institutions de haut savoir cédant lentement la place à une plus grande orientation scientifique).

8. *Période d'attente du rendement de l'éducation.* — L'aventure canadienne enseigne que tant qu'une nation n'est pas devenue complètement industrialisée, elle peut ne pas être en mesure ou ne pas éprouver le désir d'accorder à l'éducation la primauté requise pour consacrer une large partie de ses maigres ressources à certains perfectionnements humains susceptibles de produire, dans quelques décennies, d'intéressants résultats dans le domaine économique. Dans le domaine de l'éducation, la période d'attente du rendement est beaucoup plus longue que dans le domaine social ou dans celui des affaires. Il semble qu'une des principales raisons pour lesquelles le Canada, durant les huit premières décennies, n'a consacré à l'éducation qu'une petite partie de son revenu national brut, soit le peu d'importance qu'on lui a attaché; mais dans les deux dernières décennies, les idées ont évolué. La planification à long terme nous a conduit à miser avec une insistance croissante sur le capital humain, malgré les périodes plus étendues d'attente du rendement.

9. *Démarrage en éducation.* — Sans prétendre que l'expérience canadienne s'applique aux autres nations en voie de développement par suite des grandes différences qui existent dans la culture, les traditions, le système politique et les autres domaines non économiques, ainsi que l'état du développement économique, qu'on nous permette l'énoncé suivant : le rythme du progrès économique et de l'accroissement de la productivité semble imposer à tout pays des limites à sa capacité d'accélérer l'amélioration de ses ressources humaines par l'éducation. Bien que le progrès très accéléré puisse être attribué à la fois à l'aide venue de l'extérieur et à la grande importance attachée à l'éducation, il n'en reste pas moins vrai que la période initiale d'attente du rendement de l'éducation et de l'entrainement professionnel est longue, et que la transformation d'une société à économie traditionnelle en une nation industrialisée capable d'absorber les produits de l'éducation et de les rénumérer raisonnablement, requière beaucoup de temps. Il ressort de l'aventure canadienne que le progrès de l'éducation et l'accroissement économique marchent de pair durant les quatre premiers stades du développement économique, et que le véritable démarrage en éducation survient au stade de la maturité technologique et de la consommation de masse. Durant la seconde moitié du XXᵉ siècle, les pays moins développés vont avoir à relever

un défi : décider s'ils doivent réduire l'écart de cinquante ans qui existe entre ce qu'elles veulent faire et ce qu'elles peuvent réaliser dans le domaine de l'éducation et du progrès économique, et comment elles doivent s'y prendre. Dans leurs efforts pour ajuster leurs aspirations à la réalité, ces pays méritent la compréhension et l'aide des nations à l'aise.

10. *Inscriptions plus nombreuses dans les écoles, dans l'ensemble.* — Durant le dernier siècle le taux moyen annuel d'accroissement des inscriptions d'élèves dans les écoles publiques primaires et secondaires a été de 2%. Les taux d'accroissement ont été relativement bas durant le 2ᵉ stade, celui de la préparation au départ, 1867-1896, soit 1,3%, et durant le 4ᵉ stade, celui de la poussée vers la maturité, 1914-1950, soit 1,2%. Ces taux furent un peu plus élevé durant la période d'immigration en masse, au début du siècle, coïncidant avec le 3ᵉ stade, celui du démarrage, 1896-1914, soit 2,2%, et ils ont atteint leur plus haut point durant le 5ᵉ stade, l'ère de la consommation de masse, 1950-1968 (encore en cours), soit 4,6%.

11. *Inscriptions plus nombreuses de la population d'âge scolaire dans les écoles.* — Les statistiques disponibles pour la période de 1921 à 1961 indiquent une tendance à procurer une éducation plus poussée aux jeunes. Durant cette période, les inscriptions dans les écoles publiques primaires et secondaires se sont accrues selon les taux moyens annuels suivants : groupes d'âges de 5 à 9 ans et de 10 à 14 ans, environ 2%; de 15 à 19 ans, environ 4%; et de 20 à 24 ans, environ 4,6%.

12. *Durée plus longue de la scolarité.* — Les statistiques suivantes montrent que le Canada a accru de deux cinquièmes le capital éducationnel de ses travailleurs durant le dernier demi-siècle. De 6,60 qu'il était en 1911, le nombre moyen des années passées à l'école s'est élevé à 9,15 en 1961.

13. *Plus grande assiduité à l'école.* — La moyenne quotidienne des présences à l'école, de 53% qu'elle était en 1867, s'est accrue à 93% en 1967. A l'époque de la Confédération, chaque élève était présent à l'école moins de 100 jours par année en moyenne; en 1967, 186 jours en moyenne. Cette assiduité presque doublée semble avoir été un facteur important de l'accroissement du capital éducationnel.

14. *Plus grande importance attachée au haut savoir.* — Entre 1911 et 1961, le nombre des travailleurs de sexe masculin entre 24 et 65 ans ayant fréquenté l'université s'est accru plus rapidement que celui de tout autre groupe ayant un degré inférieur d'éducation, comme le montre la statistique suivante donnant divers taux annuels d'accroissement : personnes n'ayant pas dépassé la 8ᵉ année d'école primaire, 0,8% ; personnes ayant fréquenté l'école secondaire durant 1 à 4 années, 3% ; personnes ayant fréquenté l'université quelque temps (y compris celles qui ont terminé la 13ᵉ année), 5,7% ; personnes ayant obtenu un grade universitaire, 3,5%.

15. *Qualité accrue de l'enseignement.* — La proportion entre le nombre des élèves et celui des professeurs pourrait nous fournir un indice de l'amélioration de la qualité de l'enseignement. Le nombre moyen d'élèves par classe est descendu de 60 en 1867 à 40 en 1896, à 34 en 1914, à 27 en 1950 et à environ 24 en 1967. Le nombre des instituteurs comparé au nombre total des salariés illustre les changements survenus à différentes périodes dans l'utilisation des ressources en faveur de l'éducation : en 1867, 1,14% ; en 1896, 1,54% ; en 1915, 1,60% ; en 1950, 1,75% ; en 1967, 2,78%. Cet accroissement durant la période de maturité technologique et de consommation de masse, 1950-1967, est tout à fait spectaculaire.

16. *Effets sur les gains passés.* — Durant la période de 1911 à 1961, l'accroissement du revenu moyen par personne dû à l'augmentation de la durée des études au Canada, fut de 12%. Le taux de l'accroissement entre 1951 et 1961 ne fut que d'environ 2¼%. Comment expliquer cette lenteur dans l'amélioration du revenu malgré que le Canada ait connu une amélioration rapide dans le domaine de l'éducation en rapport avec l'accroissement du produit national brut, en termes de la valeur réelle ? Cela prend beaucoup de temps avant que les placements dans les ressources humaines ne produisent une amélioration de la productivité et, par suite, une augmentation du revenu national soit dans l'ensemble, soit par personne.

17. *Effets sur les revenus prévus.* — Les calculs fondés sur le recensement de 1961 permettent de prévoir les différents niveaux suivants de revenus qui pourraient être accumulés la vie durant, avant déduction des impôts, par l'ouvrier canadien moyen de sexe masculin, âgé de 15 à 64 ans, ne travaillant pas sur la ferme :

	Total en dollars (milliers de dollars)	Total escompté à 5% (milliers de dollars)
École primaire, 5 à 8 ans	152	48
École secondaire, 4 à 5 ans	222	64
Grade universitaire	356	92
Pourcentage de différence entre la scolarité et le grade universitaire	134	92

18. *Rendement des placements dans l'éducation.* — En utilisant des méthodes semblables à celles que Gary S. Becker et W. Lee Hansen ont élaborées, compte tenu des dépenses encourues par les particuliers en vue de l'éducation ainsi que des revenus prévus, on peut estimer que le rendement des placements en éducation se situe entre 16 et 20% selon le niveau d'éducation atteint. Si l'on y ajoute les dépenses encourues par la société, le rendement se situe entre 10 et 15%. Même calculé avant toute déduction d'impôts, ce rendement est supérieur à celui des placements en valeurs matérielles ou financières.

19. *Gain net dans les placements pour l'éducation en rapport avec l'immigration et l'émigration.* — Si l'on compare l'exode du capital éducationnel avec l'apport de l'immigration, le Canada a enregistré un gain net durant la plus grande partie du siècle dernier. La statistique suivante illustre le gain net durant la période de 1951 à 1961, quant au coût total à l'étranger pour l'entraînement des immigrants et au Canada pour celui des émigrants.

	Immigrants (millions de dollars)	Émigrants (millions de dollars)	Gain net (millions de dollars)
Personnel professionnel	1.403	336- 594	809-1.067
Autres travailleurs	2.924	313- 555	2.369-2.611
Total pour les travailleurs	4.327	649-1.149	3.178-3.678
Membres de la famille	1.563	330- 580	983-1.233
Total	5.890	979-1.729	4.161-4.911

20. *Édification du capital éducationnel au Canada et aux États-Unis.* — Durant la plus grande partie du XX° siècle, le produit national brut par tête du Canada est demeuré inférieur à celui des États-Unis dans la proportion d'environ 25%. Le capital éducationnel a été édifié aux États-Unis plus rapidement qu'au Canada. Voici quelques exemples : 1° de 1910 à 1960, le nombre moyen d'années pendant lesquelles un tra-

vailleur de sexe masculin a fréquenté l'école s'est accru d'environ 9 à 10% par décennie aux États-Unis, tandis qu'il ne s'est accru que de 5 à 8% au Canada; 2° en 1961-1962, la moyenne des années de scolarité des travailleurs de sexe masculin âgés de 25 à 54 ans était de 20 à 25% plus élevée aux États-Unis qu'au Canada; 3° en 1960-1961, environ 11% des travailleurs de sexe masculin aux États-Unis avaient obtenu un grade universitaire, alors que le pourcentage n'était que de 5,5 au Canada; et l'écart semblait vouloir s'élargir, si l'on considère que 45% des personnes âgées de 25 à 34 ans avaient reçu une éducation secondaire ou supérieure aux États-Unis, alors que la proportion n'était que de 24% au Canada; 4° entre 1911 et 1961, le revenu individuel, si on ne tient compte que d'ouvriers ayant le même niveau scolaire, a augmenté deux fois plus vite aux États-Unis, soit 21,2% comparé à 12% au Canada. L'effet cumulatif de ces écarts est particulièrement sensible durant la période de 1951 à 1961, alors que le revenu individuel des travailleurs, tenant compte d'ouvriers ayant atteint le même niveau de scolarité, a augmenté de 4,7% aux États-Unis et de 2,3% au Canada, soit plus du double.

21. *Répercussions au Canada des réalisations aux États-Unis dans le domaine de l'éducation.* — L'éducation aux États-Unis a exercé une double influence sur le progrès au Canada: négative et positive. Parmi les effets négatifs on compte l'exode massif de personnel instruit, le retard dans la recherche et dans le progrès scientifique qui s'ensuivit et la diminution des possibilités d'amélioration de la productivité. Les effets positifs comprennent « le témoignage » des réalisations dans l'éducation, le partage des connaissances résultant de la recherche, théorique et appliquée, l'opportunité offerte à plusieurs Canadiens de profiter directement des progrès réalisés par les États-Unis dans l'éducation. On pourrait objecter qu'il n'est pas nécessaire qu'un petit pays comme le Canada marche de pair avec les progrès des États-Unis en éducation, et qu'il serait plus convenable qu'il progresse à son allure propre. Mais par suite de la diffusion internationale de l'éducation et de l'influence croissante du « témoignage », les Canadiens ont jugé nécessaire, durant la dernière période, d'intensifier leurs efforts pour diminuer l'écart qui existe entre le Canada et les États-Unis dans le domaine des réalisations en éducation, et ces efforts se continuent.

22. *Effets sur la croissance économique.* — En se basant sur les méthodes élaborées par Edward F. Dennison, des statistiques ont été préparées sur l'apport de l'éducation au progrès économique, au Canada et aux États-Unis de 1929 à 1957 :

	Canada (pourcentage)	États-Unis (pourcentage)
Rapport du progrès dans l'éducation		
à la productivité, par personne employée	20,0	42,0
a'ı revenu national réel	11,4	23,0

Les statistiques indiquent que les ressources moindres consacrées par le Canada à l'éducation ont fourni au progrès économique de ce pays un apport deux fois moindre qu'aux États-Unis. Cependant, cet état de choses est en train de changer et il semble que le Canada va réussir durant la décennie de 1965 à 1975, à diminuer l'écart passé entre ses réalisations en éducation et celles des États-Unis.

23. *Lacunes de cette analyse.* — Cette étude comprend un certain nombre de statistiques annuelles embrassant la période de 1867 à 1967, données dans l'appendice A. Afin de compléter les données provenant de sources officielles, à partir de 1925 jusqu'à nos jours, nous avons ajouté des statistiques pour la période de 1867-1925, quelquefois pour chaque année, d'autres fois pour des intervalles de cinq ou dix ans. Les sources, la qualité et les lacunes de ces statistiques sont décrites dans l'Appendice B. Mises à part les imperfections des statistiques, cette étude s'attache aux aspects économiques de l'apport de l'éducation au progrès et met ainsi de côté plusieurs facteurs sociaux, culturels et politiques très importants. Cette étude constitue le stade préliminaire de l'enquête sur les répercussions économiques de l'éducation sur le progrès au Canada. Les calculs ont été fondés principalement sur des méthodes élaborées aux États-Unis. Les méthodes d'analyse dans ce domaine n'en sont encore qu'au début de leur élaboration, malgré les travaux remarquables de Théodore W. Schultz et d'Edward F. Dennison. Il est à espérer que le progrès dans ce domaine sera accéléré, afin que les experts en sciences sociales puissent apporter bientôt à cette question urgente, une réponse appuyée sur un fondement méthodique et théoriquement cohérent : Quelle contribution l'éducation peut-elle apporter à la progression de l'ère de la pénurie à l'ère de l'abondance, pour l'individu, pour la nation et pour la communauté mondiale ?

24. *Conclusion.* — On peut tirer six conclusions générales mettant en rapport l'éducation et le progrès économique. 1. L'éducation est un facteur de progrès économique. La société peut obtenir un meilleur rendement des placements dans le capital humain que dans le capital matériel. 2. L'éducation et la croissance économique sont intimement liés. Une plus grande croissance économique permet une meilleure éducation et une meilleure éducation accélère le rythme du progrès économique. 3. L'éducation est un des principaux moyens de briser les barrières qui entravent l'évolution économique et le progrès social. Si on la fait progresser sagement et si on l'utilise à bon escient, l'éducation permet de remplacer l'ignorance restrictive par la connaissance lumineuse et prévoyante. 4. L'éducation, en contribuant à augmenter les connaissances et à valoriser le capital humain, peut augmenter la disponibilité de ce capital humain et sa possibilité de substitution au capital physique, et vice versa. 5. L'éducation contribue aux changements de structures, à partir de l'enchevêtrement industriel jusqu'au partage du rendement national entre les différents usages et les différents usagers. A leur tour, les changements dans les structures économiques peuvent affecter l'éducation. 6. L'éducation ouvre de nouveaux horizons au progrès humain. Elle rend aussi l'homme plus conscient des limites de ses capacités à tel moment donné. Se rendre de plus en plus compte de ses limites, comporte pour l'homme l'avantage de vaincre les trois grandes faiblesses de la fragilité humaine : l'insuccès, la crainte et la frustration. C'est un défi à son ingéniosité et à son génie créateur. Plus l'homme est éduqué, mieux il est préparé à comprendre sa destinée et à prendre conscience de ses capacités.

Basic Tabular Material

TABLE 1. — POPULATION, LABOUR FORCE, EMPLOYMENT, GROSS NATIONAL PRODUCT IN CURRENT AND CONSTANT DOLLARS, AND IMPLIED PRICE INDEX, CANADA, 1867-1967.

YEAR	POPULATION[1] Thous.	LABOUR-FORCE[2] Thous.	EMPLOYMENT[2] Thous.	GROSS NATIONAL PRODUCT $ Mill.			GROSS NATIONAL PRODUCT IN CONSTANT DOLLARS	
				Current Dollars[3] Mill.	Constant Dollars[3] Mill.	Implied Price Index[4]	Per Capita	Per Person Working
1867	3,463	1,104	1,060	365[5]	1,535	23.8	443	1,448
1868	3,511	—	—	—	1,537[5]	—	438	—
1869	3,565	—	—	—	1,567[5]	—	439	—
1870	3,625	1,166	1,119	390[5]	1,647	23.7	454	—
1871	3,689	—	—	—	1,697	—	460	—
1872	3,754	—	—	—	1,426	—	380	—
1873	3,826	—	—	—	1,567	—	410	—
1874	3,895	—	—	—	1,888	—	485	—
1875	3,954	—	—	—	1,828	—	462	—
1876	4,009	—	—	—	1,838	—	458	—
1877	4,064	—	—	—	1,888	—	465	—
1878	4,120	—	—	—	1,858	—	451	—
1879	4,185	—	—	—	2,179	—	521	—
1880	4,255	1,429	1,343	564[5]	2,420	23.3	569	1,802
1881	4,325	—	—	—	2,752	—	636	—
1882	4,375	—	—	—	2,732	—	624	—
1883	4,430	—	—	—	2,682	—	605	—
1884	4,487	—	—	—	2,953	—	658	—
1885	4,537	—	—	—	3,274	—	722	—
1886	4,580	—	—	—	2,953	—	645	—
1887	4,626	—	—	—	2,963	—	641	—
1888	4,678	—	—	—	3,113	—	665	—
1889	4,729	—	—	—	3,033	—	641	—
1890	4,779	1,675	1,591	719[5]	3,113	23.1	651	1,957
1891	4,833	—	—	—	3,626	—	750	—
1892	4,883	—	—	—	3,545	—	726	—
1893	4,931	—	—	—	3,455	—	701	—
1894	4,979	—	—	—	3,425	—	688	—
1895	5,026				3,615		719	
1896	5,074	1,780[5]	1,704[5]	875[5]	3,957	22.1	780	2,322
1897	5,122	—	—	—	3,445	—	673	—
1898	5,175	—	—	—	4,077	—	788	—
1899	5,235	—	—	—	3,907	—	746	—
1900	5,301	1,861	1,787	999[5]	4,078	24.5	769	2,282
1901	5,371	—	—	—	4,489	—	836	—
1902	5,494	—	—	—	4,811	—	876	—
1903	5,651	—	—	—	4,951	—	876	—
1904	5,827	—	—	—	5,042	—	865	—
1905	6,002	—	—	—	5,423	—	904	

TABLE 1. — POPULATION, LABOUR FORCE, EMPLOYMENT, GROSS
NATIONAL PRODUCT IN CURRENT AND CONSTANT DOLLARS,
AND IMPLIED PRICE INDEX, CANADA, 1867-1967. *(Continued.)*

YEAR	POPULA-TION [1] Thous.	LABOUR-FORCE [2] Thous.	EMPLOY-MENT [2] Thous.	GROSS NATIONAL PRODUCT $ Mill.			GROSS NATIONAL PRODUCT IN CONSTANT DOLLARS	
				Current Dollars [3] Mill.	Constant Dollars [3] Mill.	Implied Price Index [4]	Per Capita	Per Person Working
1906	6,097	—	—	—	5,735	—	941	—
1907	6,411	—	—	—	5,765	—	899	—
1908	6,625	—	—	—	6,016	—	908	—
1909	6,800	—	—	—	6,689	—	984	—
1910	6,988	2,801	2,717	2,059	6,819	30.2	976	2,510
1911	7,207	—	—	2,335	7,412	31.5	1,028	—
1912	7,389	—	—	2,477	7,552	32.8	1,022	—
1913	7,632	—	—	2,644	8,185	32.3	1,072	—
1914	7,879	3,090 [5]	2,900 [5]	2,546	7,693	33.1	976	2,653
1915	7,981	—	—	2,509	7,924	34.4	993	—
1916	8,001	—	—	3,169	8,275	38.3	1,034	—
1917	8,060	—	—	3,907	8,456	46.2	1,049	—
1918	8,148	—	—	4,405	8,537	51.6	1,048	—
1919	8,311	—	—	4,996	8,938	55.9	1,075	—
1920	8,556	3,229	3,164	5,355	8,486	64.1	992	—
1921	8,788	3,318	3,126	4,281	7,713	55.5	878	2,467
1922	8,919	3,385	3,235	4,240	8,346	50.8	936	2,580
1923	9,010	3,437	3,327	4,470	8,868	50.3	984	2,665
1924	9,143	3,506	3,348	4,456	8,858	50.3	969	2,646
1925	9,294	3,584	3,427	4,777	9,240	51.7	994	2,696
1926	9,451	3,663	3,555	5,152	10,043	51.3	1,063	2,825
1927	9,637	3,762	3,695	5,549	10,962	50.6	1,137	2,967
1928	9,835	3,866	3,801	6,046	11,996	50.4	1,220	3,156
1929	10,029	3,969	3,853	6,134	12,027	51.0	1,199	3,121
1930	10,208	4,066	3,695	5,728	11,525	49.7	1,129	3,119
1931	10,376	4,156	3,675	4,699	10,041	46.8	968	2,732
1932	10,510	4,216	3,475	3,827	9,026	42.4	859	2,597
1933	10,633	4,280	3,454	3,510	8,438	41.6	794	2,443
1934	10,741	4,343	3,712	3,984	9,463	42.1	881	2,549
1935	10,845	4,407	3,782	4,315	10,201	42.3	940	2,697
1936	10,950	4,472	3,901	4,653	10,648	43.7	972	2,730
1937	11,045	4,532	4,121	5,257	11,708	44.9	1,060	2,841
1938	11,152	4,595	4,073	5,278	11,781	44.8	1,056	2,892
1939	11,267	4,658	4,129	5,636	12,665	44.5	1,124	3,067
1940	11,381	4,714	4,291	6,743	14,470	46.6	1,271	3,372
1941	11,507	4,762	4,567	8,328	16,557	50.3	1,439	3,625
1942	11,054	4,961	4,826	10,327	19,633	52.6	1,776	4,068
1943	11,705	5,207	11,088	11,088	20,345	54.5	1,728	3,907
1944	11,946	5,327	5,264	11,850	21,085	56.2	1,765	4,006
1945	12,072	5,256	5,183	11,835	20,583	57.5	1,705	3,971
1946	12,292	4,954	4,791	11,850	20,187	58.7	1,642	4,214
1947	12,551	4,977	4,867	13,165	20,439	64.4	1,628	4,200
1948	12,823	5,024	4,911	15,120	20,821	72.6	1,624	4,240
1949 [6]	13,447	5,100	4,958	16,343	21,626	75.6	1,608	4,362

TABLE 1. — POPULATION, LABOUR FORCE, EMPLOYMENT, GROSS
NATIONAL PRODUCT IN CURRENT AND CONSTANT DOLLARS,
AND IMPLIED PRICE INDEX, CANADA, 1867-1967. *(Continued.)*

YEAR	POPULA-TION [1] Thous.	LABOUR-FORCE [2] Thous.	EMPLOY-MENT [2] Thous.	GROSS NATIONAL PRODUCT			GROSS NATIONAL PRODUCT IN CONSTANT DOLLARS	
				Cur-rent Dol-lars [3] Mill.	Con-stant Dol-lars [3] Mill.	Im-plied Price Index [4]	Per Capita	Per Person Work-ing
1950	13,712	5,216	5,029	18,006	23,114	77.9	1,686	4,596
1951	14,009	5,300	5,174	21,170	24,531	86.3	1,751	4,741
1952	14,459	5,421	5,266	23,995	26,514	90.5	1,834	5,035
1953	14,845	5,502	5,340	25,020	27,525	90.9	1,854	5,154
1954	15,287	5,607	5,357	24,871	26,714	93.1	1,747	4,987
1955	15,698	5,727	5,481	27,132	29,018	93.5	1,849	5,294
1956	16,081	5,899	5,702	30,585	31,508	97.1	1,959	5,526
1957	16,610	6,121	5,843	31,909	31,509	100.0	1,921	5,461
1958	17,080	6,247	5,810	32,894	32,284	101.9	1,890	5,557
1959	17,483	6,348	5,975	34,915	33,398	104.5	1,910	5,590
1960	17,870	6,530	6,084	36,287	34,200	106.1	1,914	5,621
1961	18,238	6,642	6,176	37,471	35,081	106.8	1,924	5,680
1962	18,583	6,741	6,351	40,575	37,429	108.4	2,014	5,893
1963	18,931	6,871	6,498	43,424	39,352	110.3	2,079	6,056
1964	19,290	7,053	6,729	47,393	41,876	113.2	2,171	6,223
1965	19,644	7,254	6,975	52,203	44,768	116.6	2,279	6,418
1966	20,015[7]	7,527	7,259	58,120	47,970	121.9	2,382	6,567
1967[5]	20,405	7,800	7,485	62,068	49,007	126.7	2,402	6,547

Source: DOMINION BUREAU OF STATISTICS, *Population: Estimated Population of Canada, by Province as of June 1, 1967*, Ottawa, September
1967, and earlier issues; *Census of Canada*, 1871-1921; labour force
and employment, *The Labourforce*, March 1968, and earlier bulletins,
including Special Reference Paper No. 23 (revised), DOMINION
BUREAU OF STATISTICS, 1957, *Census of Canada*, 1871-1921; Gross
National Product for period 1926 to date from DOMINION BUREAU OF
STATISTICS, *National Accounts, Income and Expenditure, 1966*, Ottawa, 1967 and earlier issues; and DOMINION BUREAU OF STATISTICS,
*National Accounts, Income and Expenditure, Fourth Quarter and
Preliminary Annual 1967*, Ottawa, April 1968; for earlier period from
O. J. FIRESTONE, *Canada's Economic Development, 1867-1953*, Lon-
don, Bowes & Bowes, 1958, and unpublished work sheets underlying
estimates prepared for this study.

[1]   As of April 1 for 1867-1901; as of June 1 for 1902-1967.
[2]   Including personnel in the Armed Forces; data for 1867-1910
relate to end of year; for 1920-1945 data relate to the beginning of June,
and for 1946-1967 represent the average for the year.
[3]   In 1957 dollars.
[4]   Implied Price Index of Gross National Expenditure. Base
1957=100.
[5]   Estimates specially prepared for this study. The estimates of
Gross National Product in current dollars for the years 1870-1925 appear
to be on the low side (see Appendix B).
[6]   Includes Newfoundland commencing in 1949.

EDUCATION AND ECONOMIC DEVELOPMENT

TABLE 2. — NUMBER OF PUPILS ENROLLED, AVERAGE DAILY ATTENDANCE AND NUMBER OF TEACHERS, PUBLICLY CONTROLLED ELEMENTARY AND SECONDARY SCHOOLS, CANADA, [1] 1867-1967.

YEAR	NUMBER OF PUPILS ENROLLED Thous.	TOTAL AVERAGE DAILY ATTENDANCE Thous.	NUMBER OF TEACHERS Thous.	NUMBER OF PUPILS ENROLLED		NUMBER OF TEACHERS PER THOUSAND PERSONS EMPLOYED	AVERAGE DAILY ATTENDANCE PER PUPIL
				Per Thousand Population	Per Teacher		
1867 [2]	726.0	387.3	12.1	210	60.0	1.14	0.53
1868	746.3	394.7	—	213	—	—	0.53
1869	752.6	409.0	—	211	—	—	0.54
1870	763.0	413.5	12.9	211	59.1	1.15	0.54
1871	781.5	427.7	—	212	—	—	0.55
1872	798.8	424.2	—	213	—	—	0.53
1873	826.0	437.9	—	216	—	—	0.53
1874	840.7	456.7	—	216	—	—	0.54
1875	838.2	466.0	14.2	212	59.0	—	0.56
1876	853.9	466.5	—	213	—	—	0.55
1877	865.6	485.6	—	213	—	—	0.56
1878	869.8	503.7	—	211	—	—	0.58
1879	869.0	500.5	—	208	—	—	0.58
1880	856.3	494.5	17.5	201	48.9	1.30	0.52
1881	852.3	493.2	—	197	—	—	0.58
1882 [2]	880.0	519.2	—	201	—	—	0.59
1883 [2]	908.0	544.8	—	205	—	—	0.60
1884 [2]	936.0	571.0	—	209	—	—	0.61
1885	964.3	598.7	19.6	213	49.2	—	0.62
1886	966.1	579.7	—	211	—	—	0.60
1887	967.9	554.3	—	209	—	—	0.57
1888	974.0	554.4	—	208	—	—	0.57
1889	983.8	570.5	—	208	—	—	0.58
1890	980.0	576.6	21.1	207	46.9	1.33	0.58
1891	991.5	583.6	—	205	—	—	0.59
1892	993.4	591.4	—	203	—	—	0.60
1893	1,006.2	600.3	—	204	—	—	0.60
1894	1,028.3	614.3	—	207	—	—	0.60
1895	1,047.8	641.3	25.7	208	40.8	—	0.61
1896	1,056.8	643.2	26.2	208	40.3	1.54	0.61
1897	1,064.3	647.5	—	208	—	—	0.61
1898	1,075.5	660.2	—	208	—	—	0.61
1899	1,078.1	657.1	—	206	—	—	0.61
1900	1,086.3	665.6	28.2	205	38.5	1.58	0.61
1901	1,092.6	666.0	—	203	—	—	0.61
1902	1,104.8	678.5	—	201	—	—	0.61
1903	1,113.8	693.2	—	197	—	—	0.62
1904	1,120.6	692.7	—	192	—	—	0.62
1905	1,149.9	724.0	30.5	192	37.8	—	0.63
1906	1,173.0	743.3	—	192	—	—	0.63
1907	1,196.0	753.9	—	187	—	—	0.63
1908	1,230.1	782.4	—	186	—	—	0.64
1909	1,272.2	815.2	—	187	—	—	0.64
1910	1,310.0	849.1	38.1	187	34.4	1.41	0.65
1911	1,361.2	870.5	—	189	—	—	0.64

TABLE 2. — NUMBER OF PUPILS ENROLLED, AVERAGE DAILY
ATTENDANCE AND NUMBER OF TEACHERS, PUBLICLY CON-
TROLLED ELEMENTARY AND SECONDARY SCHOOLS, CANADA, [1]
1867-1967. *(Continued.)*

YEAR	NUMBER OF PUPILS EN-ROLLED Thous.	TOTAL AVER-AGE DAILY ATTEND-ANCE Thous.	NUMBER OF TEACH-ERS Thous.	NUMBER OF PUPILS ENROLLED		NUMBER OF TEACH-ERS PER THOU-SAND PERSONS EM-PLOYED	AVER-AGE DAILY ATTEND-ANCE PER PUPIL
				Per Thou-sand Popu-lation	Per Teacher		
1912	1,402.6	928.9	—	190	—	—	0.66
1913	1,470.8	978.9	—	193	—	—	0.67
1914	1,555.6	1,052.0	46.3	197	33.6	1.60	0.68
1915	1,603.0	1,112.8	48.0	201	33.4	—	0.69
1916	1,626.1	1,118.5	—	203	—	—	0.69
1917	1,650.6	1,143.2	—	205	—	—	0.69
1918	1,674.9	1,161.9	—	206	—	—	0.69
1919	1,750.4	1,187.2	—	211	—	—	0.68
1920	1,826.6	1,234.0	55.7	214	32.8	1.76	0.67
1921	1,894.7	1,349.2	57.5	216	33.0	1.84	0.71
1922	1,964.9	1,436.0	59.9	220	32.8	1.85	0.73
1923	2,009.1	1,468.6	61.7	223	32.6	1.85	0.73
1924	2,029.3	1,503.3	62.9	222	32.3	1.88	0.74
1925	2,054.6	1,540.4	63.5	221	32.4	1.85	0.75
1926	2,085.5	1,563.8	64.8	221	32.2	1.82	0.75
1927	2,120.0	1,600.4	66.4	220	31.9	1.80	0.75
1928	2,153.7	1,633.3	68.5	219	31.4	1.80	0.76
1929	2,184.6	1,704.7	69.3	218	31.5	1.80	0.78
1930	2,220.4	1,746.5	70.3	218	31.4	1.90	0.79
1931	2,264.1	1,802.0	71.7	218	31.6	1.95	0.80
1932	2,285.9	1,839.8	73.4	217	31.1	2.11	0.81
1933	2,287.2	1,857.0	73.2	215	31.2	2.12	0.81
1934	2,215.7	1,873.8	73.2	206	30.3	1.97	0.84
1935	2,195.8	1,857.3	74.2	202	29.6	1.96	0.85
1936	2,189.5	1,832.4	73.9	200	29.6	1.89	0.84
1937	2,186.6	1,846.0	74.7	198	29.3	1.81	0.84
1938	2,190.7	1,868.6	74.4	196	29.4	1.83	0.85
1939	2,196.1	1,870.6	75.4	195	29.1	1.83	0.85
1940	2,164.8	1,870.6	76.1	190	28.4	1.77	0.86
1941	2,130.8	1,802.3	75.7	185	28.1	1.66	0.85
1942	2,088.4	1,785.5	76.1	189	27.4	1.58	0.86
1943	2,061.0	1,697.2	75.3	176	27.4	1.45	0.82
1944	2,060.7	1,717.7	75.4	173	27.3	1.43	0.83
1945	2,062.2	1,753.1	75.9	171	27.2	1.46	0.85
1946	2,106.4	1,804.3	77.5	171	27.2	1.62	0.86
1947	2,114.8	1,819.1	78.8	168	26.8	1.62	0.86
1948	2,151.5	1,861.7	81.0	168	26.6	1.65	0.87
1949	2,292.1	1,986.3	81.9	170	28.0	1.65	0.87
1950	2,377.5	2,065.6	85.2	173	27.9	1.69	0.87
1951	2,446.7	2,117.5	89.7	175	27.3	1.73	0.86
1952	2,567.8	2,232.0	93.3	178	27.5	1.77	0.87
1953	2,708.8	2,389.1	97.5	182	27.8	1.83	0.88
1954	2,864.1	2,562.8	102.4	187	28.0	1.91	0.89
1955	3,055.6	2,744.5	108.7	195	28.1	1.98	0.90
1956	3,211.5	2,921.3	115.6	200	27.8	2.03	0.91

TABLE 2. — NUMBER OF PUPILS ENROLLED, AVERAGE DAILY ATTENDANCE AND NUMBER OF TEACHERS, PUBLICLY CONTROLLED ELEMENTARY AND SECONDARY SCHOOLS, CANADA, [1] 1867-1967. *(Continued.)*

YEAR	NUMBER OF PUPILS ENROLLED Thous.	TOTAL AVERAGE DAILY ATTENDANCE Thous.	NUMBER OF TEACHERS Thous.	NUMBER OF PUPILS ENROLLED		NUMBER OF TEACHERS PER THOUSAND PERSONS EMPLOYED	AVERAGE DAILY ATTENDANCE PER PUPIL
				Per Thousand Population	Per Teacher		
1957	3,345.7	3,101.3	122.7	201	27.3	2.10	0.93
1958	3,495.2	3,175.0	128.6	205	27.2	2.21	0.91
1959	3,719.8	3,390.4	137.6	213	27.0	2.30	0.91
1960	3,893.6	3,559.9	143.5	218	27.1	2.36	0.91
1961	4,077.6	3,769.1	151.1	224	27.0	2.45	0.92
1962	4,278.0	4,021.1 [3]	161.0	230	26.6	2.54	0.94
1963	4,451.5	4,043.7 [3]	171.3	235	26.0	2.64	0.91
1964	4,551.7	4,280.0 [4]	178.5	236	25.5	2.65	0.94
1965	4,762.4	4,448.0 [4]	189.7	243	25.1	2.72	0.93
1966 [4]	4,929.2	4,584.0 [4]	200.8	246	24.5	2.77	0.93
1967 [4]	5,095.3	4,743.0 [4]	215.4	250	23.7	2.88	0.93

Source: For the years 1867-1886, *Historical Statistics of Canada*, M. C. URQUHART, Ed. K. A. H. BUCKLEY, Ass. Ed., Section V: "Education", by R. W. B. JACKSON, Toronto, The MacMillan Company of Canada Limited, 1965, p. 587; for the years 1887-1889, DOMINION BUREAU OF STATISTICS, *Elementary and Secondary Education in Canada, 1936-38*, Ottawa, 1940; for the years 1900-1953, DOMINION BUREAU OF STATISTICS, *Survey of Elementary and Secondary Education, 1950-1954* and *1962-1963*, Ottawa, 1959 and 1966; for the years 1964-1967, DOMINION BUREAU OF STATISTICS, *Preliminary Statistics of Education 1965-1966* and *1966-1967*, Ottawa, 1967 and 1968; DOMINION BUREAU OF STATISTICS, *Salaries and Qualifications of Teachers in Public Elementary and Secondary Schools, 1965-1966* and *1966-1967*, Ottawa, 1967 and 1968.

[1]   Covers nine provinces up to 1948 and ten provinces commencing in 1949 when Newfoundland joined Canada.

[2]   Special estimates (see Appendix B).

[3]   Revised.

[4]   Preliminary estimates.

TABLE 3. — RECEIPTS BY PUBLICLY CONTROLLED ELEMENTARY AND SECONDARY SCHOOL BOARDS, AND TOTAL EXPENDITURES ON FORMAL EDUCATION, CANADA, [1] 1867-1967.

YEAR	RECEIPTS BY SCHOOL BOARDS [2] $ Mill.	TOTAL EXPEND-ITURES ON FORMAL EDUCA-TION [3] $ Mill.	RECEIPTS OF SCHOOL BOARDS AS PER CENT OF TOTAL EXPEND-ITURES ON FORMAL EDUCA-TION	RECEIPTS BY SCHOOL BOARDS PER CAPITA	TOTAL EXPEND-ITURES ON FORMAL EDUCATION	
					Per cent Gross National Product	Per Capita
1867[4]	2.3	—	—	0.66	—	—
1870	2.9	—	—	0.80	—	—
1875	4.5	—	—	1.14	—	—
1880	4.8	—	—	1.13	—	—
1885	5.7	—	—	1.26	—	—
1890	7.0	—	—	1.46	—	—
1895	8.1	—	—	1.61	—	—
1896[4]	8.4	—	—	1.66	—	—
1900	9.6	—	—	1.81	—	—
1905	13.0	—	—	2.17	—	—
1910	22.8	—	—	3.26	—	—
1914[4]	37.8	—	—	4.80	—	—
1915	41.5	—	—	5.20	—	—
1920	71.1	—	—	8.31	—	—
1925	98.6	—	—	10.61	—	—
1926	96.5	142.4	67.8	10.21	2.7	15
1927	100.8	147.8	68.2	10.46	2.7	15
1928	99.5	157.0	63.4	10.12	2.6	16
1929	110.9	159.7	69.4	11.06	2.6	16
1930	112.1	165.3	67.8	10.98	2.9	16
1931	109.6	178.7	61.3	10.56	3.8	17
1932	105.1	163.9	64.1	10.00	4.3	16
1933	95.6	146.9	65.1	8.99	4.0	14
1934	98.1	138.9	70.6	9.13	3.5	13
1935	96.0	136.0	70.6	8.85	3.2	13
1936	98.5	140.4	70.2	9.00	3.0	13
1937	100.3	145.9	68.7	9.08	2.8	13
1938	108.8	151.5	71.8	9.75	2.9	14
1939	112.5	154.3	72.9	9.98	2.7	14
1940	115.3	157.1	73.4	10.13	2.3	14
1941	114.2	156.5	73.0	9.92	1.9	14
1942	124.7	165.7	75.3	11.28	1.6	14
1943	132.2	218.0	60.4	11.29	2.0	18
1944	139.8	172.7	80.9	11.70	1.5	14
1945	157.0	195.0	80.5	13.00	1.6	16
1946	159.5	290.0	55.0	12.97	2.4	24
1947	193.5	351.8	55.0	15.41	2.7	28
1948	226.3	372.0	60.8	17.64	2.5	29
1949	263.8	408.0	64.7	19.61	2.5	30
1950	329.6	464.5	70.0	24.03	2.6	34
1951	347.8	515.9	67.4	24.82	2.4	37
1952	398.0	583.7	68.2	27.52	2.4	40
1953	438.0	627.0	69.9	29.50	2.5	42
1954	492.8	713.2	69.1	32.23	2.9	47
1955	552.8	807.8	68.4	35.21	3.0	51
1956	626.1	908.7	68.9	38.93	3.0	57

TABLE 3. — RECEIPTS BY PUBLICLY CONTROLLED ELEMENTARY
AND SECONDARY SCHOOL BOARDS, AND TOTAL EXPENDITURES
ON FORMAL EDUCATION, CANADA, [1] 1867-1967. *(Continued.)*

YEAR	RECEIPTS By SCHOOL BOARDS [2] $ Mill.	TOTAL EXPEND-ITURES ON FORMAL EDUCA-TION [3] $ Mill.	RECEIPTS OF SCHOOL BOARDS AS PER CENT OF TOTAL EXPEND-ITURES ON FORMAL EDUCA-TION	RECEIPTS BY SCHOOL BOARDS PER CAPITA	TOTAL EXPEND-ITURES ON FORMAL EDUCATION Per cent Gross National Product	Per Capita
1957	737.5	1,088.5	67.8	44.40	3.5	66
1958	840.1	1,235.1	68.0	49.18	3.8	72
1959	978.6	1,426.5	68.6	55.97	4.1	82
1960	1,097.5	1,622.2	67.7	61.42	4.5	91
1961	1,210.9	1,873.3	64.6	66.39	5.0	103
1962	1,365.4	2,280.8	60.0	73.48	5.6	123
1963	1,523.1	2,439.0	62.4	80.46	5.6	129
1964	1,740.9	2,818.0	61.8	90.25	5.9	146
1965 [5]	1,953.8	3,277.1	59.6	99.46	6.3	167
1966 [5]	2,233.0 [5]	3,945.7	56.6	111.57	6.8	197
1967 [5]	2,500.0 [5]	4,539.0	55.1	122.51	7.3	222

Source: For the years 1870-1925 at quinquennial intervals, M. C. UR-QUHART, ed., and K. A. H. BUCKLEY, ass. ed., *Historical Statistics of Canada*, Section V: "Education", by R. W. B. JACKSON, Toronto, The MacMillan Company of Canada Limited, 1965, p. 599; for the years 1926-1967, DOMINION BUREAU OF STATISTICS, *Elementary and Secondary Education, 1950-54, Survey of Education Finance, 1963, Preliminary Statistics of Education 1966-1967*, Ottawa, 1940, 1959 and 1967; DOMINION BUREAU OF STATISTICS, *Daily Bulletin*, Ottawa, March 15, 1968, p. 5.

[1] Covers nine provinces to 1948 and ten provinces commencing in 1949 when Newfoundland joined Canada.
[2] Covers current revenues of public school boards comprising provincial government grants and revenues from local taxation. Items not covered include fees, revenues from counties and other sources which comprise only a small fraction of the total.
[3] Covers operation and capital expenditures of elementary and secondary education, teacher training outside universities, higher education, and other types of formal education, and vocational training including business colleges, private and public.
[4] Special estimates (see Appendix B).
[5] Preliminary estimates.

TABLE 4. — CAPITAL EXPENDITURES FOR SCHOOLS AND UNIVERSITIES, SOCIAL AND BUSINESS CAPITAL EXPENDITURES, TOTAL PRIVATE AND PUBLIC CAPITAL EXPENDITURES AND BUSINESS GROSS CAPITAL FORMATION, CANADA, 1926-1967.

$ Mill.

	CAPITAL EXPENDITURES					TOTAL BUSINESS CAPITAL EXPENDITURES	TOTAL PRIVATE AND PUBLIC CAPITAL EXPENDITURES	BUSINESS GROSS CAPITAL FORMATION AS PER NATIONAL ACCOUNTS
YEAR	SCHOOLS	UNIVERSITIES	SCHOOLS AND UNIVERSITIES	OTHER SOCIAL CAPITAL EXPENDITURES	TOTAL SOCIAL CAPITAL EXPENDITURES			
1926	20	4	24	312	336	581	917	702
1927	25	3	28	345	373	714	1,087	830
1928	28	2	30	383	413	883	1,296	1,007
1929	30	5	35	418	453	1,065	1,518	1,161
1930	35	9	44	417	461	826	1,287	926
1931	24	9	33	346	379	502	881	622
1932	18	2	20	217	237	254	491	319
1933	8	1	9	161	170	157	327	234
1934	6	1	7	207	214	202	416	298
1935	7	1	8	238	246	259	505	369
1936	9	2	11	256	267	323	590	458
1937	8	3	11	355	366	462	828	633
1938	8	2	10	328	338	435	773	592
1939	13	5	18	341	359	406	765	592
1940	7	2	9	457	466	582	1,048	803
1941	6	3	9	700	709	754	1,463	1,085
1942	6	1	7	737	744	798	1,542	1,064
1943	8	2	10	796	806	679	1,485	887
1944	8	2	10	566	576	733	1,309	900
1945	14	7	21	480	501	747	1,284	1,031
1946	27	12	39	672	711	992	1,703	1,388
1947	31	14	45	928	973	1,516	2,489	2,085
1948	53	12	65	1,146	1,211	1,940	3,151	2,619
1949[1]	79	12	91	1,270	1,361	2,130	3,491	3,032
1950	88	14	102	1,396	1,498	2,317	3,815	3,348
1951	111	14	125	1,286	1,411	3,166	4,577	3,959
1952	145	13	158	1,578	1,736	3,549	5,285	4,451
1953	133	17	150	1,745	1,895	3,946	5,841	4,998
1954	154	20	174	2,217	2,391	3,330	5,721	4,779
1955	188	25	213	2,438	2,651	3,593	6,244	5,210
1956	190	26	216	2,815	3,031	5,003	8,034	6,774
1957	217	43	260	2,803	3,063	5,654	8,717	7,335
1958	223	63	286	3,208	3,494	4,870	8,364	6,975
1959	235	82	317	3,299	3,616	4,801	8,417	6,894
1960	256	87	343	3,045	3,388	4,874	8,262	6,692
1961	253	112	365	3,040	3,405	4,767	8,172	6,635
1962	451	115	566	3,177	3,743	4,972	8,715	6,960
1963	477	138	615	3,315	3,930	5,463	9,393	7,591
1964	339	178	517	3,810	4,327	6,617	10,949	9,103
1965	487	256	743	4,185	4,928	7,937	12,865	10,651
1966	601	297	898	4,530	5,428	9,662	15,090	12,493
1967	694	337	1,031	4,804	5,835	9,339	15,174	12,365

Source: Data on Business Gross Capital Formation as per National Accounts for the years 1926-1967 are from DOMINION BUREAU OF STATISTICS, *National Accounts, Income and Expenditure 1926-1956,*

TABLE 4. — CAPITAL EXPENDITURES FOR SCHOOLS AND UNIVER-
SITIES, SOCIAL AND BUSINESS CAPITAL EXPENDITURES, TOTAL
PRIVATE AND PUBLIC CAPITAL EXPENDITURES AND BUSINESS
GROSS CAPITAL FORMATION, CANADA, 1926-1967. *(Continued.)*

National Accounts, Income and Expenditure by Quarters 1947-1961,
and *National Accounts, Income and Expenditure 1966,* Ottawa, 1962
et 1967; DOMINION BUREAU OF STATISTICS, *National Accounts, Income and Expenditure, Fourth Quarter and Preliminary annual 1967,*
Ottawa, April 1968; all other data are from DEPARTMENT OF TRADE
AND COMMERCE, *Private and Public Investment in Canada, 1926-1951,* Ottawa, 1951, and DOMINION BUREAU OF STATISTICS and
DEPARTMENT OF TRADE AND COMMERCE, *Private Investment Outlook
in Canada 1968,* Ottawa, April 1968, and earlier issues for the years
1947-1967.

---

[1] Includes Newfoundland commencing in 1949.

TABLE 5. — CAPITAL EXPENDITURES ON SCHOOLS AND UNIVER-
SITIES AS A PERCENT OF TOTAL SOCIAL CAPITAL EXPEND-
ITURES, TOTAL BUSINESS CAPITAL EXPENDITURES, TOTAL
PRIVATE AND PUBLIC INVESTMENT, BUSINESS GROSS CAPITAL
FORMATION PER NATIONAL ACCOUNTS AND GROSS NATIONAL
PRODUCT, CANADA, 1926-1967.

YEAR	TOTAL SOCIAL CAPITAL EXPEND-ITURES	TOTAL BUSINESS CAPITAL EXPEND-ITURES	TOTAL PRIVATE AND PUBLIC CAPITAL EXPEND-ITURES	BUSINESS GROSS CAPITAL FORMATION AS PER NATIONAL ACCOUNTS	GROSS NATIONAL PRODUCT
1926	7.1	4.1	2.6	3.4	0.47
1927	7.5	3.9	2.6	3.4	0.50
1928	7.3	3.4	2.3	3.0	0.49
1929	7.7	3.3	2.3	3.0	0.57
1930	9.5	5.3	3.4	4.8	0.77
1931	8.7	6.6	3.7	5.3	0.70
1932	8.4	7.9	4.1	6.3	0.52
1933	5.3	5.7	2.7	3.8	0.26
1934	3.3	3.5	1.7	2.3	0.18
1935	3.3	3.1	1.6	2.2	0.19
1936	4.1	3.4	1.9	2.4	0.24
1937	3.0	2.4	1.3	1.7	0.21
1938	3.0	2.3	1.3	1.7	0.19
1939	5.0	4.4	2.4	3.0	0.32
1940	1.9	1.5	0.9	1.1	0.13
1941	1.3	1.2	0.6	0.8	0.11
1942	0.9	0.9	0.5	0.7	0.07
1943	1.2	1.5	0.7	1.1	0.09
1944	1.7	1.4	0.8	1.1	0.08
1945	4.2	2.8	1.6	2.0	0.18
1946	5.4	3.9	2.3	2.8	0.33
1947	4.6	3.0	1.8	2.2	0.34
1948	5.4	3.4	2.1	2.5	0.43
1949	6.7	4.3	2.6	3.0	0.56
1950	6.8	4.4	4.4	3.1	0.57
1951	8.6	3.9	2.7	3.2	0.59
1952	9.1	4.5	3.0	3.5	0.66
1953	7.9	4.4	2.7	3.2	0.60
1954	7.3	5.2	3.0	3.6	0.69
1955	8.0	5.9	3.4	4.1	0.79
1956	7.1	4.3	2.7	3.2	0.71
1957	8.5	4.6	3.0	3.5	0.81
1958	8.2	5.9	3.4	4.1	0.87
1959	8.8	6.6	3.8	4.6	0.91
1960	10.1	7.0	4.2	5.1	0.95
1961	10.7	7.7	4.5	5.5	0.97
1962	15.1	11.4	6.5	8.1	1.39
1963	15.6	11.3	6.5	8.1	1.42
1964	11.9	7.8	4.7	5.7	1.09
1965	15.1	9.4	5.8	7.0	1.42
1966	16.5	9.3	6.0	7.2	1.55
1967	17.7	11.0	6.8	8.3	1.66

Source: Based on Tables 1 and 4 in Appendix A.

TABLE 6. — TOTAL EXPENDITURES ON FORMAL EDUCATION AND CAPITAL EXPENDITURES ON SCHOOLS AND UNIVERSITIES, IN CONSTANT DOLLARS, CANADA, [1] 1926-1967.

| YEAR | TOTAL EXPEND- ITURES ON FORMAL EDUCA- TION [2] | CAPITAL EXPEND- ITURES ON SCHOOLS AND UNIVERSITIES | | PER CAPITA | |
		TOTAL [3] $ Mill.	PERCENT OF TOTAL EXPEND- ITURES ON FORMAL EDUCA- TION	TOTAL EXPEND- ITURES ON FORMAL EDUCA- TION	CAPITAL EXPEND- ITURES ON SCHOOLS & UNIVER- SITIES
1926	277.6	59.1	21.3	29.37	6.25
1927	292.1	70.0	24.0	30.31	7.26
1928	311.5	74.0	23.8	31.67	7.52
1929	313.1	84.1	26.9	31.21	8.38
1930	332.6	109.5	32.9	32.58	10.72
1931	381.8	87.1	22.8	36.79	8.39
1932	386.6	54.6	14.1	36.78	5.19
1933	353.1	25.4	7.2	33.20	2.38
1934	329.9	19.5	5.9	30.71	1.81
1935	321.5	22.0	6.8	29.64	2.02
1936	321.3	29.7	9.2	29.34	2.71
1937	324.9	27.7	8.5	29.41	2.50
1938	338.2	25.4	7.5	30.32	2.27
1939	346.7	45.9	13.2	30.77	4.07
1940	337.1	21.6	6.4	29.61	1.89
1941	311.1	20.0	6.4	27.03	1.73
1942	315.0	14.8	4.7	28.49	1.33
1943	400.0	21.1	5.3	34.17	1.80
1944	307.3	19.6	6.4	25.72	1.64
1945	339.1	41.4	12.2	28.08	3.42
1946	494.0	74.3	15.0	40.19	6.04
1947	546.3	77.2	14.1	43.53	6.15
1948	512.4	98.2	19.2	39.95	7.65
1949	539.7	130.6	24.2	40.13	9.71
1950	596.3	138.4	23.2	43.48	10.09
1951	598.8	149.5	25.0	42.74	10.67
1952	645.0	182.7	28.3	44.60	12.63
1953	689.8	168.9	24.5	46.47	11.37
1954	766.1	194.4	25.4	50.11	12.71
1955	863.9	232.3	26.9	55.03	14.79
1956	935.9	223.6	23.9	58.19	13.90
1957	1,088.5	260.0	23.9	65.53	15.65
1958	1,212.1	279.8	23.1	70.96	16.38
1959	1,365.1	301.6	22.1	78.08	17.25
1960	1,528.9	319.4	20.9	85.56	17.87
1961	1,754.0	337.0	19.2	96.17	18.47
1962	2,104.1	508.5	24.1	113.23	27.36
1963	2,211.2	536.2	24.2	116.80	28.32
1964	2,489.4	431.9	17.3	129.05	22.39
1965	2,810.5	595.4	21.2	143.07	30.31
1966	3,327.0	692.4	21.4	161.73	34.59
1967	3,582.5	776.9	21.7	175.57	38.07

Source: Based on Tables 1, 3 and 4 in Appendix A.

[1] In 1957 dollars.

[2] Deflated by the Implied Price Index in Gross National Expenditure.

[3] Deflated by the Implied Price Index in Business Gross Fixed Capital Formation.

APPENDIX B.

Notes on Sources and Quality of Estimates

The notes that follow relate to Tables 1 - 6 in Appendix A.

TABLE 1. — POPULATION, LABOUR FORCE, EMPLOYMENT, GROSS NATIONAL PRODUCT IN CURRENT AND CONSTANT DOLLARS, AND IMPLIED PRICE INDEX, CANADA, 1867-1967.

1. *Population.* The population series is based on actual counts in the census years at decennial intervals, 1871-1961, supplemented by data from quinquennial censuses for 1956 and 1966 and for prior periods (with such censuses going back to 1906 for the three Prairie provinces). Population estimates have been prepared by the Dominion Bureau of Statistics in intercensal years using two methods: 1867-1931 by fitting smooth curves to successive sets of three decennial figures of total population, adjusted for annual fluctuation in net population growth; 1932-1967 by estimating for each year the number of births, deaths and immigration and emigration, with the resulting estimates of net increase in population added to the census base and adjusted each census date for intercensal over or under-estimation. In 1949, Newfoundland became part of Canada. In that year, Newfoundland's population numbered 345,000 and is included in the Canada total. Since all other data in this table and the other tables in Appendix A cover Newfoundland commencing with 1949, the data are comparable in territory covered for the years 1867-1948 and 1949-1967.

In making comparisons of rates of economic growth over stage 4, 1914-1950, such comparison made in terms of aggregates, say population and total Gross National Product in constant dollars includes an over-statement in the rate of growth to the extent that Newfoundland added about 2½ per cent to the population in 1950 and a somewhat lesser proportion to the Gross National Product, since Gross National Product per capita in Newfoundland was notably lower than that of the other provinces. When comparison is made on the basis of Gross National Product in constant dollars per capita or per person working, the effects of the over-statement even to the minor extent referred to above, are removed and the series are fully comparable over the period. There are small variations in the months to which the data apply, April 1 (or close to it) for the years 1867-1901 and June 1 for the period 1902-1967, but such differences have little quantitative effect on long-term growth trends and annual average compound rate increases over the four stages of economic development that can be observed over the last hundred years.

The data are from DOMINION BUREAU OF STATISTICS, *Population: Estimated Population of Canada, by Provinces as of June 1, 1967,* Ottawa, 1967, and earlier issues, published in annual issues of the *Canada Year Book* and *Census of Canada, 1871-1921.*

2. *Labour Force and Employment.* The data for the period commencing with 1945 are from *The Labour Force,* a sample survey of about 30,000 households, undertaken quarterly since November 1945 and monthly since November 1952, published by the Dominion Bureau of Statistics. The data shown relate to the beginning of June for the period 1920-1945 and they represent annual averages for the period 1946-1967. The data are a revised series based on a population weighting taken from the 1961 Census, as explained in the Special Bulletin, *The Labour Force, March 1965,* Catalogue No. 71-001. Members of the Armed Forces are included and so are persons in the labour force and employed in Newfoundland commencing with 1949. The data for the years 1920-1945 are special estimates prepared by the Dominion Bureau of Statistics, published in *Canadian Labour Force Estimates, 1931-1945,* Reference Paper No. 23 (revised), Ottawa, 1957. In the Appendix to this publication "Estimates of the Civilian Labour Force and its main Components" for the period 1921-1930 are included.

For the years 1867, 1870, 1880, 1890, 1900 and 1910, the estimates are taken from *Canada's Economic Development 1867-1953, op. cit.,* p. 58. The data relate to year end and include members of the Armed Forces. These estimates are based on decennial censuses taken at mid-year, adjusted to year end and to definitions of the labour force and persons employed, as used in the labour force surveys carried on by the Dominion Bureau of Statistics. The methods of adjustments are explained in *Canada's Economic Development, 1867-1953, op. cit.,* pp. 309 and 310.

Special estimates were prepared for this study for the years 1896 and 1914, required for the stages analysis. The technique used was to interpolate the labour force participation rates between 1890 and 1900, and 1910 and 1920, and applying these ratios to population to arrive at estimates of the labour force for 1896 and 1914. Then a ratio of persons employed to total labour force was arrived at by choosing a ratio between those applying to 1890, a year of recession and 1900, a year of prosperity by reference to data reflecting the cyclical upswing commencing in 1896.

A similar technique was employed for 1914, except that this year was a year of recession and the estimates allowed for the fact that the proportion of the number of persons unemployed to the labour force rose in that year and hence the ratio of persons employed declined. The estimate relates to June of the year.

Since reliance on data of general economic activity represents only a tentative basis of estimating the relative degree of unemployment, taking into account changes in productivity, number of hours worked per week, and the degree of part-time employment, the estimates of the unemployment ratio to the labour force are subject to significant errors for the early period. But even if the error would be as much as 25 per cent, it would not affect significantly the estimates of the number of persons employed and hence the rate of growth over the longer term.

In 1914, for example, the proportion of persons unemployed was assumed to be 6.3 per cent of the labour force. A 25 per cent error would place the unemployment ratio at 7.9 per cent, assuming under-estimation, and this would reduce the number of persons employed from 2,900,000 to about 2,850,000 or by 1.7 per cent. The effect of this error in determining a compound rate of annual growth over eighteen years, 1896-1914, is minimal. Still, the fact remains that the estimates for the period 1867-1910 are on a less firm basis than the official estimates commencing with 1920.

The shift of labour force and employment estimates from year end covering the period 1867-1910, to June for the period 1920-1945 and to the annual average for the period 1946-1967 introduces several minor breaks in the comparability of the data. But these are not of much quantitative significance in medium and long-term growth analysis.

To illustrate: Persons in the labour force including members of the Armed Forces as of June 1950 numbered 5,278,000 as compared with an annual average of 5,216,000, a difference of 1.2 per cent. Persons employed as of June 1950 numbered 5,121,000 as compared with an annual average of 5,029,000, a difference of 1.8 per cent. Using the June 1950 figure for employment yields a Gross National Product in constant dollars per person working of $4,514. This compares with the Gross National Product in constant dollars per person working on the basis of the annual average of $4,596, a difference of 1.8 per cent.

Gross National Product in constant dollars per person working in 1914 on the basis of the estimate of employment as of June is placed at $2,653. Compared with $4,514, the estimate for 1950 on the basis of employment as of June yields a total increase for the period of 70.1 per cent. This compares with an increase of 73.2 per cent on the basis of Gross National Product in constant dollars per person working, average for the year 1950, as per Summary Table 1. The compound rates of annual change over the period 1914-1950 are the same if the rate is expressed to one decimal, 1.5 per cent in both cases.

3. *Gross National Product in Current and Constant Dollars.* For the period 1926-1967, the data are from four publications: DOMINION BUREAU OF STATISTICS, *National Accounts, Income and Expenditure, 1926-1956, National Accounts, Income and Expenditure, by Quarters, 1947-1961* and *National Accounts, Income and Expenditure, 1966,* Ottawa, 1958, 1962 and 1967; and DOMINION BUREAU OF STATISTICS, *National Accounts, Income and Expenditure, Fourth Quarter and Preliminary Annual 1967,* Ottawa, April 1968.

The estimates for 1867, 1870, 1880, 1890, 1900 and annually for 1910 to 1925 are arrived at by converting the constant dollar series shown in *Canada's Economic Development, 1867-1953, op. cit.,* p. 276, into current dollars by using the Implied Price Index in Gross National Expenditure as shown in column 7 of Table 1, in Appendix A.

The current dollar estimates of Gross National Product for the latter part of the nineteenth century and the early part of the twentieth century are subject to understatement of the order between 3½ per cent and 17 per cent mainly for two reasons:

The first is that the Implied Price Index used is on a 1957 basis. It was constructed by linking price indices with three different base periods as explained below.

The second reason is that the value added technique used in another study, prepared subsequently to *Canada's Economic Development 1867-1953* yielded for two years somewhat higher and for two years somewhat lower estimates:

	E.E.D. [1] $ Mill.	C.E.D. [2] $ Mill.	D.C.E. [3] $ Mill.
1867	365	419	—
1870	390	458	459
1880	564	612	581
1890	719	815	803
1900	999	1,032	1,057
1910	2,059	2,138	—
1920	5,355	5,543	—

The differences between the C.E.D. and the D.C.E. estimates are small, between ¼ per cent and 5¼ per cent. The differences between the E.E.D. and the C.E.D. estimates ar more significant, between 3½ per cent and 17 per cent.

A choice had to be made whether to use the lower current dollar figures of Gross National Product based on the Implied Price Index with a base 1957=100 or to use the C.E.D. or D.C.E. estimates both of which were converted to current dollars by using the Implied Price Index with a base 1935-1939=100. Since the data for the period 1947 to date, published by the Dominion Bureau of Statistics, are expressed in 1957 dollars, it was considered desirable to construct a current dollar series for the earlier period, comparable to those available from official sources.

The techniques used were to convert the official series of Gross National Product for the period 1926-1946 from current dollars to constant dollars by using the Implied Price Index in Gross National Expenditure with a 1957 base, and to convert the C.E.D. estimates for the period 1867-1925 from constant dollars to current dollars on the basis of the same index.

---

[1]   As per Table 1 in Appendix A.
[2]   *Canada's Economic Development 1867-1953, op. cit.*, p. 66.
[3]   O. J. FIRESTONE, "Development of Canada's Economy, 1850-1900", in *Trends in the American Economy in the Nineteenth Century*, studies in Income and Wealth, Volume 24, National Bureau of Economic Research, Princeton, Princeton University Press, 1960, p. 225.

Allowing for the fact that there are also some differences between the C.E.D. and the D.C.E. series, generally speaking the margin of error in using the current dollar data as per Table 1 in Appendix A may be between 10 per cent and 15 per cent during the nineteenth century, reducing to about 5 per cent in the early part of the twentieth century.

Since the analysis of rates of economic growth are presented in terms of constant dollars, the assessment is unaffected by the margin of error in the current dollar estimates indicated above. To the extent that the comparison is made in terms of the ratio of educational expenditures to Gross National Product in current dollars, as per Summary Table 5, the understatement of Gross National Product in current dollars of the order of 5 per cent to 15 per cent would overstate the ratio of educational expenditures to Gross National Product.

To indicate the approximate character of the estimates, the ratios are shown in a form indicative of possible errors, less than 1 per cent for 1867, 1¼ per cent plus or minus for 1896, and 2 per cent plus or minus for 1914. There is a good deal of scope for improving Canadian economic data covering the first half of the country's history as a nation and this remains a task for future research.

4. *Implied Price Index in Gross National Expenditure.* This index with a base 1957 = 100 covering the period 1947-1967 is from DOMINION BUREAU OF STATISTICS, *National Accounts, Income and Expenditure by Quarters, 1947-1961; National Accounts, Income and Expenditure, 1966, and National Accounts, Income and Expenditure, Fourth Quarter and Preliminary Annual 1967,* Ottawa, 1962, 1967 and April 1968.

For the period 1926-1946, the index with a base 1949_100 is from *National Accounts, Income and Expenditure, 1926-1956,* Dominion Bureau of Statistics, Ottawa, 1958. For the period 1867-1925, with a base 1935-1939=100 (which was the base used in the official statistics when the estimates were prepared for the early period) the data are from *Canada's Economic Development 1867-1953, op. cit.,* p. 66 and from unpublished worksheets underlying this study.

The price indices for the periods 1867-1925 and 1926-1946 were converted to a 1957 base by a linking process. The method used was to divide all index numbers for the various years corresponding to the old base period by index number corresponding to the new base period, expressing the results in percentages.

Mathematically speaking this method is strictly applicable only if the index numbers satisfy the "circular test", i.e. $I_{j/i} = I_{j/k} I_{k/i}$, where I is the index and j and k refer to the indices corresponding to the base periods j and k respectively. The method used does not meet this circular test. As a result the aggregate price indices for the early period converted to a 1957 base show a somewhat greater differential with the more current series than if a price series with an earlier base year had been used. This has the effect of understating the current dollar values of Gross National Product for the early period, as suggested above.

The figures for 1896 and 1914 are estimates based on an interpolation using data of changes in the wholesale price index taken from *Wholesale Prices in Canada, 1890-1909*, Ottawa, Government Printing Bureau, 1910, and *Wholesale Prices, Canada,* annual 1910 to 1917, Government Printing Bureau and King's Printer, Ottawa.

TABLE 2. — NUMBER OF PUPILS ENROLLED, AVERAGE DAILY ATTENDANCE AND NUMBER OF TEACHERS, PUBLICLY CONTROLLED ELEMENTARY AND SECONDARY SCHOOLS, CANADA, 1867-1967.

1. *Pupils Enrolled.* The data relate to publicly controlled elementary and secondary schools. For the period 1867-1886, the data are from *Historical Statistics of Canada*, M. C. URQUHART, Ed., K. A. H. BUCKLEY, Ass. Ed., Section V: "Education", by R. W. B. JACKSON, Toronto, The MacMillan Company of Canada Limited, Toronto, 1965, p. 587. The data are based in the main on DOMINION BUREAU OF STATISTICS, *Historical Statistical Survey of Education in Canada, 1921,* Ottawa, 1921, and provincial annual reports of Departments of Education.

For the years 1887-1889, the data are from DOMINION BUREAU OF STATISTICS, *Elementary and Secondary Education in Canada, 1936-38,* Ottawa, 1940; for the years 1900-1953, DOMINION BUREAU OF STATISTICS, *Survey of Elementary and Secondary Education, 1950-1954 and 1962-1963,* Ottawa, 1959 and 1966; and for the years 1964-1967, DOMINION BUREAU OF STATISTICS, *Preliminary Statistics of Education 1955-1966,* and *Preliminary Statistics of Education 1966-1967,* Ottawa, 1967 and 1968.

In the early period some provinces did not issue annual reports for some of the years or they issued incomplete reports. An example would be the Province of Quebec which reported at times the enrolment in Roman Catholic schools and at times the enrolment in Roman Catholic and Protestant schools. To obtain comparable data over the period, the figures were adjusted upward to allow for non-reporting or under-reporting.

Special estimates had to be prepared for the years 1867, 1892-1894, and 1896, because of a more than usual degree of under-reporting. This was done by adding to the figures for 1867 as shown in *Historical Statistics of Canada,* additional data obtained by courtesy of Education Statistics Division, Dominion Bureau of Statistics and for 1892-1894 and 1896 by straight line interpolation. Commencing with 1949, the data include Newfoundland.

The data of pupils enrolled are subject to a number of statistical shortcomings, even after adjustments were made, as indicated above, largely because of difficulties encountered in making an adequate allowance for under-reporting and for changes in the classification between gross and net numbers. The Dominion Bureau of Statistics commented on the data in these terms:

"Because of variety in the methods of reporting, provision of comparable enrolment figures for all provinces, or even for one province for a series of years, is often difficult if not impossible. A case in point is Ontario. Before 1930, the enrolment given was the gross total of registrations in all schools for the calendar year. In 1930 this was changed to enrolment as of the last school day in May, thus eliminating duplication, and for that year the enrolment figure dropped some forty-odd thousand. A further change to 'net enrolment during the school year', beginning with the secondary schools in 1942, and the elementary ones in 1943, added a count of over 25,000 pupils of whom at least 12,000 were in secondary schools. Net enrolment is the total of all pupils registered in school during the school year with each pupil being counted only once.

There are provincial differences in the method of reporting pupils who moved from one room to another or from one school to another during the school year. Most provinces now make a systematic attempt to ensure that the enrolment and attendance of such pupils will be recorded only once. Several provinces use transfer cards which go with the pupil to his new room or school. When this system was introduced in Manitoba in 1932, the total enrolment figure for the year dropped by 1,600." [4]

Two other shortcomings of the data should be noted. One is the lack of consistency of reporting pupil enrolment from one province to another and from one year to another. The data to which the statistics apply may range from the beginning of the school year, usually September, to the end of the school year, June. Only in 1967 do the data relate to the identical point of time, the beginning of the school year, September 1967, because of improved reporting to the Dominion Bureau of Statistics.

The other shortcoming is due to the fact that the published data include in addition to pupil enrolment in public schools also students enrolled in private schools in the Province of Quebec. For 1957, the adjusted figure is 3,262,300 or 2½ per cent lower than the figure shown in Table 2 and for 1967 the adjusted figure is 5,044,100 or 1 per cent lower than the figure shown in Table 2. This difference increases generally speaking as the data go back in time mainly because of the greater relative weight of the Province of Quebec in the total school population. For most of the years over the period 1867-1956, the ratio varies between 2 per cent and 8 per cent. (Adjusted data by courtesy of Education Division, Dominion Bureau of Statistics.) Unadjusted data were used in Table 2 to ensure comparability over the one hundred year period covered.

While attempts have been made in this study to make allowance for some of the inadequacies in the basic data, the series for the early

------

    [4] DOMINION BUREAU OF STATISTICS, *Survey of Elementary and Secondary Education, 1950-54*, Ottawa, 1959, p. 31.

period remains a conglomeration of inadequate statistics coming from different government sources. But even with their shortcomings, the data permit a first impression of changes over the longer term in an analysis where differentials of rates of growth over four stages of economic development are examined rather than rates of changes per se. Further in terms of totals for Canada, the under or over-reporting does not appear to be numerically of major significance. For example, the instance referred to by the Dominion Bureau of Statistics of over-reporting for Ontario for 1930 introduces an error of about 2 per cent in the Canadian total and for 1943 about 1¼ per cent. Under-reporting for Manitoba for 1932 involves an error in terms of the Canada total of less than 0.1 per cent.

2. *Total Average Daily Attendance.* The data are from the same sources as pupils enrolled, referred to above, with similar adjustments. The figures are based for most provinces on the class as a unit. It "is calculated by dividing the aggregate actual pupil-days attendance of the class for the school year, by the number of days the class was in session. The total for a school, centre or province is then the sum of these figures. However, four provinces calculate average daily attendance differently. The school is the unit in Saskatchewan and Ontario and the province is the unit in Alberta and New Brunswick." [5]

One way of testing the comparability of the series of pupils enrolled and total average daily attendance is to examine the average daily attendance per pupil. The long-term trend is more or less continuously upward from 0.53 in 1867 to 0.93 in 1967. But from 1895 to 1897 when the source of the series is shifted from the *Historical Statistics of Canada* to statistics published by the Dominion Bureau of Statistics, there is a decline indicated from 0.62 to 0.57. Then from 1897 onwards the ratio improves almost without interruption for the next seventy years. The break in the ratio from 1895 to 1897 suggests the possibility that the number of pupils enrolled series for the period 1867-1895 may be over-stated in relation to the total daily average attendance. The estimate for 1896 was arrived at by interpolation and thus would reduce somewhat the upward bias that appears to be applicable to the series from 1867 to 1895.

As to the quality of the data, certain variations of recording attendance and calculating average daily attendance should be noted. An example of different methods of recording is the inclusion in school attendance of pupils absent from schools on religious holidays in some provinces and their exclusion in other provinces. Another example is that some provinces count all pupils as present whether they are or whether they are not attending year-end examinations while other provinces do not count attendance during the period of year-end examinations. The data include attendance of pupils enrolled in private schools in the Province of Quebec and hence are comparable with the data of the number of pupils enrolled as per Table 2.

---

5   *Ibid.*

3. *Number of Teachers.* These data for the years 1870, 1880, 1890, 1900, 1910 and 1920 to 1967 are from the sources listed above under pupils enrolled. The figures for 1867, 1896 and 1914 are estimates on the basis of trend analysis of pupils per teacher ratios.

The number of teachers covers all full-time teachers employed in publicly controlled elementary and secondary schools including "regular classroom teachers, special teachers and supervisors of special subjects or work. Inspectors and superintendents are not included." [6] The data exclude teachers in private schools. More recent investigations show that the data exclude also the number of full-time itinerants, that is teachers moving from one school to another during the school year. Revised figures are published in DOMINION BUREAU OF STATISTICS, *Salaries and Classifications of Teachers in Public Elementary and Secondary Schools, 1966-67,* Ottawa, 1968. The revised figure for 1961 is 152,500, as compared with the unrevised figure of 151,100, a difference of 0.9 per cent, and for 1967, 217,700 as compared with 215,400, a difference of 1.1 per cent. The Dominion Bureau of Statistics commented on the quality of the data:

"It must be borne in mind that the number of teachers given for any year does not mean the number teaching at one time. (A truer estimate [. . .] is [. . .] the number of classrooms in operation.) Some teachers leave the school before the end of the year and are replaced by new teachers. They may teach in on part of the province during one part of the year and in another at another; thus the same teacher may be counted more than once." [7]

In the more recent period, with the growing practice of teachers changing schools at the end of the school year rather than during the year, the possibility of over-counting has been reduced.

TABLE 3. — RECEIPTS BY PUBLICLY CONTROLLED ELEMENTARY AND SECONDARY SCHOOL BOARDS, AND TOTAL EXPENDITURES ON FORMAL EDUCATION, CANADA, 1867-1967.

1. *Receipts by School Boards.* The data relate to receipts by publicly controlled school boards covering elementary and secondary schools obtained from two main sources: provincial government grants and local assessments. For the period 1870-1925 at quinquennial intervals the data are from *Historical Statistics of Canada,* ed., M. C. URQUHART, ass. ed., K. A. H. BUCKLEY, Section V: "Education", by R. W. B. JACKSON, Toronto, The MacMillan Company of Canada Limited, 1965, p. 595. The published data were adjusted upwards for non-reporting or under-reporting, similar to the techniques employed in estimating the number of pupils enrolled, referred to above.

---

[6] DOMINION BUREAU OF STATISTICS, *Survey of Elementary and Secondary Education, 1950-54,* Ottawa, 1959, p. 67.
[7] DOMINION BUREAU OF STATISTICS, *Historical Statistical Survey of Education in Canada, 1921,* Ottawa, 1921, p. 65.

The data for the period 1926-1967 are from DOMINION BUREAU OF STATISTICS, *Elementary and Secondary Education in Canada, 1936-38, Survey of Elementary and Secondary Education 1950-54, Survey of Education Finance, 1963, Preliminary Statistics of Education, 1966-67*, Ottawa, 1940, 1959 and 1968; and DOMINION BUREAU OF STATISTICS, *Daily Bulletin*, Ottawa, March 15, 1968, p. 5.

The figures for 1867, 1896 and 1914 are special estimates based on trend analysis. The figures for 1966-1967 are preliminary estimates based on partial data.

School board revenues represent the bulk of total revenues, about 99½ per cent out of a total of $1.8 billion in 1964, the balance consisting of fees and other revenues. Total school board revenues approximate total operating and capital expenditures by school boards, covering operating and capital costs financed from current revenues. In 1964, total school board expenditures amounted to $1,772 million or 99½ per cent of total school board revenues of $1,781 million. The figures include Newfoundland commencing with 1949.

The Dominion Bureau of Statistics commented on the quality of the figures of revenues of school boards: These figures represent "the closest approach to a comparable statement" and the data "permit a reasonably accurate comparison of school costs as between provinces". [8] Annual estimates are available from Dominion Bureau of Statistics sources for the period 1914-1925 in the *Annual Survey of Education 1934* but annual estimates commencing with 1926 only are presented in Table 3.

2. *Total Expenditures on Formal Education*. These data are estimates prepared by the Dominion Bureau of Statistics for the period 1926-1967, covering all funds raised for educational purposes by different levels of governments and from private organizations and individuals. Thus the estimates cover operating and capital expenditures of elementary and secondary schools, teacher-training outside universities, higher education and other types of formal education, and vocational training including business colleges, private and public.

The data for 1926-1963 are from *Survey of Education Finance, 1963*, Dominion Bureau of Statistics, Ottawa, 1967. Data for 1964-1967 are from *Preliminary Statistics of Education, 1965-1966, and 1966-1967*, Dominion Bureau of Statistics, Ottawa, 1967 and 1968. The totals include Newfoundland commencing with 1949. The data relate to the school year ending June 30.

During 1926-1967, the ratios of receipts of publicly controlled school boards vary for most years between 60 and 70 per cent of total expenditures on formal education with the notable exception of the war and immediate postwar years when special training programmes during the

---

[8] DOMINION BUREAU OF STATISTICS, *Elementary and Secondary Education in Canada, 1936-38*, Ottawa, 1940, p. 68.

war and the Federal Government's educational grants to veterans in 1946 and 1947 particularly affected the ratio significantly.

TABLE 4. — CAPITAL EXPENDITURES FOR SCHOOLS AND UNI-
VERSITIES, SOCIAL AND BUSINESS CAPITAL EXPENDITURES,
TOTAL PRIVATE AND PUBLIC CAPITAL EXPENDITURES AND
BUSINESS GROSS CAPITAL FORMATION, CANADA, 1926-1967.

Except for the series on business gross capital formation as per National Accounts, the data for the period 1926-1946 are from DEPART-MENT OF TRADE AND COMMERCE, *Private and Public Investment in Canada, 1926-1951*, Ottawa, 1951. The data for the period 1947-1967 are from DOMINION BUREAU OF STATISTICS and DEPARTMENT OF TRADE AND COMMERCE, *Private and Public Investment in Canada, Outlook 1968*, Ottawa, 1968 and earlier issues.

The data of business gross capital formation as per National Accounts for the period 1926-1967 are from DOMINION BUREAU OF STATISTICS, *National Accounts, Income and Expenditure 1926-1956; National Accounts, Income and Expenditure by Quarters 1947-1961; National Accounts, Income and Expenditure, 1966, and National Accounts, Income and Expenditure, Fourth Quarter and Preliminary Annual, 1967*, Ottawa, 1962, 1967 and April 1968.

The data for capital expenditures in schools include vocational schools as well as all elementary and secondary schools, both public and private. The data of capital expenditures of universities cover all institutions of higher learning involving expenditures on new construction and purchase of new machinery and equipment but excluding purchases of land and existing assets, obtained from current revenues as well as from borrowing.

TABLE 5. — CAPITAL EXPENDITURES ON SCHOOLS AND UNIVER-
SITIES AS A PERCENT OF TOTAL SOCIAL CAPITAL EXPEND-
ITURES, TOTAL BUSINESS CAPITAL EXPENDITURES, TOTAL
PRIVATE AND PUBLIC INVESTMENT, BUSINESS GROSS CAPITAL
FORMATION PER NATIONAL ACCOUNTS AND GROSS NATIONAL
PRODUCT, CANADA, 1926-1967.

These computations are based on Tables 1 and 4 in Appendix A.

TABLE 6. — TOTAL EXPENDITURES ON FORMAL EDUCATION
AND CAPITAL EXPENDITURES ON SCHOOLS AND UNIVERSI-
TIES, IN CONSTANT DOLLARS, 1926-1967.

These computations are based on Tables 1, 3 and 4 in Appendix A. The data on total expenditures on formal education are deflated by the Implied Price Index in Gross National Expenditures and the data on Capital Expenditures on schools and universities by the Implied Price Index of Business Gross Capital Formation, on the basis of 1957=100, with the price indices converted to a common base. The data are from

DOMINION BUREAU OF STATISTICS, *National Accounts Income and Expenditure 1926-1956; National Accounts, Income and Expenditure by Quarters 1947-1961, National Accounts, Income and Expenditure 1966,* and *National Accounts, Income and Expenditure, Fourth Quarter and Preliminary Annual, 1967,* Ottawa, 1958, 1962, 1967 and April 1968.

It bears emphasis that the technique used expresses the expenditures on formal education in terms of the general purchasing power as it applied to 1957 and the capital expenditures on schools and universities in terms of the capital cost index applicable to all capital expenditures, with 1957 as a base and on the basis of weighting between major types of capital expenditures as shown in the National Accounts. The indices used are general price indexes and therefore do not reflect the specific cost increases applicable to total educational expenditures and to capital expenditures for education.

LIST OF TABLES

SUMMARY TABLE   PAGE

1. Percent Changes of Population, Labour Force, Employment and Gross National Product in Constant Dollars, Totals for Five Periods and Annual Rates, Canada 1867-1967 _____ 123

2. Changes in Industrial Structure, Agriculture, Manufacturing and Services, Output and Employment, Canada, 1870-1966 ____ 129

3. Consumer Expenditures on Goods and Services, Essential and other, Canada, 1870-1966 _____ 133

4. Population, School Enrolment, Total Expenditures on Formal Education and Capital Expenditures on Schools and Universities, Canada, 1950 and 1967 _____ 174

5. Expenditures on Formal Education, Totals and Per Capita, and Rates of Economic Growth, Canada, 1867-1967 _____ 185

6. Capital Expenditures on Schools and Universities Compared with Capital Formation, Social, Business and Total, and Gross National Product, Canada, 1926, 1950 and 1967 _____ 191

7. Enrolment, Attendance, and Teachers, Publicly Controlled Elementary and Secondary Schools, Canada, Selected Years, 1867-1967 _____ 198

8. Enrolment, Attendance and Teachers, Publicly Controlled Elementary and Secondary Schools, Totals for Five Periods and Annual Rates, Canada, 1867-1967 _____ 199

9. Population and School Enrolment, Males, Aged 5-24, Canada, 1921-1961 _____ 202

10. Male Labour Force, 25-64 Years, by Years of Schooling, Canada, 1911-1961 _____ 206

11. Average Earnings of Non-Farm Labour Force, by Level of School, Age and Sex, Canada, 1961 _____ 212

12. Average Lifetime Earnings by Occupational Group and Level of Education, Male Non-Farm Labour Force, Aged 25-64, Canada, 1961 _____ 215

13. Average Life-Time Earnings, Total and Discounted, by Levels of Education, Male Non-Farm Labour Force, Canada, 1961 ____ 216

14. Return on Private Investment in Education, by Levels of Education, Male Non-Farm Labour Force, Canada, 1961 _____ 220

15. Population, Immigration and Emigration, Canada, by Decades, 1861-1961 _____ 224

16. Total Years of Education and Costs of Education, Immigrants and Emigrants, Canada, 1951-1961 _____ 227

TABLE IN APPENDIX A   PAGE

1. Population, Labour Force, Employment, Gross National Product
   in Current and Constant Dollars, and Implied Price Index,
   Canada, 1867-1967 _____ 261

2. Number of Pupils Enrolled, Average Daily Attendance and
   Number of Teachers, Publicly Controlled Elementary and
   Secondary Schools, Canada, 1867-1967 _____ 264

3. Receipts by Publicly Controlled Elementary and Secondary
   School Boards, and Total Expenditures on Formal Education,
   Canada, 1867-1967 _____ 267

4. Capital Expenditures for Schools and Universities, Social and
   Business Capital Expenditures, Total Private and Public Capital
   Expenditures and Business Gross Capital Formation, Canada,
   1926-1967 _____ 269

5. Capital Expenditures on Schools and Universities as a Percent
   of Total Social Capital Expenditures, Total Business Capital
   Expenditures, Total Private and Public Investment, Business
   Gross Capital Formation per National Accounts and Gross
   National Product, Canada, 1926-1967 _____ 271

6. Total Expenditures on Formal Education and Capital Expenditures on Schools and Universities, in Constant Dollars,
   Canada, 1926-1967 _____ 272

Index of Subjects

Academic freedom, 170
Adams, Howard, 190
Advertising, 95
Affluence, 128, 131, 156, 247
Age distribution, 198, 200, 208
Agriculture, 5, 6, 21, 24, 126, 128, 129, 130
Aircraft industry, 28, 34, 35, 38, 111, 112
Aitken, Hugh G. J., 15, 78
Alberta, 37, 182
Aluminum industry, 34, 35
Anderson, C. Arnold, 144, 163, 164
Anderson, Walton, J., 160
Argentina, 46
Asimakopoulos, A., 22
Aspiration(s), 143, 144, 247
Assets, 52, 53, 58, 59, 63, 64, 65, 130, 148
Atkinson, Edward, 11
Australia, 46, 114
Austria, 48
Automation, 246
Automobile industry, 26, 57, 74
Autonomous variables, 147

Balance of payments, 39, 61, 62, 65, 66, 116
Bannock, Graham, 47
Becker, Gary S., 209, 221, 222, 240
Beckerman, W., 164
Beland, Richard, 163
Belgium, 48
Benians, E. A., 27, 100
Bennett, R. B., 70
Bereday, George Z. F., 240
Bertram, Gordon W., 22, 201, 203, 204, 205, 211, 229, 230, 231, 235, 241, 244, 245
Beverage industry, 58
Birthrate, 173
Blanchet, Joseph, 178
Black, Edwin R., 235, 236
Blaug, Mark, 240
Bonar, James, 1
Boulding, Kenneth E., 94, 95, 149
Bowman, Mary Jean, 144, 163, 217, 240

Brady, A., 27, 79
Brain-drain, 143, 194, 223, 225, 236
Brewery industry, 21, 26
Britain, 3, 15, 22, 26, 34, 46, 47, 48, 100, 105, 112, 113, 126, 132
British Empire Preferential System, 33, 112
British North America Act, 75, 173
Brown, T. M., 92
Business cycle, 40, 102, 109, 113, 118, 184

Canada Development Corporation, 74
Capacity
  to consume, 156
  to produce, 157, 158
Capital, 6, 8, 13, 16, 24, 26, 33, 55, 59, 60, 61, 62, 67, 79, 90, 91, 92, 96, 97, 99, 104, 105, 107, 116, 117, 122, 127, 135, 137, 147, 187, 210, 218, 234, 237
  cost allowances, 73
  equipment, 25, 50, 108
  expenditures, 40, 93, 146, 171, 183, 187
  formation, 93, 109, 126, 127, 130, 131, 135, 148
  goods, 5, 37, 42, 146, 159
  human, 144, 147, 160, 195, 209, 218, 221, 245, 246
  inflow, 228
  intensity, 234
  investment, 48, 52, 171, 187, 221, 235
  physical, 144, 147, 218, 221, 222, 246
Cartter, Allan M., 163
Cheal, John E., 179, 182, 194
Chemical industry, 5, 26, 34, 35, 37, 45, 57, 58, 73, 111, 112
Chiswick, Barry R., 240
Church, 177, 181
Civil War, 17
Clark, Colin, 89, 126
Class(es), 208
  rooms, 172, 175

Clergy, 177, 214

Coal industry, 15, 58

College, 181, 205, 206
  business, 175, 205
  junior, 170

Commercial system, 118

Commonwealth Caribbean Assistance Programme, 153

Commonwealth Scholarship and Fellowship Plan, 153

Communication industry, 7, 16, 18, 105, 129, 140, 193

Competition, 13, 23, 42, 43, 44, 45, 47, 48, 50, 51, 68, 69, 80, 194, 237, 239

Computers, 175

Concentration, 233

Confederation, 10, 15, 18, 21, 23, 25, 69, 70, 100, 101, 106, 182, 204

Constitutional system, 9

Construction industry, 22, 28, 129

Consumer
  assets, 157
  choice, 157
  expenditures, 93, 95, 115, 116, 138, 149, 156, 157
  goods and services, 5, 25, 94, 108, 115, 125
  liabilities, 157
  needs, 156
  preferences, 95
  satisfaction, 90, 94, 96, 156, 157, 158
  sovereignty, 115, 149, 150
  values, 156
  wants, 157
  welfare, 96

Consumption, 96, 101, 115, 127, 138, 145, 146, 147, 148, 156, 157, 166, 196, 221

Corporations and Labour Unions Return Act, 51, 52, 53, 57, 58, 63

Cost benefit analysis, 151, 164

Cost-push pressures, 237

Crown companies, 36

Culture (al), 190
  absorption, 235
  attitudes, 246
  factors, 159, 162, 235
  variables, 182

Curriculum, 150, 190, 207

Dalhousie University, 179

De Champlain, Samuel, 103

De la Roche, Marquis, 103

Demonstration effect, 156, 237, **238**

Denison, Edward F., 211, 238, **239**, 240, 241, 242, 244, 245

Depression, 22, 27, 32, 33, 41, **106**, 122, 184

De Roberval, Sieur, 103

Devaluation, 39, 45, 116

Diefenbaker, The Right Hon. John, 61

Diminishing returns, 218

Distillery industry, 21

Diversification, 41

Division of labour, 42, 44

Domar, Evsey D., 158

Douglas, W. A., 19

Drive to maturity, 184, 192, **193**, 198, 200, 213

Duality, 155, 164, 239

Duesenberry, James S., 156

Du Gua de Monts, Pierre, 103

Earnings, 12, 148, 161, 162, **165**, 197, 211, 213, 214, 216, **217**, 218, 219, 221
  foregone, 219
  life-time, 215, 217

Easterbrook, W. T., 15, 78

Economic
  aid, 8
  choice, 138, 139, 169
  control, 235
  dependence, 17
  development, 18, 19, 26, 55, **61**, 65, 69, 72, 78, 89, 90, 91, **92**, 93, 94, 95, 96, 97, 99, **101**, 102, 113, 114, 117, 118, **119**, 120, 124, 125, 127, 130, **133**, 141, 144, 145, 148, 151, **152**, 155, 159, 160, 161, 162, **163**, 175, 177, 189, 193, 195, **196**, 204, 228, 229, 237, 238, **239**, 245, 246

expansion, 22, 110, 116, 117
growth, actual, 246
  general, 3, 8, 15, 18, 23, 31, 38,
    39, 40, 53, 59, 68, 77, 78, 80,
    89, 90, 91, 93, 95, 96, 97, 100,
    101, 105, 110, 117, 119, 122,
    125, 126, 133, 139, 140, 141,
    142, 143, 144, 145, 148, 151,
    155, 158, 159, 165, 167, 181,
    183, 187, 196, 209, 217, 221,
    234, 237, 239, 241, 242, 245,
    246, 247
  potential, 246
  planning, 19
  policy, 33, 70, 72, 91, 101, 105,
    134, 144, 150, 152, 156
  power, 68
  progress, 4, 8, 9, 12, 38, 70, 78,
    89, 93, 94, 95, 96, 97, 101,
    104, 107, 116, 122, 138, 145,
    150, 151, 152, 158, 162, 166,
    234, 237, 239, 246
  rationale, 143
  scale, 140
  stages, 89, 99, 101, 117
Economic Council of Canada, 45,
    97, 192, 201, 208, 209, 217,
    221, 223, 225, 229, 232, 233,
    234, 242, 243, 244
Edding, Friedrich, 244
Education, 9, 79, 97, 105, 118, 122,
    124, 125, 126, 127, 128, 131,
    132, 133, 134, 135, 137, 139,
    140, 141, 143, 144, 145, 148,
    150, 151, 153, 155, 156, 157,
    158, 159, 160, 163, 164, 165,
    173, 177, 178, 181, 182, 184,
    189, 193, 197, 200, 201, 203,
    205, 208, 209, 213, 217, 218,
    219, 221, 222, 223, 227, 228,
    230, 235, 241, 245, 246
  adult, 141, 172
  attainments, 214, 231, 237
  budget, 164
  compulsory, 169
  continuing, 141, 166
  costs, 182, 221
  denominational, 181
  elementary, 192
  formal, 183, 197, 228
  free, 169, 178

industry, 125, 126, 127, 140, 169,
    171, 172, 173, 175, 239, 240
  objectives, 189
  secondary, 181
  standard, 171
  stock, 209, 223
  technical, 173, 192
Educational
  advancement, 232
  attainments, 157, 160, 162, 165,
    192, 203, 210, 217, 221, 223,
    225, 226, 229, 232, 233, 234,
    235, 236, 238, 243
  capital, 144, 150, 165, 194, 197,
    198, 200, 201, 204, 206, 208,
    209, 222, 225, 226, 228, 231,
    236, 244
  development, 180, 236
  differentials, 233
  expenditures, 161, 164, 186, 187,
    189, 192, 193
  explosion, 173, 186
  growth model, 144
  improvements, 241
  investment, 147, 165, 217, 221,
    223
  opportunities, 235
  performance, 170
  planning, 150, 163
  policy, 143, 164, 222
  progress, 200, 204, 238
  standards, 232, 235
  take-off, 196
Electrical equipment industry, 31,
    57, 58, 111
Electronics industry, 38, 112
Employment, 5, 6, 11, 19, 23, 24,
    27, 28, 38, 39, 40, 68, 72, 90,
    97, 102, 106, 108, 113, 117,
    119, 122, 127, 128, 135, 158,
    159, 163, 205, 208, 209, 210,
    211, 216
  full, 117, 142, 247
  under-, 210
Emulation, 165
Endogenous variables, 147
Entrepreneur, 67, 113, 157, 158
Enterprise, 72, 96
Expectation, 157

Exports, 3, 7, 8, 10, 11, 15, 16, 18, 22, 25, 27, 40, 41, 42, 43, 45, 46, 49, 66, 73, 99, 100, 106, 108, 112
  credit insurance, 73
  financing, 50
External economies, 140

Fabricant, Solomon, 240
F.A.O., 153
Farm implement industry, 26, 31, 111
Finance, 7, 130
Firestone, O. J., 10, 21, 28, 38, 107, 109, 110, 114, 188, 276
Fiscal
  concessions, 116
  incentives, 73
  policy, 36, 55, 62, 95, 157
  responsibilities, 17
  soundness, 8
Fishery industry, 129
Flour milling industry, 21, 26
Fogel, Walter, 163
Food industry, 58
Footwear industry, 26
Foreign
  control, 55, 56, 57, 60, 64, 66, 67, 71, 235
  exchange, 16
  ownership, 55, 58
Forestry industry, 105, 129
Foster, Sir George E., 13
France, 3, 47, 48
Free trade, 17, 68, 100
Fullerton, D. H., 13
Furniture industry, 21, 58

Galbraith, J. K., 95
Gap, 230, 232, 235, 236
Germany, 180
Goldsmith, Raymond, 102
Gordon, The Hon. Walter, 50, 61, 67, 74
Gourlay, Robert, 179
Government
  spending, 171
  services, 130
Griffin, Watson, 13

Gross Domestic Product, 3, 39, 40, 130
Gross National Expenditure, 186, 190, 246
Gross National Product, 5, 10, 11, 24, 27, 29, 40, 91, 92, 93, 94, 95, 96, 102, 106, 107, 108, 109, 110, 113, 114, 116, 117, 119, 121, 122, 130, 132, 139, 148, 151, 152, 161, 162, 171, 173, 182, 183, 184, 186, 187, 189, 190, 193, 194, 200, 213, 228, 229, 232, 241, 243, 246
Growth
  path, 149
  quality of, 224
  theory, 96
Guidelines, 62, 63, 66

Hagen, Everett E., 91, 163
Hall-Dennis Report, 190
Hampson, H. A., 13
Hansen, W. Lee, 219
Harbison, Frederick H., 167
Harris, Seymour E., 218
Harrod, Roy F., 158
Health, 9, 141, 147
Heavy equipment industry, 112
Henripin, J., 22
Higgins, Benjamin, 94, 96, 135
High mass consumption, 99, 114, 115, 116, 124, 173, 192, 193, 198, 208, 213, 229
Hopkins, J. Castell, 12
Hours worked, 6, 7, 10, 12, 24, 92, 95, 96
Howe, The Right Hon. Clarence Decatur, 71, 72, 73, 78
Hudson's Bay Company, 103
Hudson River, 103
Hydro-electric power, 26, 111

Illing, Wolfgang M., 201
Illiteracy, 247
I.L.O., 153
Immigration, 100, 109, 134, 143, 165, 223, 225, 226, 228
Imperfect market, 166, 169
Imports, 66, 70

Income, 5, 7, 17, 19, 24, 38, 72, 77, 90, 93, 94, 127, 128, 139, 146, 147, 149, 158, 159, 162, 163, 167, 182, 209, 210, 211, 213, 217, 218, 226, 230, 231, 233, 234, 236
  discretionary, 131, 132
  distribution, 95, 138
  foregone, 221
  personal disposable, 128, 138, 157
  redistribution, 9, 247

Industrial
  advancement, 78
  development, 1, 4, 9, 16, 23, 25, 26, 27, 31, 38, 59, 60, 65, 70, 71, 72, 73, 74, 75, 77, 79, 80, 100, 111, 127, 180, 200
  diversification, 24, 113
  expansion, 36, 72
  integration, 112
  maturity, 120, 124, 126, 184, 186, 213, 225, 228, 235, 239
  progress, 18, 49, 77, 111, 115, 134
  structure, 16, 35, 89, 91, 92, 93, 111, 112, 239, 246, 247
  take-off, 196

Industrial Development Bank, 73

Industrial Revolution, 15

Industrialization, 8, 13, 16, 41, 68, 70, 72, 77, 78, 90, 105, 111, 128, 181, 194, 196

Infra-structure, 18, 77, 92, 101, 104, 105, 109, 124, 134, 159, 193, 246

Innovations, 92, 104, 131, 139, 141, 142, 156, 157, 158, 169, 238, 246,

Input-output, 135

Insurance, 7, 188

International
  indebtedness, 55
  lending, 22

Investment, 22, 31, 32, 35, 36, 59, 60, 62, 67, 79, 91, 96, 97, 111, 116, 122, 125, 127, 130, 145, 146, 148, 149, 150, 151, 164, 166, 209, 213, 218, 219, 221, 222, 228, 237, 246

  human, 195
  physical, 147
Iron and steel industry, 5, 15, 25, 26, 28, 34, 35, 37, 42, 108, 111, 237
Italy, 3

James, H. Thomas, 193
Japan, 3, 42, 119
Johnson, Harry G., 151
Jolly, Richard, 144

Kendrick, John W., 148, 164, 240
Kindleberger, Charles P., 93
Knight, R., 164
Kuznets, Simon, 89, 90, 102, 119, 121, 122, 126, 129, 130, 132, 148

Labour market, 141
Lag, 180, 208
Language laboratories, 175
Laurier, Sir Wilfrid, 12, 70
Laval University, 179
Lawerys, Joseph A., 240
Layard, P. R. G., 163
Leather industry, 58
Leisure, 91, 94, 95, 138 139, 152 155, 166
Less developed countries, 8, 15, 45, 96, 142, 145, 153, 196
Lewis, W. Arthur, 142, 143, 177
Literacy, 144, 192
Local assessments, 177, 183
Lower, A. R. M., 100
Lumber industry, 21, 22, 26
Lundberg, Erik, 244
Lyons, Raymond F., 163

MacDonald, Sir John A., 70
Machinery industry, 31, 45, 58, 111
Mackenzie, William Lyon, 180
Malinvaud, Edmond, 244
Managerial
  advances, 112
  competence, 158
  cxpcrience, 29, 59
  know-how, 34, 108, 127, 134
  talent, 238
Manpower
  planning, 142, 150, 163, 164
  projections, 164

Manufacturing industry, 4, 5, 6, 7, 8, 10, 11, 12, 13, 24, 27, 28, 31, 32, 35, 38, 39, 40, 41, 43, 44, 45, 50, 53, 56, 57, 59, 60, 63, 65, 69, 75, 108, 126, 128, 129, 214

Marginal product, 143

Marion, Gérald, 163

Mass communications, 165, 169

Matriculation, 172

Maturity, 92, 99, 101, 112, 113, 114, 115, 116, 119, 162

McGill University, 169

Meat packing industry, 26

Mechanization, 246

Metal fabricating industry, 58, 111

Middle class, 187, 188, 189

Miller, William L., 245

Minimum wage laws, 210

Mining industry, 7, 56, 60, 63, 65, 106, 116, 129

Mobility, 137, 143, 160, 166, 171, 243, 246

Model, 144

Monetary policy, 157

Monopoly, 181

Mortality, 226

Motivation, 146

Motor car industry, 31, 111, 115, 237

Myers, Charles A., 167

Myint, H., 240

Nation-building, 101

National
   income, 10, 21, 39, 110, 135, 209, 213, 217, 239, 242, 243
   survival, 80

National Policy, 23, 70, 71, 105

Nationalism, 19, 69, 235

Nationhood, 104

Natural gas industry, 37, 42, 56, 113

Navigation laws, 17

Netherlands, 48

New Brunswick, 16, 178

Newton, A. P., 27, 100

Non-ferrous metals industry, 37, 42, 108, 112

Non-metallic minerals industry, 42, 58, 111

Nova Scotia, 16, 178

Obsolescence, 166, 169

Occupations, 143, 146, 149

Oil industry, 37, 42, 43, 113

Ontario, 16, 25, 100, 178, 179

Parent Report, 190

Pay-off, 195, 196

Peel, Sir Robert, 100

Phillips, Charles E., 178

Pigou, A. C., 147

Planning, 150, 163, 195

Plastics industry, 45

Podoluk, J. R., 214, 217, 218, 219

Political
   independence, 236
   absorption, 236

Polymer Corporation, 73

Population, 3, 10, 11, 21, 90, 91, 102, 106, 108, 109, 110, 113, 115, 117, 119, 120, 125, 126, 152, 160, 163, 165, 170, 173, 182, 183, 184, 189, 198, 200, 204, 208, 226, 229, 232

Porter, Richard C., 164

Poullier, Jean-Pierre, 245

Poverty, 178, 247

Preconditions for take-off, 99, 104, 105, 131, 181, 183, 193, 197, 198

Pre-Confederation, 181

Pre-industrial society, 118

Price(s), 12, 16, 22, 24, 29, 94, 106, 108, 149, 166, 184, 186, 188, 234
   system, 166, 170, 221

Primary metals industry, 58

Printing and publishing industry, 58

Priorities, 134, 162, 164, 169, 193, 195, 198, 232, 239, 244, 247

Product alternatives, 170

Productivity, 5, 7, 9, 24, 27, 36, 43, 47, 48, 50, 59, 65, 73, 74, 79, 89, 91, 92, 93, 96, 97, 109, 117, 120, 121, 122, 139, 141, 143, 147, 152, 158, 165, 167, 194, 195, 210, 213, 225, 229, 230, 234, 236, 237, 241, 242, 243, 244, 247

Professors, 214

Profits, 6, 7, 8, 18, 52, 53, 58, 59, 79, 107, 218

Property and civil rights, 75

Public utilities, 6, 129

Pulp and paper industry, 5, 25, 26, 31, 42, 58, 111

Pupils, 197, 207

Quebec, 16, 100, 103, 160, 177, 179, 182, 189

Rado, E. R., 164

Railway building, 22, 25, 28, 105, 108

Rate of return, 245

Rationalizing, 68

Raw materials, 46

Raynaud, André, 115, 163

Real estate, 7, 130

Recession, 27, 31, 38, 53, 101, 111, 113, 116, 117

Reciprocity Treaty, 17

Research, 34, 50, 61, 73, 75, 79, 126, 132, 151, 165, 171, 172, 186, 200, 223, 229, 235, 236, 237, 238, 240

Residual factor, 239, 243, 244

Resources
  allocation, 127
  development, 64, 105, 108, 110
  human, 213
  industries, 111
  natural, 3, 4, 9, 37, 43, 56, 59, 60, 68, 69, 96, 97, 152, 234

Ricardo, David, 138

Risks, 51, 57, 72, 79, 96, 105, 158

Roberts, B. C., 164

Rose, J. Holland, 100

Rostow, W. W., 89, 92, 99, 101, 102, 103, 104, 105, 107, 110, 112, 113, 114, 115, 118, 121, 165, 181, 192, 213, 229

Royal Commission on Canada's Economic Prospects, 13

Royal Commission on Dominion-Provincial Relations, 17, 22, 23, 25, 28, 29

Rubber industry, 34, 35, 57, 58, 73

Sacrifice, 96

Saigal, J. C., 163

St. Lawrence, 18, 100, 103, 104

Salt works, 21

Samuelson, Paul A., 91

Sandee, J., 244

Savings, 24, 59, 105, 130, 147, 148, 149, 150

Scale of operations, 170, 237

School, 146, 157, 173, 182, 198, 200, 205, 230
  age, 197
  attendance, 149, 181, 198, 200, 203, 204, 205, 219, 230
  boards, 171
  denominational, 181, 182
  elementary, 169, 170, 171, 175, 177, 181, 183, 190, 192, 197, 210, 211, 215, 216, 217, 219
  enrolment, 197, 200, 201, 205, 209, 232
  free, 179
  high, 181, 200, 214, 218, 219
  leaving age, 208
  non-sectarian, 178
  primary, 144, 187, 192, 207, 208
  public, 137, 147, 177, 182, 190, 205
  retention rates, 209
  secondary, 144, 169, 170, 171, 175, 177, 183, 187, 190, 192, 197, 205, 207, 208, 210, 222
  separate, 181, 182
  year, 204

Schultz, Theodore W., 127, 145, 147, 151, 162, 240

Scott, Anthony, 91

Security, 188

Seers, Dudley, 144

Service industries, 70, 77, 113, 116, 126, 130
Sheffield, Edward F., 172
Shoe factories, 21
Shipbuilding industry, 21, 28, 34, 38, 111
Shortt, Adam, 100
Siegel, Barry N., 95
Skelton, O. D., 9, 24, 78
Smith, Arthur J. R., 97
Smith, J. H., 164
Social
    alienation, 163
    capital, 171, 187, 195, 200, 239
    costs, 143
    income, 221
    investment, 147, 148, 166
    justice, 95
    responsibility, 150
    returns, 150, 160, 222, 235
    security, 9, 95, 116, 137
    structure, 91
    welfare, 115
Solow, Robert M., 240
Sovereignty, 235
Special Commonwealth African Assistance Plan, 153
Specialization, 205, 234, 237, 243
Standard of living, 3, 8, 36, 47, 72, 77, 78, 79, 89, 92, 94, 97, 104, 115, 116, 122, 138, 156, 234, 247
Stone, Richard, 144
Structure (al), 5, 29, 49, 52, 55, 134, 142, 247
    of industry, 210
    changes, 90, 124, 125, 126, 128, 130, 133, 134, 192, 246
Student(s), 172, 181, 232
    counselling, 150
    power, 175
Sugar factories, 21
Substitution, 94
Sweden, 48

Take-off
    in economic development, 99, 101, 107, 109, 110, 113, 118, 162, 184, 193, 198, 229
    in education, 195

Tariffs, 23, 33, 50, 70, 73, 100, 105
Taxes, 8, 127, 132, 170, 219, 221
Teachers, 126, 140, 145, 146, 159, 161, 169, 171, 172, 175, 178, 179, 182, 197, 207, 208
    quality, 170
    training, 175
Technological maturity, 127, 131, 142, 161, 186, 192, 193, 196, 229
Technology, 4, 15, 37, 59, 67, 74, 78, 91, 92, 103, 108, 110, 111, 112, 113, 114, 115, 120, 122, 126, 127, 132, 133, 134, 135, 137, 141, 144, 150, 158, 160, 165, 166, 169, 181, 184, 189, 194, 198, 221, 239, 243, 247
Television industry, 38, 175
Textile and clothing industry, 26, 45, 58
Thayer, V. T., 177
Tilley, The Hon. Samuel L., 69
Tobacco industry, 58
Trade
    barriers, 44, 45
    international, 42, 44, 45, 46, 71, 100, 104, 110, 130, 194, 200, 234
    policies, 69
    preferences, 17
    retail, 7
    terms of, 46
    wholesale, 7
Traditional society, 99, 100, 101, 103, 104, 118, 120, 196
Training, 150, 157, 158, 159, 161, 165, 166, 172, 175, 181, 197, 206, 209, 210, 226, 244, 246
Transfer payments, 116
Transportation
    industry, 7, 16, 18, 21, 45, 58, 105, 129, 193
    problem, 170
Tremblay, Marc-Adélard, 160

Unemployment, 17, 27, 32, 37, 39, 116, 209
U.N.E.S.C.O., 153
United Nations, 8

United Nations Development Programme, 153
United Nations Training and Research Institute, 153
United States, 3, 10, 11, 15, 17, 19, 23, 25, 27, 33, 34, 36, 38, 42, 43, 46, 47, 48, 56, 57, 62, 66, 68, 78, 79, 80, 97, 103, 105, 111, 112, 116, 126, 132, 141, 148, 163, 165, 175, 177, 178, 181, 193, 201, 221, 223, 225, 226, 227, 228, 229, 230, 231, 232, 233, 234, 235, 237, 238, 239, 241, 242, 245
University, 147, 161, 170, 172, 173, 175, 179, 180, 181, 187, 200, 203, 205, 206, 210, 211, 214, 215, 216, 217, 218, 219, 222, 225, 230, 231, 232, 233
University of Toronto, 179
Urbanization, 9, 107, 111, 205, 207, 208
U.S.S.R., 3, 34, 120

Vaizey, J., 147, 156, 164, 240
Vocational, 173
    institutions, 206
    schools, 205
    training, 171

Wage parity, 237
Waines, W. J., 195
Walras, Leon, 95
Wants, 156, 157, 246
Watkins, Prof. Melville H., 67
Welfare, 95, 116
    economics, 94
Western Germany, 3, 46, 47, 48
Wheat, 5, 42, 108
Wilkinson, Bruce W., 226
Winters, The Hon. Robert H., 63, 65, 66, 67
Williams, C. H., 222
Wood products industry, 58
Woodhall, Maureen, 164

Zsigmond, Zoltan E., 201

PRINTED BY

LECLERC PRINTERS LIMITED

HULL, CANADA

JANUARY 12, 1969